TIRPITZ

TIRPITZ

Hunting the Beast

John Sweetman

SUTTON PUBLISHING

This book was first published in 2000 by
Sutton Publishing Limited · Phoenix Mill
Thrupp · Stroud · Gloucestershire · GL5 2BU

This paperback edition first published in 2004

British Library Cataloguing in Publication Data
A catalogue record for this book is available from the
British Library.

ISBN 0 7509 3755 6

Typeset in 10.5/12pt Iowan.
Typesetting and origination by
Sutton Publishing Limited.
Printed and bound in Great Britain by
J.H. Haynes & Co. Ltd, Sparkford.

CONTENTS

ACKNOWLEDGEMENTS

I am greatly indebted to a large number of people for their invaluable assistance in the preparation of this book, the following in particular: Lt Cdr R.M. Griffiths (Fleet Air Arm Officers' Association); Sqn Ldr T.C. Iveson (Chairman, Bomber Command Association); R.M. Owen (Official Historian, 617 Squadron); Major K. Store (former Curator, Royal Norwegian Air Force Museum); Dr N. Young (Research and Information Office, Imperial War Museum).

The staff of the following libraries and archives have supplied me with material and patiently answered a multitude of questions:

British Library
Department of Aviation Records, RAF Museum Hendon
Fleet Air Arm Museum, Yeovilton
Imperial War Museum: Department of Documents, Department of Photographs, Sound Archive
Ministry of Defence, Air Historical Branch
Public Record Office, Kew
Royal Military Academy Sandhurst

I readily acknowledge permission to use the information that they have produced and I particularly thank the Controller of Her Majesty's Stationery Office for permission to reproduce photographs and to quote from records under Crown copyright and the Imperial War Museum for allowing reproduction of photographs held there.

Many of those involved in the different operations

against *Tirpitz* have generously given of their time, corresponded at length and made available to me a wide range of documents, photographs and sketches, including:

Fleet Air Arm: Cdr N.H. Bovey, Lt Cdr R. Fulton, Cdr S.G. Orr, Cdr J.W. Powell, H.K. Quilter, Rear-Admiral I.G.W. Robertson, Lt Cdr J.H. Stenning, Lt Cdr F.R.A. Turnbull
9 Squadron RAF: J.F.E. Brookbank (Squadron Association Hon. Sec.), R.J. Harris, P.J. Parsons, J.C. Pinning, J.D. Melrose
10 Squadron RAF: G.M. Dickson
35 Squadron RAF: A. Abels
511 Squadron RAF: G. Briggs
617 Squadron RAF: T. Bennett, A.W. Cherrington, F.E. Cholerton, G. Cole, L.W. Curtis, C.B.R. Fish, D.E. Freeman, S.V. Grimes, F.E. Howkins, T.C. Iveson, B.F. Kent, R.E. Knights, H.C. Knilans, A.J. Lammas, J.H. Leavitt, J.D. Phillips, H.J. Riding, J.A. Sanders, J. Soilleux, Gp Capt J.B. Tait (former CO), F.L. Tilley, D.H. Vaughan, E.A. Wass (Squadron Association Hon. Sec.), H. Watkinson.

The following have also provided valuable assistance, and to them I am extremely grateful:

L. Arneberg (Curator, Tromso Museum); B.N. Boorer (colleague of Sir Barnes Wallis); Dr A.H. Clayton and P.A. Warner (former colleagues at The Royal Military Academy Sandhurst); Mrs M. Dove (daughter of Roy Chadwick); P. Elliott (RAF Museum Hendon); Lt Col C.G.O. Hogg (Regimental Secretary, King's Own Scottish Borderers); P.T. Jacobsen (former Norwegian SIS member); T.W. Jameson and P. Rix (Barnes Wallis Memorial Trust); Mrs S. Le Clerq; C.E. Mackay; J. Reed; Herr K. Rymus; Dr M.R. Stopes-Roe and B.W. Wallis (children of Sir Barnes & Lady Mary Wallis); Herr A. Zuba (*Tirpitz* survivor). Sarah Harris has given special assistance with German correspondence and translation. Nor should I forget my sons Paul and Mark for their (constructive) criticism.

GLOSSARY AND ABBREVIATIONS

Note: In the text, Germany ranks have been Anglicised with one exception. Gross Admiral is the equivalent of Admiral of the Fleet. However, 'Grand Admiral' often appears in British Literature and that has been used throughout this book

AA	anti-aircraft
A&AEE	Aeroplane and Armament Experimental Establishment, Boscombe Down
A/B	able-bodied seaman
A/C	aircraft
ACAS (Ops)	Assistant Chief of the Air Staff (Operations)
ACAS (P)	Assistant Chief of the Air Staff (Policy)
Adm	Admiralty
Air Cdre	air commodore
amatol	explosive
AOC	air officer commanding
AOC-in-C	air officer commanding-in-chief
AP	armour piercing (bomb) or aiming point
API	air position indicator
A/S	anti-submarine
A/T	anti-torpedo
BC	Bomber Command
BCFU	Bomber Command Film Unit
Brawn	codename for FAA operation against *Tirpitz*
BST	British Summer Time (GMT+1)
CAP	combat air patrol
Capt	captain, kapitän zur see, hauptmann
CAS	Chief of the Air Staff
Catechism	codename for RAF operation against *Tirpitz*
Cdr	commander, fregatten-kapitän
CIU	Central Interpretation Unit
CO	commanding officer

CRD	Controller of Research and Development, Ministry of Aircraft Production
CS	capital ship (bomb)
DB Ops	Director Bombing Operations, Air Ministry
DBST	Double British Summer Time (GMT+2); BDST sometimes
DCAS	Deputy Chief of the Air Staff
DFC	Distinguished Flying Cross
DNC	Director or Directorate of Naval Construction
DR	dead reckoning
DSC	Distinguished Service Cross
DSO	Distinguished Service Order
ETA	estimated time of arrival
FAA	Fleet Air Arm
Fg Off	flying officer
Flt Lt	flight lieutenant
F/Sgt	flight sergeant
GAF	German Air Force
Gee	navigational aid
Glycol	coolant liquid
GMT	Greenwich Mean Time
Goodwood	codename for four FAA operations against *Tirpitz*
GP	general purpose (bomb)
Gp Capt	group captain
GST	German Summer Time
HC	high capacity (bomb)
HE	high explosive
H/F	high frequency or heavy flak
Highball	codename for 'bouncing bomb' in Mosquito
HQ	headquarters
IAS	indicated air speed
IFF	identification friend or foe
JPS	Joint Planning Staff (before 1941, Joint Planning Sub-Committee of the Chiefs of Staff Committee)
JSM	Joint Services Mission, Washington
JW	Johnny Walker (mine)
km	kilometre
knot	sea mile
LT	local time
Lt	lieutenant, kapitän-leutnant, oberleutnant
Lt Cdr	lieutenant-commander, korvetten-kapitän
Maj	major
MAP	Ministry of Aircraft Production
Mascot	codename for FAA operation against *Tirpitz*
MC	medium capacity (bomb)
met.	meteorological
Midshipman	faenrich
MO	medical officer
mph	miles per hour

GLOSSARY AND ABBREVIATIONS

MPI	mean point of impact
NCO	non-commissioned officer
NID	Naval Intelligence Division
Obviate	codename for RAF operation against *Tirpitz*
OC	officer commanding
Oiled	codename for RAF operation against *Tirpitz*
Op	operation
ORB	operations record book
Paravane	codename for RAF operation against *Tirpitz*
Planet	codename for FAA operation against *Tirpitz*
Plt Off	pilot officer
PR	photographic reconnaissance
PRU	photographic reconnaissance unit
QFE	Q code: barometric pressure at destination
RAAF	Royal Australian Air Force
RAF	Royal Air Force
RAS	rectified air speed
RCAF	Royal Canadian Air Force
RDF	radio direction finding (radar)
RDX	Research Department Explosive
rev(s)	revolution(s)
RM	Royal Marines
RN	Royal Navy
RNZAF	Royal New Zealand Air Force
RNZN	Royal New Zealand Navy
RNZNVR	Royal New Zealand Navy Volunteer Reserve
rpm	revolutions per minute
R/T	radio-telephony
SABS	stabilised automatic bomb sight
SAP	semi-armour piercing (bomb)
SASO	senior air staff officer
SBNO	senior British naval officer
Seaman	matrose
Servant	codename for Highball operation against *Tirpitz*
Sgt	sergeant
SIS	Secret Intelligence Service (Norway)
SOE	Special Operations Executive
Source	codename for RN X-craft/midget submarine attack on *Tirpitz*
Sqn Ldr	squadron leader
Sub Lt	sub-lieutenant, leutnant zur see
TAG	telegraphist air gunner
TBR	torpedo bomber reconnaissance (aircraft)
Tiger Claw	codename for FAA operation against *Tirpitz*
Thrustful	codename for FAA operation against *Tirpitz* changed to Tungsten
Title	codename for RN 'chariot' operation against *Tirpitz*
Torpex	underwater explosive
TOT	time over target

Tungsten	codename for FAA attack on *Tirpitz*
TV	terminal velocity
U/S	unserviceable
USAAF	United States Army Air Force(s)
USN	United States Navy
USSR	Union of Soviet Socialist Republics
VA2 HF	Vice-Admiral, Second-in-Command Home Fleet
VC	Victoria Cross
VCNS	Vice-Chief of the Naval Staff
VHF	very high frequency
WA	Western Air (plans)
Wg Cdr	wing commander
WO	War Office or warrant officer
W/Op	wireless operator
W/T	wireless telegraphy

PREFACE

HUNTERS AND PREY

'Last night's raid successful. *Tirpitz* sunk.' The terse words, with which Air Vice-Marshal the Hon. R.A. Cochrane opened his morning staff conference at Bomber Command's No. 5 Group near Grantham, Lincolnshire, on 13 November 1944, signalled the climax of a prolonged, and often costly, series of attempts by the Royal Air Force and Fleet Air Arm to destroy the massive enemy warship. Ever since her pre-war launch, the battleship's formidable main armament and menacing potential had cast a baleful influence over Allied strategy, far beyond the confines of the North Sea. Not any more.

The story of the break-out, chase and cornering of *Bismarck* in the Atlantic during May 1941, heightened by her spectacular annihilation of the 'mighty' battlecruiser *Hood* and further illustrated by the dramatic film, *Sink the Bismarck*, continues to capture popular imagination.

The fate of her sister ship is considerably less well known. Nevertheless, without ever passing the Denmark Straits or taking part in a major naval engagement, *Tirpitz* had much greater long-term impact on British political and military thinking during the Second World War. The spectre of her emerging into the Atlantic to wreak havoc along trade routes and among troop transports or to join powerful enemy warships in French ports, presented a truly terrifying image.

TIRPITZ

At times, *Tirpitz* put the international Allied alliance under direct strain. For, simply by her presence within range, she threatened the critical Arctic convoys to the Soviet Union, which thus needed strong protection. The Royal Navy was obliged to keep in home waters a formidable assembly of battleships, aircraft carriers, cruisers, destroyers and support vessels, supplemented from mid-1942 by American units. On several occasions, news that *Tirpitz* might either be at sea or about to sail practically demonstrated her latent ability to create chaos. Fear that she would shortly be steaming over the horizon in July 1942 caused dispersal and ultimate devastation of unprotected merchant ships in the Murmansk-bound PQ17 convoy. This débâcle and, at other times, the interruption of the entire convoy programme because naval escorts were more urgently required to cover the invasion of Sicily or for D-day duty, put Winston Churchill under fierce pressure from both Franklin D. Roosevelt and Joseph Stalin, who wanted sailings to continue regardless.

From the outbreak of war in September 1939, during her fitting-out and subsequent trials at Wilhelmshaven and Kiel, RAF Bomber Command frequently tried to sink *Tirpitz*. But her defences were too strong and British bombs too flimsy to scratch the armoured giant. Magnetic mines optimistically dropped in the hope that her keel would be more vulnerable also proved woefully inadequate.

Recognition that bombers might pose a terminal threat to battleships had only slowly and tortuously evolved. Single-engined biplanes, which in the words of a contemporary observer 'staggered' across the English Channel to France at 60mph in August 1914, four years later had given way to specialised multi-engined reconnaissance, fighter and bomber machines. Ranges, speeds and size of bomb-loads mushroomed. In November 1918, the Handley Page V/1500 four-engined bomber, carrying 2,000lb of bombs and capable of travelling from England to Berlin and back at 85mph, was in service. By the Armistice, the bomber had proved itself an integral and valuable part of each country's military arsenal.

PREFACE: HUNTERS AND PREY

Although the Royal Naval Air Service (which during the First World War unilaterally broke free from the Royal Flying Corps) did use bombers and the Royal Air Force, once formed in 1918, developed aircraft carriers, many admirals and government ministers discounted bombers as a threat to battleships. In the United States, William Mitchell, an air power enthusiast who had exercised tactical command of American squadrons with the US First Army on the Western Front, publicly disagreed. He was appointed Assistant Chief of the infant Army Air Force post-war and during bombing trials in July 1921 his aeroplanes sank the anchored former German battleship *Ostfriesland* and cruiser *Frankfurt*. Two months later they dealt similarly with the obsolete American battleship, *Alabama*. In 1923, Mitchell's bombers despatched *Virginia* and *New Jersey*. Battleships, he declared, were indisputably vulnerable to bombs and aerial torpedoes. His critics dismissed the trials as worthless. The hulks had been undefended. No guns opposed the attackers and Mitchell disregarded the agreed rules by using 2,000lb bombs. In turn, he defended his views in copious articles, to which his opponents reacted even more vigorously. The Secretary of the Navy, Josephus Daniel, declared that Mitchell would be 'blown to atoms long before he gets close enough to drop salt upon the tail of the enemy'. *Ostfriesland* had sunk in 21 mins, but when the incomplete hull of the new battleship *Washington* was bombed in August 1924, it proved a much tougher proposition: a finished, well-defended version would allegedly be impossible to sink.

Polarised opinion likewise appeared in Britain during the House of Commons' debate on the 1922 Air Estimates. A succession of speakers drew attention to the implications of Mitchell's experiments for future warfare, only for naval supporters to reiterate that the American trials were unrealistic and that contemporary warships were considerably better constructed and equipped to withstand air attack than the old ones. Shortly before the Second World War, Gp Capt A.T. Harris served in London on the Chiefs of Staff Inter-Service Joint Planning Sub-Committee with Capt T.S.V. Phillips RN, who confidently maintained that capital ships were invulnerable to air attack. Harris had long been convinced about the ability of RAF bombers to immobilise warships. 'The trouble with you, Tom', he said, 'is that when you're hit by a bomb, you'll say it's a bloody great mine.' Commanding Force Z aboard the ill-fated *Prince of Wales*, Phillips would tragically discover the truth of Harris's assertion at the hands of Japanese bombers in the South China Sea on 10 December 1941. Curiously, on 5 November Churchill told Dominion prime ministers that, if *Tirpitz* seemed likely to break into the Atlantic, *Prince of Wales* might be recalled to Britain en route to Singapore.

Before the catastrophe in the Far East, the Fleet Air Arm had sunk three Italian battleships in Taranto harbour on 11 November 1940 and on 7 December 1941 Japanese aircraft devastated the American Pacific fleet at Pearl Harbor. Both attacks achieved complete surprise. However, to prove Mitchell's (and Harris's) point with *Tirpitz*, British airmen would need to annihilate a well-equipped, modern battleship, specifically constructed to resist aerial torpedoes and bombs, and fully expecting air raids.

Having avoided destruction in German ports, in January 1942 *Tirpitz* sailed for Norway. For the next three years at four different locations (Trondheim, Narvik, Alten Fjord and Tromso), punctuated by most gallant Royal Navy operations with two-men 'chariot' torpedoes and midget submarines plus attempts to lure *Tirpitz* into a fleet action, aircraft of the Fleet Air Arm, RAF Coastal Command and RAF Bomber Command sought to sink the battleship. To do so, the bombers and on occasions their fighter escorts, flew in the face of a blistering array of flak, smoke canisters and the warship's own 15in guns. Enemy fighters stationed in the vicinity of the German battleship's different anchorages posed a dangerous further threat. Fourteen air attacks were mounted, several others cancelled due to the fickle weather, forecasting of which proved particularly hazardous; and Soviet bombers were credited with carrying out at least one independent night operation.

PREFACE: HUNTERS AND PREY

A bewildering collection of ambitious, even bizarre, schemes, which never attained operational status, emphasised the increasing desperation of planners. The prospect of using American B-17 Flying Fortresses to bomb the enemy battleship often appeared – ultimately fruitlessly – on the military agenda. Hampden torpedo bombers were sent to bases in the northern Soviet Union in 1942, but *Tirpitz* uncooperatively failed to sail within range and the venture was abandoned. That same year, Beauforts were flown from the English coast to north Scotland, before commonsense prevailed and an extremely dubious operation was called off. Suicidally, crews had been expected to attack the target, then (with insufficient fuel to regain friendly territory) bale out, take to their dinghy and await arrival of Air-Sea Rescue services in the freezing wastes of the northern North Sea. Range, in reality, was a crucial factor, especially after the target moved north of Trondheim. This made a return flight from Scotland hazardous, if not impossible, even for aircraft with greater endurance than the Beaufort. In 1943, two ideas for using Mosquitoes (one involving a smaller version of Barnes Wallis's bouncing bomb, the other flying off aircraft carriers) were shelved, partly due to the eternal range problem.

Like the 1940–1 attacks on *Tirpitz* in German ports, the limited effect of existing bombs undermined the bravery and skill of crews, who flew into an aerial Valley of Death time and again. In 1944, a viable weapon came into production. Four years earlier, Barnes Wallis had put forward comprehensive plans for a 10 ton bomb, which would penetrate the earth beside a target to burrow beneath it before exploding. The 5 ton version, codenamed Tallboy and within the carrying capacity of a Lancaster, could perhaps achieve similar results if dropped beside a battleship. Moreover, it had a much better chance of slicing through deck armour than the 500lb SAP or even 1,600lb AP bombs previously used. And so it proved. Tallboys dropped by Lancaster bombers on 15 September, 29 October and 12 November 1944 at last accounted for the enemy's principal surface threat.

TIRPITZ

Throughout the months and years that the Fleet Air Arm and RAF attempted to eliminate the German battleship, despite poor weather which often frustrated their efforts, photo-reconnaissance pilots supplied invaluable information about her precise whereabouts, defences and movements. Contemporary references to the pivotal nature of agents' activities and the testimony of prisoners of war should be treated with caution. In practice, much important information was gleaned from Ultra decrypts of German Enigma machine messages. Delays in breaking code variations or, for example during part of December 1943 and September 1944, inability to do so at all caused consternation. Nor should dedicated Norwegian patriots, who risked their lives to transmit clandestine radio reports, be overlooked. For, without accurate intelligence, the planners and aircrew were effectively blind.

Later, when isolated in a Norwegian fjord, *Tirpitz* acquired seductive nicknames like 'Lonely Queen' or 'Lone Wolf', even 'Solitary Dinosaur' and 'Poor Old Lone Tirpitz'. From the outset, infinitely less romantically, Winston Churchill dubbed her 'this brute' or, simply, 'the beast' for which the hunt must proceed with all speed.

1

PINPRICKS, 1939-41

On 1 April 1939, a vast crowd gathered in the naval dockyard at Wilhelmshaven in Jade Bay on the German North Sea coast. Civilian employees and their families joined local officials, high-ranking officers, Nazi Party dignitaries and a host of other invited guests. Reichsführer Adolf Hitler boasted that to bring people by train from all over Germany, Austria and Czechoslovakia was 'the best propaganda'. After acknowledging acclaim from the massed ranks of sailors and cheers of the waving spectators from the back of an open car as he was driven slowly towards an elevated podium, Hitler adroitly used the stage-managed occasion once more to trumpet the merits of Teutonic military might.

Above the throng towered the hull of an enormous battleship ('the pride of the German navy' to one ebullient newsreel commentator) without turrets or superstructure but impressively dressed overall in colourful bunting. The launching ceremony was performed by Frau Ilse von Hassell, wife of the German ambassador in Rome and elder daughter of Grand Admiral Alfred von Tirpitz, the architect of German naval power at the turn of the century. As the traditional bottle of wine smashed against the bow and Hitler ostentatiously saluted, workmen lowered two signs from the deck to reveal in Gothic script the name of the great vessel, 'Tirpitz'. This newest battleship brashly

1

reaffirmed that Nazi ambitions were not confined to European land conquest. Another naval arms race was gathering pace; in the eighteen months prior to December 1941, between them Britain, France, the United States, Italy, Japan and Germany would complete ten battleships.

Tirpitz was the latest in a burgeoning miscellany of vessels designed to create a modern German navy, and signal the death knell of the tonnage restriction imposed on it by the victorious allies after the First World War. By 1939, three 14,000 ton 'pocket battleships' (Panzerschiffe) with six 11in (280mm) guns and a speed of 26 knots; two nominally 26,000 (in fact, 31,000) ton battlecruisers with nine 11in guns; two 8in gun heavy cruisers; six 6in gun light cruisers; thirty-four destroyers; and fifty-seven U-boats had been launched. Two 35,000 ton battleships (Schlachtschiffe F and G) were under construction. Hitler's aim was to build a fleet powerful enough to challenge Britain in 1944.

Without fuel or ammunition *Tirpitz* displaced 41,700, fully laden 52,600 tons. 828ft (250.5m) long, 119ft (36m) broad with a 36ft (11m) maximum draught, she had double and transverse internal bulkheads to guard against torpedo attack, the effects of mines and bombs falling close-by. Externally, like a tortoise's shell, hardened steel protected the ship's sides from forward of the front turret to aft of the rear, 12.5in (320mm) thick at 6.5ft (2m) below the waterline up to the battery deck, then 5.6in (145mm) to the upper deck. This shield sought to withstand 15in shells from 20km. Beyond it, more reinforced steel up to 5.9in (150mm) forward and 3.5in (90mm) aft completed the ship's outer skin. The upper deck itself was covered with 2in (50mm) strengthened plate, designed to detonate contact-fused bombs and frustrate plunging shells fired from a distance. Some 20ft underneath, the deck immediately above sensitive machinery and magazines had been reinforced with armour between 4.7in (120mm) and 3.9in (100mm) thick to stop bombs or shells that did get through the upper deck. The sides of this main armoured deck were 120mm thick and sloped almost to the bottom of the armoured belt, thus giving even more protection to vital machinery and other control systems within the ship.

Additionally, sixteen 4.1in (105mm) quick-firing guns on twin mountings, four each side, with a 11 miles (18,000m) range, sixteen 37mm and sixteen (later reputedly increased to ninety) single, twin and quadruple-mounted 20mm close-range flak guns were installed to cope with air attacks. The main armament comprised eight 15in (38cm) guns in four turrets – Anton and Bruno forward, Cesar and Dora aft – with a 22.4 miles (36,200m) range; twelve 5.9in (15cm) guns in six double turrets, three either side amidships, constituted the secondary armament with a range of 14.2 miles (23,000m). All turrets, gunnery control and command posts were further individually protected with yet more armour although the light flak positions lacked overhead cover, which would result in heavy casualties during air attacks. Two quadruple 21in (53.3cm) torpedo mountings on deck and four Arado 196a seaplanes, principally for reconnaissance but armed with three 7.92mm machine-guns and two 20mm cannon for defence and capable of carrying one 110lb (50kg) bomb under each wing to discourage hostile submarines from remaining on the surface, completed the protection for a crew of 2,340 officers and men. With a maximum speed of 30.8, normal 28 knots, *Tirpitz* had an endurance of 8,125 miles (13,000km) at 19 knots. Contemporary claims made her capable of 34 knot bursts. She was thus theoretically faster, better equipped and more heavily protected than any of her potential adversaries. To Admiral A.G. Golovko, C-in-C the Soviet Northern Fleet, she was a 'huge, modern floating fortress . . . an awesome machine'. German writers called her 'a behemoth'.

Post-war, with the findings of several investigations to hand and German large-scale drawings at his disposal, the Admiralty's Directorate of Naval Construction concluded that there was 'nothing sensational about the design of the *Tirpitz*. She was merely a very large battleship, designed on conventional lines, propelled by three screws driven by steam turbines.' Her main armament was distributed 'in the conventional way'; two turrets forward and two aft, not in weight-saving 'triple and quadruple arrangements'. There were separate low-angle and high-angle secondary batteries, not dual purpose mountings. Moreover, *Tirpitz*'s much-vaunted underwater protection on inspection proved 'inferior' to that of contemporary Allied battleships, her broad beam built for stability not protection. 'Fine watertight subdivisions . . . [were] a complete myth. . . . Her watertight integrity was in several ways subordinate to requirements of convenience', for instance with the provision of spacious engine rooms. Every transverse bulkhead 'was pierced by watertight doors on the lower and middle platform decks, a menace which had been eliminated from H.M. ships for many years'. It appeared, though, the battleship could exceed 31 knots in short bursts, and despite the perceived relative shortcomings remained a 'formidable' fighting unit 'capable of defeating attacks by heavy shell and all but the heaviest bombs'. Even in retrospect, the British Naval Staff referred to 'this German mastodon'; a tribute to her great strength.

The contract for Schlachtschiff G (*Tirpitz*) was placed in January 1936, but construction could not commence until 24 October, three weeks after the battlecruiser *Scharnhorst* left the slipway. Completed in November 1940, *Tirpitz* was commissioned on 25 February 1941 with Capt Karl Topp in command, and would be the largest warship to see action during the war outside of the Pacific.

The British had good reason to be concerned. Grand Admiral Erich Räder, the German navy's commander-in-chief, acknowledged on 3 September 1939 that it was 'in no way adequately equipped for the great struggle with Great Britain': fleet action was out of the question. But 'the pocket battleships . . . if skilfully used should be able to carry out cruiser warfare on the high seas for some time', in effect, acting as independent commerce raiders. He was echoing the Battle Instructions for the German navy issued in May: 'merchant raiders' would roam the high seas, avoiding combat to preserve maximum effectiveness, while

U-boats combed the coasts and the Luftwaffe attacked enemy ports. *Admiral Graf Spee*'s forays into the Indian and Atlantic oceans, which accounted for nine merchantmen until the warship was cornered in the River Plate in December 1939, proffered a grave warning. By the end of September 1940, five 'disguised raiders' had accounted for thirty-six merchant ships, totalling 235,000 tons; and, in the first quarter of 1941, the battlecruisers *Scharnhorst* and *Gneisenau*, pocket battleship *Admiral Scheer*, heavy cruiser *Admiral Hipper* and other surface raiders together despatched another 300,000 tons of Allied shipping. Breaking into the northern Atlantic from the North Sea in May 1941, *Bismarck* not only sank *Hood* but forced the Admiralty to strip escorts from convoys and deploy 7 battleships, 2 aircraft carriers, 12 cruisers, 27 destroyers and 6 submarines to challenge her. To President Roosevelt, Churchill expressed relief that a joint sortie by *Bismarck* and *Tirpitz* had been averted, but *Tirpitz* alone might still harry Atlantic shipping or menace Arctic convoys taking much-needed supplies to the Soviet Union. Like the German High Seas Fleet during the First World War, she could commit significant numbers of Allied warships to a defensive, watching role by simply remaining in port, in Churchill's words creating 'a general fear' by threatening 'all points at once'.

Prior to *Bismarck*'s demise, her sister ship had certainly not been ignored. Pre-war contingency plans, in particular Western Air Plans WA 7(a) and WA 7(b), provided for air attacks on German naval vessels in port and, nearing completion in Wilhelmshaven, *Tirpitz* attracted particular attention. However, pessimistic prospects for successful bombing operations from high or low level by Blenheims, Harrows and Whitleys examined by Air Staff planners in January 1939 were reinforced in the light of experience: on 25 November, No. 4 Bomber Group concluded that it was 'only possible to distinguish between warships and merchant ships on a bright moonlit night with a clear sky'.

In the opening phase of the war, photographic reconnaissance slowly became organised. On 22 November

1939, the Special Survey Flight flew its first successful Spitfire mission, expanded to become the Photographic Reconnaissance Unit (PRU) in July 1940 and by 1945 would have four squadrons operational in Europe. But, when war broke out, essentially reconnaissance rested with individual bomber groups. On 4 September 1939, therefore, a 2 Group Blenheim flew over Wilhelmshaven and thereafter similar 'photographic and visual' operations were carried out by single aircraft or small groups of Blenheims, Whitleys and Wellingtons. They recorded the presence and position of enemy warships, including *Tirpitz*, but establishment of a dedicated photographic organisation brought more systematic cover. Between 8 April and 25 September 1940, twenty PRU sorties reported the battleship in Bauhafen, those of 19 May noting 'guns are in turrets but less complete than Bismarck' and 6 June 'outwardly appears nearly complete'. On 28 September and 1 October, the enemy warship was seen in the floating dock of Scheerhaven, before nine reports between 10 October 1940 and 2 January 1941 put her again in Bauhafen, on the latter date 'emitting steam'. The next sortie on 29 January found the ship at Scheerhaven, before she returned once more to Bauhafen and remained there on 26 February, the day following her commissioning ceremony. Shortly afterwards, the berth was empty, and it soon became clear that *Tirpitz* had left Wilhelmshaven.

Until the German invasion of France and the Low Countries on 10 May 1940, aggressive action against Wilhemshaven and other naval ports was forbidden. The first specific operation against the battleship, as distinct from more general raids on the dockyard area which might incidentally include her, involved eleven 5 Group Hampdens during the night of 9/10 July. Bomber Command recorded, 'owing to the searchlight activity, darkness and haze, results of attacks were not observed' – in fact, they missed the target. Then, on 24/25 July, two 4 Group Whitleys 'proceeded to attack the battleship *Tirpitz* at Wilhelmshaven. . . . No results were observed owing to weather conditions', which forced twelve others

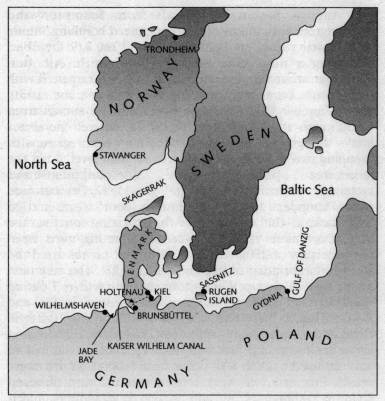

Tirpitz: Area of trials and early attacks, 1939–41

to abort the operation. Lack of success prompted Winston Churchill to goad senior officers into more effective action. On 2 August 1940, he sent a sharp memo to the Admiralty, presumably with carrier-borne operations in mind: 'Please let me have a report of the possibility of air attacks on *Bismarck* and *Tirpitz*. This seems to be one of the most vital steps to take.' Two days later, he wrote in similar vein to the Air Ministry emphasising that these warships were 'targets of supreme importance'.

No Fleet Air Arm action took place, but another inconclusive attack by 5 Group Hampdens occurred on

5/6 August. Seventeen aircraft from Scampton and Waddington, both in Lincolnshire, reported bombing '*Tirpitz* in a floating dock at Wilhelmshaven' on 8/9 October, heralding a mini blitz on her that month. All nine Waddington aircraft reported attacking the target, seeing their bombs burst but not being able to assess the results due to 'intense flak'. Two days later, fourteen aircraft from Waddington and Lindholme, Yorkshire, secured 'no direct hits' – though the three from Lindholme were credited with dropping twelve 500lb GP bombs from 'high level . . . in the target area . . . [in] a bright moon . . . [despite] intense and systematic defensive AA barrage'. On 11/12 October four more Hampdens from Lindholme in 'poor' weather tried their luck, as the 'majority' of the attacking force turned back. Once more 'no accurate results were observed' from the collection of 250lb GP and 500lb SAP bombs amid the strong concentration of flak and searchlights. The very next night, forty 3 Group Wellingtons and thirty-five 5 Group Hampdens set out for *Scharnhorst* and *Gneisenau* in Kiel and *Tirpitz*. Due to 'very bad weather conditions' – 10/10ths cloud and 'severe icing' – only four Hampdens even located Wilhelmshaven and just one from Lindholme claimed to have dropped a 500lb SAP bomb from 9,000ft on the target vessel. Precisely one week later it was the turn of seven 3 Group Wellingtons: 'All bombs seen to straddle Bauhafen and the Tirpitz and many large fires and explosions', Bomber Command noted. Disappointingly, though, 'no direct hits were reported on the battleship'. On 25/26 November, five 4 Group aircraft from 51 and 78 squadrons bombed in 'impossible conditions' of 10/10ths cloud by aiming at the 'concentration of flak and searchlights'. Unfortunately, none of these various attacks before the close of 1940 significantly damaged *Tirpitz*.

The new year brought scant improvement. The battleship constituted a special target for seven Wellingtons of 75 Squadron from Feltwell, Lincolnshire, on 8/9 January 1941. 3 Group's ORB recorded: 'Pleasantly surprising success was scored . . . majority of the aircraft found the target and some hits or near misses were claimed on the ship.' On

11/12 January 1941, sixteen aircraft from 49 and 83 squadrons took off from Scampton for *Tirpitz*, 'still alongside in the Bauhafen at Wilhelmshaven'. Two 'made attacks from below broken cloud and claim some success', eight 'from above cloud, and in consequence no definite results were seen'. Operational conditions throughout January 1941 were scarcely ideal. Some days 9in of snow had to be cleared from station runways, visibility rarely exceeded 1,500yds during the day, at night 500yds. In the laconic words of the monthly meteorological summary, the weather was 'generally bad for flying'. Thus eight 83 Squadron Hampdens endured 'intense cold' on 16/17 January en route for the enemy warship, causing two to return early and one to ditch in the North Sea with engine trouble. During the same operation only two of the ten aircraft from RAF Waddington attacked the target, with 'no results observed owing to cloud'. Twenty-five 3 Group Wellingtons were detailed to bomb *Tirpitz* on 29/30 January. Although they reached the Wilhelmshaven area and did drop their bombs, none reported having done so on the primary target. On 9 February, thirteen aircraft from 83 Squadron at RAF Scampton took off for Wilhelmshaven, briefed 'to cause maximum destruction and disturbance' to *Tirpitz*, but like the five survivors of the mid-January operation failed to hit her. Of the thirty that took off to do so, twenty-six Wellingtons from 40, 115, 214 and 218 squadrons based at Wyton (Cambridgeshire), Marham (Norfolk) and Stradishall (Suffolk) attacked the ship on 27/28 February, but 3 Group reported that 'weather interfered greatly with the success of the operation' with no reliable observation of results. The following night, twenty-three 5 Group aircraft left Scampton and Waddington, four from 49 Squadron carrying two 2,000lb AP bombs, but 10/10ths cloud down to 9,000ft in the target area 'coupled with ground haze' made identification impossible. 'Nobody' saw the target and only four machines bombed 'the position of the ship'. Three of these were from the eleven that took off from RAF Waddington. In fact, the battleship would soon be on the move, and the last attempt to sink her in Wilhelmshaven had gone. A gloomy Air Ministry summary reflected that twin-engined aircraft, even when dropping 2,000lb AP bombs, enjoyed 'no success'. Attempts 'to run "M" mines underneath', when the battleship was fitting out in the Bauhafen, were unsuccessful and, enigmatically, 'this type of attack was too costly to be continued', presumably in terms of overall effort as few bombers had been lost while attacking *Tirpitz*.

By early March 1941, the battleship had negotiated the Kaiser Wilhelm Canal to reach Kiel and prepare for sea trials in the Baltic. On 12 and 13 March, PRU aircraft found her in the southern floating dock; five days later she had vanished. Other intelligence sources confirmed that *Tirpitz* had entered the Baltic. Not until 28 May was she photographed in the southern floating dock in Kiel once more and two days later she had berthed at the Deutsche Werke. However, on 3 June that anchorage was empty. PRU did not find her alongside the north wall of the Scheerbauen (Wik) until 17 June, where six subsequent sorties placed her until 10 July. Within two days, though, the warship had returned to the southern floating dock, where she still lay on 20 and 25 July 'camouflaged with netting'. A PRU sortie on 2 August discovered that berth empty, but four days afterwards the battleship was identified 'at south wall of entrance to Inner Harbour (Naval Arsenal)', where by 19 August camouflage netting had been draped over her. The following day, two floating cranes were seen working alongside, apparently in connection with the main turrets, and an anti-torpedo boom had been put around the ship. On 29 August, she had moved to Wik Commercial Harbour, as yet uncamouflaged, but with cranes again in attendance. Two days later the anti-torpedo boom could be clearly seen in position. None the less, *Tirpitz* was soon on the move again. On 1 September she was gone from Wik, to be observed steaming off Holtenau 'towards the port'. Three days later she was berthed at the entrance to the Inner Dockyard Basin, where the main turrets were still being attended to. On 9 September she was manoeuvring in Kiel

Fjord north-east of Strander Bucht. Another sortie on 12 September located her in Strander Bucht. Preceded by an armed motor vessel, on 13 September *Tirpitz* was noted in Kiel Fjord, the following day once more berthed at the entrance to the Inner Dockyard Basin. However, on 15 September she had left harbour, and was not discovered back in Kiel until 9 November, berthed at the Southern Yard Quay of the Deutsche Werke. By 29 November, the battleship had moved to the entrance to the Inner Dockyard Basin. The next sortie on 10 January failed to find her. *Tirpitz* had already left Kiel, this time for good.

The battleship's many absences from Kiel had been spent in the Baltic. On 1 April and 15 May, she was reported by intelligence sources to be at Gydnia, where Hitler inspected her on 5 May and Capt Topp requested that his command might accompany *Bismarck* on her forthcoming foray into the Atlantic – in vain. Räder insisted on completion of sea trials. So, in the ensuing months, flak guns fired on towed targets, torpedoes were discharged, damage-control drills and launches of the seaplanes carried out, tankers and merchant ships took part in re-supply exercises. On 3 June testing of the main and secondary armament against the pre-Dreadnought battleship *Hessen* was observed off Rugen Island, after which *Tirpitz* returned to Kiel. The British naval attaché in Stockholm reported on 2 July: 'Certain guns replaced and alterations made after recent trials, which had not been satisfactory.' By 15 September, *Tirpitz* was at sea once more and shortly afterwards she was identified in company with *Admiral Scheer*, several cruisers and destroyers in the vicinity of Sassnitz. Two separate intelligence reports noted her main armament being fired on 20 and 21 September north-east of Rugen, which must have proved satisfactory. For, with the Baltic a potential battle zone as German troops advanced up the coastline towards Leningrad, from 26 to 29 September the battleship joined a powerful assembly of German warships off the Aaland Islands to deter the Soviet fleet from venturing out of Kronstadt. Back in the western Baltic, between 10 and 18 October anti-torpedo trials were conducted, followed by further exercises with two cruisers. By the end of October, *Tirpitz* was in Kiel, where she remained for most of November. On 6 December, another report from Stockholm revealed that more 'gunnery exercises' had been carried out recently between Lübeck and Gotenhaven, and it soon emerged that her final fleet exercises, involving *Admiral Hipper*, took place 13–20 December, with anti-mine degaussing trials off Hela on 28 December. An Ultra intercept of 2 January 1942 disclosed that a faulty diesel generator would be replaced at Wilhelmshaven in mid-January. This gives some credibility to the claim that, when *Tirpitz*'s chief engineer protested that the ship would sail with defects and lack of spares, Topp told him that to remain in port would be to invite renewed, dangerous air attacks. On completion of all her final sea trials, Räder inspected *Tirpitz* on 6 January. Four days later, Topp declared her fully operational.

Meanwhile, Winston Churchill fretted that *Tirpitz* was preparing to 'paralyse our North Atlantic trade', intensifying pressure for decisive air action against her. Attacking the battleship at sea, especially in the confines of the Baltic within range of the shore-based Luftwaffe, was not viable. Bombing her in Kiel – where, unlike Wilhelmshaven in 1939 and 1940, she frequently changed berth and unpredictably left port – had to be tried. Several general operations were mounted on Kiel harbour and the dockyard area early in 1941. Then, on 3 June, poor weather caused cancellation of a 63-bomber attack on *Tirpitz* by 3 Group. But on 20/21 June 5 Group Hampdens did take off for her, 'a difficult target for a non-moonlit night, and 10/10ths cloud between 1,000ft and 3,000ft made it impossible'. Accurate bombing could not, therefore, be achieved: officially twenty-two aircraft dropped six 2,000lb AP, fifty-six 500lb SAP and twenty-eight 250lb SAP bombs on the estimated position 'of the town', not the specific target. Eight times between 24 June and 2 November, 5 Group aircraft bombed 'Kiel dockyards' (*sic*) without singling out the battleship. Similarly, bombers from 3 and 4 Groups, whose battle order had now been strengthened by the arrival of four-engined Stirlings and Halifaxes, carried out eighteen attacks on repair and shipbuilding facilities in the Kiel dockyards between 11 March and 6 November. Some operations, though, did attempt specifically to find *Tirpitz*. For instance, on 28/29 May the battleship was the primary target for fourteen Whitleys of 4 Group's 58 and 78 squadrons. However, 'owing to 10/10ths cloud, severe icing and electrical storms . . . with lightning playing round the fuselage, wing tips, leading edge of wing and the aircrews . . . precluding use of the wireless in some cases, it was quite impossible to identify the target or pin-point its position, and the results of any attacks were unknown'. And, of the eleven aircraft from Linton, Yorkshire, and Middleton St George, Durham, sent to attack the ship on 25/26 June 1941, only seven unsuccessfully did so.

On 14 June 1941, the War Cabinet received a comprehensive review of future strategy from inter-Service Joint Planning Staff, which underlined that 'the threat to our sea communications is second only to the threat of invasion'. More specifically, 'intelligence information' on 9 December suggested that German naval units were preparing to break into the Atlantic. Those might well include *Tirpitz*, which was then nearing the end of its trials and in a month would be declared fully operational. Failure to sink her in Wilhelmshaven or Kiel meant that infinitely more difficult operations, involving the RAF and Fleet Air Arm, would be necessary once she left German waters.

2

NORWEGIAN LAIR, 1942

Already perturbed that the First Sea Lord (Admiral of the Fleet Sir Dudley Pound) insisted on retaining three battleships of the *King George V* class (35,000 tons, ten 14in main armament and sixteen 5.25in secondary armament) in home waters to ensure that two would always be ready to counter enemy capital ships in the North Sea, early in 1942 Churchill displayed further irritation to the First Lord of the Admiralty. He complained vigorously that the (inaccurate) practice of referring constantly to 'Admiral von Tirpitz' in correspondence, records and signals represented a waste of time and energy: 'Surely *Tirpitz* is good enough for the beast.'

Loss of *Bismarck* forced the Germans to think carefully about *Tirpitz*. Concerned about the amount of fuel required and the fate of *Bismarck*, Räder advised against entering the Atlantic, opting instead to send the battleship to Norway. Unnerved by commando raids along the Norwegian coast, lest they presaged a full-scale Allied invasion and conscious of the need to retain the ice-free port of Narvik for the transportation of critical Swedish iron ore throughout the year, Hitler concurred. The decision was confirmed on 29 December, with 10 January 1942 as the operative date, the Nazi leader underlining his fear that loss of Narvik 'might be of decisive importance for the outcome of the war'. This echoed the naval staff's appreciation three years previously that, with the British likely to opt for open blockade, the northern area of the North Sea would be 'the decisive point of the war at sea'.

Before *Tirpitz* sailed, Räder made quite clear that she was going to Trondheim, roughly half-way between the Skagerrak and the northern port of Narvik, 'to protect our position in the Norwegian and Arctic areas by threatening the flank of enemy operations against the northern Norwegian areas, and by attacking White Sea convoys . . . to tie down enemy forces in the Atlantic, so that they cannot operate in the Mediterranean, the Indian Ocean or the Pacific'. He did not anticipate a purely passive role: 'The operational objective can be attained fully only by actual operations', which might include attacking Arctic convoys, bombarding points of military significance or 'interference with enemy operations'. In the event, the battleship left for Norway five days later than planned, not via the Skagerrak, where in the narrows hostile eyes might spot and report her progress (as Räder rightly suspected had happened with *Bismarck*) but through the canal from Kiel to Wilhelmshaven.

PRU surveillance had last located the warship on 29 November 1941 in Kiel. Her position thereafter remained obscure until Ultra picked up a message from 'Gydnia Arsenal' to *Tirpitz* on 6 January 1942 confirming that 'exchange of gyro-compass transformer is possible'. This strongly suggested that the enemy vessel was in the Baltic. A corrupt transmission six days later from the battleship to Navy Group North included 'onward passage at 1700', which might reasonably be associated with signals earlier that day and the previous one detailing escort and mine-sweeping duties 'for passage of our forces proceeding from East to West' in the Baltic on 12 January. *Tirpitz* anticipated reaching Holtenau, at the eastern end of the Kiel canal at 0700 on 13 January. There she duly off-loaded unnecessary stores and equipment for the journey through the canal. Even so, her masts only just cleared the bridges. Later that day, she anchored at Brunsbüttel at the western end of the canal to take on fuel, together with the material that had been put ashore and transported independently from Holtenau. At 0832 on 14 January, the battleship signalled Wilhelmshaven Naval Dockyard: 'Arrival Wilhelmshaven on the evening of 14/1 at H.W. [high water] Slack water intended. Request confirmation regarding lock, tugs at Buoy Z, berth and commencement of work on Diesel-Electrics early on 15/1.' Later that day, at 1627, Navy Group North enquired whether enemy aircraft had flown over her 'on passage to the Jade', clearly implying that she had indeed sailed from Brunsbüttel to Wilhelmshaven.

However, different German records, quoted post-war by British naval intelligence, show *Tirpitz* leaving Brunsbüttel directly for Trondheim on 14 January. Other Ultra intercepts of messages from her during the evening, requesting the opening and illumination of the Schillig Roads boom at 2330 on the 14th and Heligoland Boom on the 15th at 0200, also suggest this. Nor is this disproved by a long signal to *Tirpitz* from Navy Group North at 2329 on 14 January, which incidentally highlighted fears of aerial detection and attack: 'On 15/1 good visibility is to be expected in the North Sea although weather will be bad over central England and Scotland with poor take-off conditions. Reconnaissance from there is not therefore very probable. Improved flying weather for the North Sea is to be expected on 16/1.'

Without doubt, though, intercepted wireless traffic, not all decoded but almost invariably designated 'immediate', between Navy Group North, the battleship, shore defences, U-boats and surface vessels along the route to Norway, indicated that she was at sea on 15 January. In the early afternoon, at 1349, Navy Group North summarised weather conditions in 'Western Skagerrak' for her, adding: 'Conditions of taking-off are bad from the Midlands to the north of England', revealing once more fear of aerial detection. At 1643, *Tirpitz* was told: 'If aircraft fly over you before 1730hrs proceed to the Skagerrak through the Hanstholm Boom Gap', presumably to abort the passage.

Relying on its own wireless interception service, at 1745 on 15 January Navy Group North warned that, despite the weather forecast, reconnaissance aircraft from RAF Leuchars, Fife, were active in the Jutland/Stavanger area. Encouragingly, however, there was no hint that *Tirpitz*'s passage was suspected, and no increased activity had been detected by the British Home Fleet. At 2037, Naval Group North warned patrolling U-boats, repeating the signal to *Tirpitz*: 'Own warships on passage along west coast of Norway', followed swiftly by orders not to fire on any warship while remaining west of 03 40E. The headquarters was more specific three hours later: 'Our warships on passage to Trondheim.'

It was by no means clear from the intercepted traffic that this would be the German warship's final destination. Messages during 16 January might indicate rather, given her known operational range, that she would acquire more escorts there before sailing further north, possibly even into the Atlantic. At 0919, Navy Group North informed *Tirpitz* that only 'very slight' activity had been noticed from No. 18 Group RAF's reconnaissance bases, with 'nothing unusual in W/T'. So far, so good. Six hours later, the naval headquarters signalled even more optimistically that, with a marked absence of relevant RAF W/T transmissions, 'we have remained unobserved'. Shortly afterwards, at 1548, a signal was logged that was worrying for the British. It came from Navy Group North to the battleship and the 5th Destroyer Flotilla: 'six hours notice for steam'. Further orders from Navy Group North to *Tirpitz* and the flotilla at 1928 required both to maintain a listening watch. At 1837 (repeated 1958) *Tirpitz* asked the Naval Communications Office at Trondheim 'that various degrees of air alarms be transmitted without delay', which indicated both that she had anchored close-by and feared air attack. On the basis of intercepted messages, an aggressive sortie with destroyer protection could not be ruled out.

Decoding of the various transmissions took time, but at 0850 BST on 17 January, Admiral Sir John Tovey (C-in-C Home Fleet) learnt that *Tirpitz* had been at sea the previous day, and at 1642 he was told her arrival at Trondheim with four destroyers on the evening of 16 January. She had

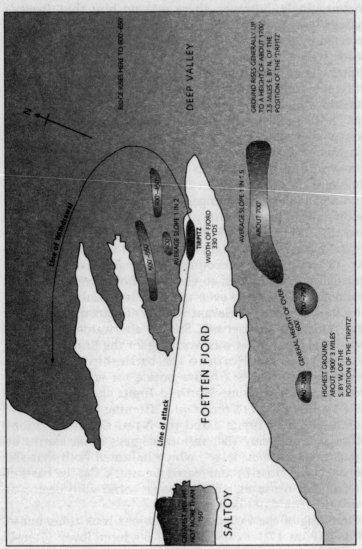

Foetten Fjord, 15 miles east of Trondheim, Norway, from Air Ministry files

entered Trondheim Fjord between shore batteries situated at its entrance, passed the port of Trondheim 40 miles east, and berthed another 15 miles further on, at the head of Foetten Fjord, a cul-de-sac finger off Aasen Fjord (or Aasfjord), in turn a branch of the main waterway. It was ¾ mile wide, surrounded on three sides by steep cliffs and only 30 miles from the Swedish frontier. *Tirpitz*'s grey camouflage merged easily with the surrounding high ground and additional flak positions were quickly established ashore. Anti-submarine nets were already stretched across the entrance to the main fjord, and Capt Topp set about installing more protective booms at the entrance to Foetten Fjord and around the battleship, as well as camouflage over her superstructure.

On 17 January, Topp noted high-flying aircraft above the fjord. Unknown to him, RAF aerial reconnaissance was 'unfortunately incomplete' and confirmation of *Tirpitz*'s position not secured until six days later. No. 1 PRU with Spitfire IVs, stationed at RAF Wick on the north-east coast of Scotland and controlled by Coastal Command, was well-placed for aerial surveillance. At 1250 on 23 January 1942, Flt Lt A.P. Fane landed back at base with photographs of a 'suspected large naval unit' in Foetten Fjord. Developed quickly, they confirmed that *Tirpitz* had anchored close inshore on the north side of the inlet under a steep cliff (approximately a 1 in 2 incline), 'with floating camouflage round bows, and A/T boom in position' at 63 32N 10 54E. Further study of Fane's photos revealed that the ground immediately to the north undulated between 200 and 250ft, with a 650ft ridge approximately 650ft to the north-west. At the end of Foetten Fjord, a deep valley ran eastwards towards 1,700ft high ground approximately 2½ miles away. To the south, the 1/1.5 slope quickly rose to 750ft and reached 1,900ft 3 miles from the warship. The only feasible line of approach was from the North Sea, past Trondheim to skirt or cross Saltoy island, which dominated the entrance to Foetten Fjord. After an attack, turning to starboard or flying straight on towards Sweden were not viable options. So the only chance for withdrawal was to port, avoiding the prominent ridge to the north-west. The pilot of another PRU flight on 25 January did not photograph the berth, but reported 'no major unit visible' which prompted an appended comment by the interpreter, '?camouflage too good'. Even for interpreters, camouflaged vessels photographed from high level were notoriously difficult to discern.

Norwegian resistance members reported *Tirpitz*'s arrival on 16 January, but their distorted radio messages failed to get through. Soon, however, a network of agents infiltrated from Britain and local patriots began to amass detailed information about the battleship, which was successfully transmitted to Britain either by radio or via a clandestine ferry service of former fishing vessels to and from Norway dubbed 'the Shetland bus'. Bjorn Rorholt, a Norwegian officer who had secretly returned to the Trondheim area, was instrumental in organising a surveillance network, including an agent in the Agnes fortress at the entrance to Trondheim Fjord to gather information about the movement of *Tirpitz* and other German vessels. Among the prominent wireless operators, who like Rorholt took enormous personal risks, were Hans Hansen and Egil Lindberg.

News that *Tirpitz* had left Germany gave rise to serious debate in Britain. The C-in-C Home Fleet, Admiral Sir John Tovey, postponed sailing of the Murmansk-bound convoy PQ9, lest the enemy warship be bound for the Arctic. All operations along the Norwegian coast were aborted and cruisers sent to patrol south of Iceland to watch for a break-out into the Atlantic. Winston Churchill particularly pinpointed the implications for the Arctic convoys, reminding the Secretary of State for Air that 'exact and punctual deliveries to Russia are of the utmost importance'. Indeed, in October 1941, the War Cabinet had committed itself to sending a convoy every ten days 'to Russia'. Writing to the First Sea Lord, the Prime Minister anticipated decisive air action: 'Crippling this ship would alter the entire face of the naval war and . . . the loss of 100 machines and 500 airmen would be well compensated for' – a bleak prospect, nevertheless, for aircrew. After *Tirpitz* had been discovered, writing to Major-General Hastings Ismay, Secretary of the Chiefs of Staff Committee on 25 January, the Prime Minister underlined that 'the destruction or even crippling of this ship is the greatest event at sea at the present time. No other target is comparable to it.' Possibly with acute friction between the two Services over air power during the First World War and inter-war years in mind, he added: 'There must be no lack of cooperation between Bomber Command and the Fleet Air Arm and aircraft carriers. A plan should be made to attack both with carrier-borne aircraft and with heavy bombers by daylight or at dawn.' He doubted that the necessary accuracy could be obtained at night, even in moonlight. Heavily underscoring the gravity of the situation, he argued: 'The whole strategy of the war turns at this period on this ship', which was tying down 'four times the number of British capital ships . . . to say nothing of the two new American battleships retained in the Atlantic.' He regarded 'the matter of the highest urgency and importance', intending to raise it at meetings next day of the War Cabinet and of the Defence Committee on the following. At the War Cabinet meeting on Monday 26 January, in answer to a question from the Prime Minister, the First Sea Lord and Chief of the Air Staff assured him 'that the possibility of attacking the *Tirpitz* . . . had been exhaustively examined and it was hoped that an attack would be made as soon as weather conditions were favourable'. Churchill reiterated 'that it was of the utmost importance strategically that the *Tirpitz* should, if possible, be disabled or sunk'.

Ideally, a raid on *Tirpitz* should be carried out before too much flak had been concentrated around her and other defences were in place. However, met. conditions over Norway were liable to pose serious difficulties for any bombing operation. Low stratus cloud usually covered coastal regions, relieved only about three days a month when a south-easterly wind prevailed. A discouraging analysis by the Air Staff of probable conditions between May and July illustrated this problem. Winds exceeding Force 4 could frequently be expected, 'Force 7 or more' were not unusual. During May the wind direction tended to be 'N. to N.E. . . . with S.W. as a "runner up", while in June and July S. to S.W. is more prevalent than the next most frequent direction – N.E.'. That was not all. 'The further you go up the fjord, the lighter, though somewhat squallier, become the winds.' These months were 'the foggiest time of the year' and 'the further North the more generally cloudy do the skies become'. A crucial added difficulty involved forecasting the local weather once bombers had completed their long journey across the North Sea. Fine conditions at take-off might well become impossible in the target area. Lack of daylight during winter months (principally late November to late January) further complicated the planning process. Moreover, coastal radar stations would provide ample time for a smoke-screen to be activated around *Tirpitz*. Adverse weather at home, which had frustrated many planned attacks on the battleship in Wilhelmshaven and Kiel, was no less important for Norway, especially as operations would be flown from northern Scotland.

Despite Churchill's reservations, the Air Staff opted for a night attack, when a moon and light winds were forecast. The next moon period was at the end of January. Operation Oiled was therefore quickly put together. At the Air Staff conference of 25 January, it was decided to mount the operation during the night of 29/30 January 'or the first suitable night following, up to and including the night of the 3/4 February, by a force of up to 30 heavy bombers'. Coastal Command would be responsible for surveillance of the target and the Fleet Air Arm approached to launch a carrier-borne attack 'at first light following the night attack' – though the latter would not, in the event, take place. 'Full security measures are to be taken, prior to, during and after' the operation. Thus, sixteen Stirlings from 15 and 149 squadrons of 3 Group and ten Halifaxes from 10 and 76 squadrons of 4 Group, accompanied by groundcrew in Transport Command aircraft, were ordered to RAF Lossiemouth on 28 January. All did not go strictly to plan. One Stirling from 149 Squadron at Mildenhall,

Suffolk, was unserviceable; one from 15 Squadron at Wyton crash-landed on the beach after being severely damaged in bright sunshine by anti-aircraft fire from a 'friendly' convoy near Whitley Bay, prompting the caustic observation from an air gunner that 'aircraft recognition did not seem to be the Navy's strong suit'. Landing on Lossiemouth's grass runway 'on a cold bleak winter's day', another 15 Squadron Stirling hit a patch of frozen snow and irreparably damaged its tail. In all, only twenty-four (thirteen Stirlings and eleven Halifaxes) arrived safely. Furthermore, their groundcrew had to scrounge additional equipment from Fleet Air Arm stores on the base, and soon 'looked like Eskimos' servicing their bombers on the exposed hard stands.

Poor weather in Norway had curtailed PRU cover, and equipment malfunction on the 25 January flight exacerbated problems. But two sorties on 29 January confirmed that *Tirpitz* was still in Foetten Fjord, with extra camouflaged rafts placed at the bow and stern in an attempt to disguise her outline. That day, the bomber crews learnt their target, as the met. forecast for the early hours of the next day was favourable. Eighteen aircraft were each fuelled with 2,000 gallons, and loaded with 2,000lb AP and 500lb SAP bombs: two 76 Squadron Halifaxes, for example, carried fifteen 500lb; three had two 2,000lb and three 500lb bombs – all with a 12sec delay fuse. From Lossiemouth, the aircraft were routed out via Hetteren and back via Hetteren, Rundo and Sumburgh. Two suffered engine malfunction, but in sub-zero temperatures at 0030 on 30 January, seven Stirlings began to take off on the first raid against *Tirpitz* in Norway. The bombers were scheduled to reach the warship after 3½hrs and be back at Lossiemouth four hours later. Quickly encountering cloud from sea level to 20,000ft and finding de-icing equipment of limited use, the Stirlings were unable to climb to clearer conditions; and, contrary to the forecast, the weather did not improve over Norway. Only one Stirling reported even glimpsing *Tirpitz*'s masts but could not reach the necessary 8,000ft to release its armour-piercing bomb-load. Another overshot on landing and was written off. Taking off between 0204 and 0234 BST, the nine Halifaxes fared no better. All four from 10 Squadron turned back through lack of fuel. Of the five from 76 Squadron, four reported reaching the target area in 5/10ths cloud, but could not find *Tirpitz* and did not bomb. The fifth aimed at the middle of the flak concentration in the hope of hitting the battleship. One Halifax crashed in the sea off Aberdeen on the return flight, the crew being rescued. 'A fiasco, due to the terrible weather both at Lossiemouth and also en route', one participant tartly observed. Bomber Command more soberly concluded that 'owing to 10/10ths cloud this operation proved to be abortive. . . . No aircraft were missing, and no combats or encounters were reported'.

Local records show that Trondheim had an air-raid alert 0512–0645 on 30 January, and at 0557 *Tirpitz* logged six four-engined aircraft entering Trondheim Fjord, flying towards Aasen Fjord in 5/10ths cloud. Flak opened up and the aircraft appeared to have difficulty locating their target. Engines were heard above the clouds intermittently for about fifteen minutes, but no mention was made of bombs being dropped. In Scotland, Wg Cdr J.C. Macdonald, OC 15 Squadron, was keen to try again, but weather conditions prevented another operation for five days, during which one Stirling refuelling for an air test caught fire on the ground. A decision to cancel further action for the present was taken, and the remaining aircraft were ordered back to their home bases.

Between 31 January and 28 February, seventeen PRU reports were received. Most located the battleship in the same position. However, occasional steaming exercises were noted too, suggesting that the battleship might be preparing to emerge into the North Sea. On 5 February, she was observed underway, but unescorted, on a north-easterly course in Norvik Sundet. Four days later she was seen in Foetten Fjord with her bows pointing east into the cul-de sac. Twice on 14 February, while at anchor, *Tirpitz* was identified 'emitting smoke' and the following day 'remarkable low oblique photographs from 1500ft' were obtained, which showed '15" gun barrels camouflaged white. Fine camouflage netting draped from shore to side of ship'. At midday BST on 19 February, the reconnaissance Spitfire found her travelling north-east at high speed (later calculated as 28 knots) in Trondheim main fjord. This was particularly worrying, because on 18 February Ultra had reported reinforcement of Luftwaffe units in southern Norway and two days later concluded: 'All indications point to a very early passage, probably to-day, of a unit or units from Germany to Trondheim.' There was special concern because the Germans were using extensively the 'Offizier cypher', which had not been broken, and the PRU sortie on 20 February discovered *Tirpitz* still in Trondheim Fjord. Two days later, she was back in Foetten Fjord, but two flights on 24 February noted absence of adjacent camouflage rafts and movement of the turrets, which suggested ammunitioning. The implication was that she might well be planning an operation, and on the following day she was again in Trondheim Fjord steaming west. However, the warship did not emerge from the fjord and by 28 February was back in her normal berth. The reason for this manoeuvring soon became clear.

Intelligence reports that German warships in Brest were planning a break-out deeply worried Tovey, who feared that they might penetrate the Iceland–Faeroes gap to join *Tirpitz*. News came that during the night of 11/12 February *Scharnhorst* and *Gneisenau* had instead dashed through the Channel. Although both ships were severely damaged by mines, Tovey still dreaded concentration of 'a considerable battle fleet' in Norway, from which 'no disposition of the Home Fleet could adequately protect both the Russian convoys and the northern passages' into the Atlantic. Intelligence sources reported *Tirpitz* carrying out firing practices 17–20 February, and Ultra intercepted heavy traffic between Navy Group North, the Admiral Commanding Battleships and 5th Destroyer Flotilla during 20 and 21 February, much of it unbreakable.

In fact, *Tirpitz* had left her berth to rendezvous with the pocket battleship *Admiral Scheer*, the heavy cruiser *Prinz Eugen* and their destroyer escort in heavy snow and poor visibility. If she had done so, Tovey's nightmare might have been realised. But *Tirpitz* did not venture into the North Sea after *Prinz Eugen* had been torpedoed approaching Trondheim Fjord. The 8in cruiser managed, nevertheless, to reach her appointed position in Lo Fjord close to Foetten Fjord with two attendant destroyers shortly before midnight on 23 February. The pocket battleship with three destroyers had preceded her, so an extremely powerful naval force had now concentrated.

PRU cover confirmed serious damage to *Prinz Eugen*, but there were signs that the other German ships might be about to act aggressively. During the afternoon of 24 February, *Tirpitz* signalled: 'Shall be at immediate notice at 1500 except for tugs to be cast off', responding to an earlier request from the Admiral Commanding Battleships to 'all fleet units in Trondheim area' to report when they were at immediate readiness to put to sea. Shortly after midday on 24 February, the commander of the 5th Destroyer Flotilla berthed near Trondheim, having previously warned of need for oil, drinking water and bread on arrival. Once more, an impending sortie might be inferred. But nothing transpired, and the British could settle once more to planning *Tirpitz*'s destruction at anchor.

Meanwhile, using evidence brought back by PRU cameras, a somewhat bizarre operation had been put in motion. Between 15 and 19 February 1942, an advanced party from 217 Squadron concentrated at RAF Skitten, preparatory to stripping all unnecessary equipment from a detachment of the squadron's Beauforts when they arrived at nearby RAF Wick. The operational plan required aircrews to fly to Trondheim, attack *Tirpitz* then either fly east to the Swedish border, bale out and leave the aircraft to crash or, even less attractively, retrace their outward track to ditch (through lack of fuel) some 60 miles from the nearest land and await rescue. Suicidal seemed the least offensive term for the second option. This uninviting enterprise seems to have survived until mid-March, using

RAF Leuchars instead of Wick, until wiser counsels prevailed. No more was heard of this fantasy; the personnel and equipment of 217 Squadron returned south.

Churchill remained keen to deal with *Tirpitz*, reiterating to the Defence Committee on 3 March 1942 that she was 'the most important vessel in the naval situation to-day, and her elimination would profoundly affect the course of the war'. During the first week of March, five PRU flights successfully covered the Trondheim area. On 7 March, *Tirpitz*'s berth was empty. The battleship was nowhere in the vicinity, and would not be found in Foetten Fjord again until 18 March. In the meantime, she would not be idle.

Flying the flag of Vice-Admiral Otto Ciliax, the German warship left Trondheim Fjord at noon on 6 March in a heavy swell, evading submarines deployed at its entrance, and steamed north with three destroyers. Early that evening, the submarine *Seawolf* sighted the force. But not until after midnight did its report via the Admiralty reach Admiral Sir John Tovey (C-in-C Home Fleet) who was at sea with two battleships, a battle cruiser and cruiser, twelve destroyers and the aircraft carrier *Victorious* to cover the convoys PQ12 to the USSR and QP8 from Murmansk. Tovey was aware via Ultra interceptions that PQ12 had been sighted by the Luftwaffe, so anticipated an attack by *Tirpitz*. Meanwhile, the battleship and her escort had steamed north-east along the Norwegian coast, before turning north at midnight on 6 March. In Operation Sportpalast, the German force aimed to attack south of Jan Mayen island, but not to engage superior forces. Should 'equal forces' be encountered, they would only be engaged if 'the main purpose, namely the destruction of the convoy' remained feasible. During the morning of 7 March, the warship flew off two Arados in a vain effort to locate the convoy, and detached her destroyers to search independently. That evening, boiler trouble reduced her maximum speed to 28 knots.

Bad weather, principally fog, prevented *Victorious* from launching reconnaissance aircraft throughout 7 March, during which *Tirpitz* was unprotected by her escorts. In a storm of snow and hail both convoys (one unlucky straggler from QP8 was sunk by a detached destroyer) safely eluded the enemy, and by the morning of 8 March, shortage of fuel had obliged all three German destroyers to return to Norway, leaving *Tirpitz* alone. At 0715 she discontinued her fruitless search and at 0850 received orders to make for Norway. Incredibly, at 2000, a further order was received to search, only for another to countermand this at 2149. *Tirpitz* should make for Narvik forthwith. The delay was almost fatal.

For during 8 March, Ultra revealed that *Tirpitz* was actually north of Tovey, who had retired westwards during the late morning of that day believing all hope of contact with the enemy had gone. At 1730 BST the Admiralty sent this new information to the C-in-C Home Fleet, who immediately turned north-east towards Bear Island. A further signal at 0230 on 9 March revealed that *Tirpitz* was now steaming south to Norway, expecting to meet her destroyers off the Lofoten Islands.

Tovey quickly set off in pursuit – in Ludovic Kennedy's later graphic quip following his success against *Bismarck* in May 1941 attempting 'the Spring double'. He aimed to be in position to despatch torpedo bombers against the German battleship at dawn on 9 March. At 0316, Tovey passed to *Victorious* further information from the Admiralty, indicating her expected position off the Lofotens at 0700, with a pithy: 'Report proposals'. *Victorious* had on board 817 (Lt Cdr P.G. Sugden) and 832 (Lt Cdr W.J. Lucas) Squadrons of Fairey Albacore bombers. A set drill, established and practised in manoeuvres since pre-war, required a torpedo bomber to attack at 6,000–9,000ft from ahead, dive to 200ft, level out at 50ft and release a torpedo 1,000yds from the target. To cover any evasive turn, a squadron would divide into four sub-flights of three and attack port and starboard bows to give 90 degrees cover. Six Albacores on the British carrier had air to surface vessel (ASV) radar. *Victorious* therefore replied to Tovey at 0537: 'Propose fly off searching force of six aircraft at 0630 to depth of 150 miles sector 105 to 155 degrees. Fly off striking force of 12 as soon as ranged about 0730.' *Victorious* would maintain her present course until 1000, then turn to 315 degrees at 26 knots.

Crews of the Albacore striking force were roused at 0530 BST, and at 0645 *Victorious* began to launch the reconnaissance Albacores, three from each squadron. Despite intermittent snow showers, visibility was generally good with 7/10ths cloud at 2,000ft, and at 0803 *Tirpitz* was sighted west of the Lofoten Islands steaming south for Trondheim. Not until shortly after 0830 did the battleship alter course eastwards to seek refuge in West Fjord, through the narrow, dangerous Moskenes Strait immediately south of the Lofotens. One of her Arado seaplanes (identified as a Ju 87 by the British, her floats mistaken for its gull-like fixed wheels) then bravely attacked three reconnaissance Albacores, succeeding in wounding one observer in the legs before running short of fuel and heading for Bodo naval base, claiming that it had shot down the British machine. Strangely, *Tirpitz*'s formal request for fighter assistance from the Luftwaffe airfield, close-by on the eastern shore of West Fjord, apparently arrived 2½hrs later, long after the action was over. Not for the last time, an arthritic, byzantine chain of command appeared responsible.

Meanwhile, at 0721, Tovey had signalled: 'A wonderful chance which may achieve most valuable results. God be with you.' In the words of *Victorious*'s captain, 'it was a chance they had dreamed and prayed for, and, they knew only too well, it was a chance that might not come again'. At 0735, *Victorious* flew off the twelve torpedo-carrying Albacores (seven from 832 and five from 817 Squadrons) under Lucas as strike leader on a course of 135 degrees true. Each aircraft carried a Mark XII torpedo, with a speed of 40 knots, depth setting of 25ft and impact-fuse. The striking force heard at 0815 that *Tirpitz* had been sighted initially steaming south. The reconnaissance Albacores thereafter reported her position, change of course and speed so accurately that at 0842 from 20 miles Lucas visually pinpointed the battleship now steaming a course of 82 degrees on a bearing from him of 142 degrees. The

Albacores had hitherto flown at 500ft to avoid radar detection, but with visibility 30 miles and the cloud base at 4,000ft he ordered them into cloud. The enemy warship was steaming at an estimated 30 knots, the laden bombers flying at 130 knots into a 35-knot headwind. So the attackers were only very slowly overhauling their quarry. Fully aware of this, worried about icing conditions and having lost visual contact with the other sub-flights, Lucas signalled them to carry out .individual attacks, which surrendered the advantage of coordination. At 0917 BST, the British broke cloud to find Lucas on the port beam, the other three sub-flights to starboard of the target. Lucas decided on an immediate attack, not waiting to get ahead of the battleship: the official conclusion would be that 'a break in the cloud revealed his position at a critical moment, forcing him to attack from a disadvantageous tactical position'. A minute later, Lucas's 832 Squadron sub-flight (4A, 4B, 4C) therefore turned to starboard, dived and at 0920½ released their three torpedoes; the squadron diary claims from 1,000yds, *Victorious*'s captain double that range.

The battleship put up a vigorous barrage and all the torpedoes passed astern, the closest 150yd away. Lucas noted no deviation of course by *Tirpitz*, which indicates that the torpedoes may have been released too far away and the battleship simply outpaced them. Meanwhile, 817 Squadron's second flight (5M, 5H, 4G) had crossed to port, and like Lucas launched a broadside attack at 0921½; again without success. To present the aircraft with the maximum deflection shot, the battleship had 'made a large [course] alteration, estimated at 100degs to port [virtually due north], which was very soon altered to starboard'. *Tirpitz* was now back on an easterly track. However, the deviation of course had allowed the other two sub-flights under Sugden still to starboard to anticipate that the target would resume her original dash for West Fjord and effectively cut a corner 'to synchronise an attack from ahead'. *Tirpitz*'s second change of course foiled them. A surviving pilot, Lt Cdr J.H. Stenning, later recalled: 'As we dived from our low height into a 30-knot wind she [*Tirpitz*] altered course to

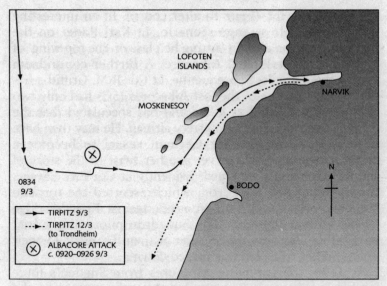

LOFOTEN
ISLANDS

NARVIK

MOSKENESOY

0834
9/3

BODO

N

→ TIRPITZ 9/3
---▶- TIRPITZ 12/3
(to Trondheim)
⊗ ALBACORE ATTACK
c. 0920–0926 9/3

Fleet Air Arm action off Narvik, 9 March 1942

starboard, so we had to chase her and with shots from her coming all round us I dropped my torpedo at almost extreme range.' Two Albacores – 4P (832) and 5C (817) – were shot down and the remaining four torpedoes from 5L, 5B, 4M, and 4R released at 0925½ all missed. Post-war, the Naval Intelligence Division explained: 'It was intended to work to windward of the target and then come down through the clouds to attack ahead. As they approached, a large gap in the clouds revealed their presence.' This entailed loss 'of the advantage of surprise . . . and the sudden change of plan', as a result of which 'TIRPITZ was able to escape undamaged'. From the attacking force, only Albacore [4R] brought back photographic evidence of release at 2,100yds from the target. This led the captain of *Victorious* to conclude that 'all aircraft were deceived by *Tirpitz's* large size and dropped their torpedoes at too great a range'.

A legend has persisted that one survivor from a British aircraft in the water ahead of the battleship successfully waved his cap for *Tirpitz* to alter course. In an interesting variation of this strange scenario, Lt Karl Räder on the battleship saw an airman 'sitting helpless on the top wing' of a crashed, waterlogged Albacore. A further conundrum adorns this episode. Subsequently, Lt Cdr R.M. Griffiths has discovered that one of the lost Albacores (5C) had only two crew members listed as killed and has speculated that the missing observer was the mystery airman. He may then have been rescued by another German vessel to become a prisoner of war. Post-war, yet another twist to the story of the Albacore attack emerged. Evidently Lt Cdr E.G. Savage, commanding 809 Squadron, which escorted the torpedo bombers, proposed a head-on attack against *Tirpitz*'s bridge by his Fulmar fighters: 'The Squadron pilots didn't [*sic*] favour this idea very much', one of them recalled. To their intense relief, 'the plan was turned down'.

At 1100, the surviving Albacores from Sugden's force landed on *Victorious*. Thus ended the only attempt by the Fleet Air Arm to torpedo *Tirpitz* on the high seas, but not the recriminations. Capt H.C. Bovell RN of *Victorious* blamed Lucas for attacking too soon from a poor position, contrasting this unfavourably with Sugden's effort. Later writers have also pointed to Lucas's inexperience with the squadron, of which he had only recently assumed command. Stenning did reflect 'that he briefed us to carry out the attack in a different formation to what we had always done previously'. But had Lucas not attacked, forcing *Tirpitz* to take evasive action, Sugden would never have had the opportunity to attempt a standard head-on attack. Furthermore, *Tirpitz* would report torpedoes launched considerably closer than 2,000yds. More sympathetic than Bovell, the Admiralty concluded: 'It was intended to work to windward of the target and then come down through the clouds to attack ahead. As they approached a large gap in the clouds revealed their presence. Having lost the advantage of surprise the A/C made immediate attack. In the hurry necessitated by the sudden change of plan their efforts were unsuccessful and *Tirpitz* was able to escape undamaged.' Undeniably, though, this was a courageous operation. As German records would reveal, it came within 30ft of success.

Tirpitz's log, acquired after the war, showed that three shadowing Albacores had been detected at 0910 LT, 12 miles away. Fifteen minutes later, as the battleship steamed at 27 knots on a course of 130 degrees, intercepted transmissions from these aircraft indicated an imminent attack. At 0932, *Tirpitz* flew off her seaplanes, two minutes later altered course to 82 degrees and increased speed to 29 knots. Actions stations sounded at 0942. At 1015, allegedly *Tirpitz* was attacked 'from both sides by about 25 Swordfish torpedo bombers', an understandable mistake as the biplane Albacores were unfamiliar. Diving from 3,000ft to 100–200ft, the bombers dropped their torpedoes 400–1,200yds from the warship, 'a few' apparently approaching to 200yd. The first torpedo was picked up at 1020 and passed 170yds astern. The sequence of events, according to the log, was then difficult to determine: 'further contacts of torpedoes increased on both sides and were actually detected round the entire horizon. . . . After dropping torpedoes, the aircraft attacked the bridge with machine guns.' Each Albacore supposedly launched two torpedoes, and one [from the second wave] passed about 10yds off the starboard bow. This assertion and that of *Victorious*'s captain on 15 March that *Tirpitz* had time to 'comb the second lot of torpedoes' suggests that the battleship may have made a further adjustment of course to starboard to avoid them. After studying British and German documents post-war, the Directorate of Naval Construction concluded that 'the torpedoes appear to have been dropped at an excessively long range which enabled *Tirpitz* "to comb the tracks", turning sharply first to port and then to starboard'. In his operational report, Capt Bovell wrote that the two sub-flights 'were unable to attack as intended' and had to do so 'with *Tirpitz* swinging rapidly to starboard'. This raises the possibility that the four torpedoes passed in front of her as she carried out her wide swing to starboard, the last only 10yds from the bow.

Admiral Ciliax wrote of 'the good God's intervention

between the *Tirpitz* and the deadly British weapons'. More practically, he awarded Capt Topp an Iron Cross. During the nine-minute action, *Tirpitz*'s 105mm flak guns fired 345 rounds, 37mm 897, and 20mm 3,372. In addition, the main 15in armament discharged 2 long-range broadsides, 16 rounds barrage and 12 rounds nose-fused. Three bombers were reputedly shot down and several more damaged – a fairly accurate assessment. At 1957, now protected by three destroyers, *Tirpitz* anchored in Bogen Fjord (Bogenbucht) near Narvik as British submarines gathered at the entrance to West Fjord and along the coast towards Trondheim.

This attempt by the Fleet Air Arm to sink *Tirpitz* (officially declared 'disappointing' though described in an intercepted German signal as 'most courageous') failed, but it had a profound impact on Hitler. He apparently ruled that the battleship should on no account make another sortie against a convoy until British carriers had been located and neutralised. To this end, Fw 200C long-range reconnaissance aircraft of 1/KG 40 were moved to Trondheim. In addition, by the time that PQ13 sailed in March, Luftflotte 5 had bombers (Ju 87, Ju 88 and He III) at Bardufoss, Banak and Kirkenes poised to attack. The British reacted too, Pound advising suspension of Arctic convoys during the summer months. Mindful of the political implications with the Soviet Union of such a move, President Roosevelt promised a battleship and two cruisers in support of the Home Fleet.

Extremely concerned that she might be bottled up in West Fjord with totally inadequate defence against air attack, at 2355 LT on 12 March *Tirpitz* weighed anchor and by dawn 13 March with five destroyers she had negotiated the fjord's exit in bad visibility and begun to race south close inshore, to the consternation of her navigating officer: 'It was both a fear and a nightmare for me', especially as several drifting mines were seen and 'a number of explosions in the water were heard not far from the ship'. He would have been even more agitated if he had known that four Allied submarines and seven destroyers were looking for the battleship. She moored back in Foetten Fjord at 2200, her presence signalled to Britain by an agent, but not confirmed by PRU until 18 March: 'A/T boom and camouflage rafts in position.' Two days later 'no change' was reported. Then on 21 March *Admiral Hipper* joined her, and a powerful force once more lay near Trondheim. The PRU summary of 28 March referred to 'a remarkable low oblique photograph taken from a height of 300ft', and flights on the three successive days confirmed *Tirpitz*'s position, though the post-operational photograph on 31 March proved 'poor', with 'no statement possible'.

Despite the Air Staff's concern about the lack of heavy bomber bases in Scotland, operations against her were still being actively mooted. Early in March, Coastal Command noted that Bomber Command 'considered the only hope . . . a low flying attack by moonlight with big calibre blast bombs, to be followed by a high-level day attack'. On 13 March, the Chief of the Air Staff (Air Chief Marshal Sir Charles Portal) informed the Prime Minister that fourteen heavy bombers had been standing by in northern Scotland with the hope of hitting *Tirpitz* at sea, presumably during the passage to Trondheim after her attempt on PQ12. In the absence of a suitable opportunity, with the First Sea Lord's agreement, they had now returned to their own bases. The projected operation involved seven 10 Squadron Halifaxes, which landed at Lossiemouth on 9 March, one having defective brakes due to the zealous attention of gunners from another 'friendly' east coast convoy – a replacement aircraft was flown up. The Halifaxes, which had intended to use 4,000lb HC bombs, returned to RAF Leeming, West Yorkshire, four days later without seeing action. Portal further explained to Churchill, curiously in view of Coastal Command's earlier contention, that Harris agreed 'a day attack on the ship when at Trondheim would stand no chance of securing a hit, and would be certain to incur heavy casualties'. During the next moon period, Portal revealed, Bomber Command hoped to make use of a special weapon to 'do serious underwater damage'. Planning for this operation was in hand.

Lack of effective weapons had hitherto represented a major handicap. 500lb SAP, 2,000lb AP and 4,000lb blast bombs designed to detonate on impact would not penetrate *Tirpitz*'s armoured decks, and torpedoes could not be successfully used, given the existence of protective nets and the narrowness of Foetten Fjord, which precluded a beam attack. Bomber Command's new acquisition – modified naval Mk XIX spherical contact mines – offered a better prospect of success. Their casings had been strengthened for air use and the amatol explosive content raised from 100 to 770lb (making a total weight of 1,000lb). Mooring mechanisms and the external horns had been removed, together with much of the internal fitting. The 31in diameter weapon, equipped with a Mk XIV hydrostatic pistol set at 14–18ft, could fatally damage the battleship's hull if dropped accurately. During the first fortnight in March 1942, 10 Squadron aircraft flew from RAF Leeming to carry out low-level practice drops off the Outer Hebrides, but blast from the explosions caused acute discomfort to tail gunners. This was confirmed in more trials at Filey Bay bombing range off the Yorkshire coast, with the weapon described by one pilot as 'a gigantic football'. Because this spherical weapon had an unpredictable trajectory, release from 4,000–10,000 ft proved unsatisfactory. Heights as low as 150ft were tried and, at length, an operational altitude of 600ft agreed. However, a steady approach to the target was also required, an unattractive proposition at that height and in the face of determined enemy gunners.

On 21 March, 4 Group Operation Order No. 9 was circulated to 10, 35 and 76 squadrons at Leeming, Linton and Middleton St George. It noted that 'for some time past' *Tirpitz* had used 'Aasfiord . . . as a base for raiding activity against convoys in the Atlantic [*sic*] or on the way to N. Russian ports. . . . This capital ship is one of the most powerful war vessels afloat and its presence in these [Norwegian] waters, apart from the constant menace to our convoys, had a widespread influence on the strategical situation at sea.' The destruction of, or serious damage to, the German battleship, especially at a time when supplies to 'the Russian Armies' were crucial, 'would have a profound effect on the whole course of the war, the importance of which cannot be over emphasised'. Alternative targets were *Admiral Scheer* and *Prinz Eugen* in nearby Lo Fjord. However, enemy defences around Trondheim were by no means negligible. In the area, 'but mainly at Vaernes aerodrome' 17 miles east of Trondheim, there were an estimated eighteen Ju 88s of KG/30 and nine Fw 200s of KG/40 and, more ominously, thirty Messerschmitt Bf 109 and thirty Bf 110 fighters from I Gruppe. 'Up to 2 staffel . . . [of] coastal units' were also thought to be close-by – altogether a formidable Luftwaffe array. Long-range RDF (radar) stations were liable to detect aircraft flying above 5,000ft at 80 miles, over 1,500ft at 50 miles, beyond the Norwegian coast. A supplementary chain 30 miles inland could identify aircraft at even lower heights. 'The intention is to attack the *"Tirpitz"* in the Aasfiord with heavy bomber aircraft of No. 4 Group . . . this operation being co-ordinated with an attack by Lancasters of No. 5 Group on VAERNES aerodrome' on 29/30 March or 'the first suitable night thereafter'.

Ten Halifaxes from 10, twelve from 35 and ten from 76 squadrons were to fly respectively to Lossiemouth, Kinloss and Tain in Scotland on the afternoon of 27 March, two 97 Squadron Lancasters to Elgin. The Station Commander at RAF Leeming, Gp Capt S. Graham, would direct the operation from Lossiemouth. All 10 Squadron aircraft and ten from 35 Squadron would carry four modified mines and ninety 4lb incendiaries, with the remaining two 35 Squadron Halifaxes having a full load of 50lb incendiaries. From Tain, 76 Squadron aircraft would take one RDX-filled 4,000lb HC bomb plus four 500lb or 250lb GP bombs. The 10 Squadron mines were to be dropped in sticks at 100ft intervals, those of 35 Squadron at 200ft intervals, with the 50lb incendiaries from the two designated 35 Squadron Halifaxes 50ft apart. Every aircraft would take 1,632 gallons of petrol, except those of 76 Squadron with No. 6 tanks and 1,872 gallons. The distance involved would be approximately 1,300 miles and the whole operation last 8–8½hrs.

The attack would be carried out in two phases. The first between 2145 and 2230 BST involved 76 Squadron, coinciding with the Lancaster attack on Vaernes. The Halifaxes would fly up Trondheim Fjord at 4,000–5,000ft 'straight to the Aasfiord', on arrival identifying the target with flares if necessary. 'Precision' bombing would then take place (also at 4,000–5,000ft) 'from the general direction East to West or West to East at the discretion of Captains of aircraft'. Once the 4,000lb bombs had been released, 500lb and 250lb bombs would deal with 'any active "flak" or searchlights in the neighbourhood'. The second phase would be executed by 10 and 35 squadrons between 2235 and 2315 BST, with mines and incendiaries released at 600ft. Like first phase aircraft, these Halifaxes would fly up Trondheim fjord at 4,000–5,000ft, but then approach *Tirpitz* 'on the glide from an easterly direction, making away towards the open water of the main Trondheim Fiord'. Ideally, the two aircraft with 50lb incendiaries should attack first, but other machines were not to wait for them. Coordination of the two phases was crucial. Neither 4,000lb bombs nor flares were to be dropped after 2230 and first phase aircraft were to be clear of the area by this time, so as not to interfere with the mining bombers. After outlining further administrative instructions, the operation order closed by underlining need for strict security. Details must be revealed only to essential personnel. During the operation, three destroyers would be stationed along the planned route for rescue duties, backed up by two seaplane tenders at Burghead, near Kinloss, and two high-speed launches at Buckie, east of Lossiemouth.

Almost immediately problems arose. One of the Lancasters crashed on take-off from Woodhall Spa, Lincolnshire. Having reached Lossiemouth, not Elgin as originally planned, the other returned to base on 28 March, 'owing to the operation being cancelled due to grounding of aircraft'. In fact, it had been delayed, not abandoned. Meanwhile, the Halifax squadrons (35 Squadron's complement increased to twelve), each with a spare aircraft, had duly reached the operational stations to meet groundcrew, who had travelled ahead by road and rail. On 29 March, Air Vice-Marshal C.R. Carr, AOC 4 Group, addressed crews at the three stations, the day after Flt Lt A.P. Fane had flown at 300ft across Foetten Fjord to confirm that *Tirpitz* remained at anchor there.

At 1800 on 30 March the Halifaxes began filing towards the runways, now without any Lancasters to attack Vaernes. Thick, overcast weather was to baulk them. The cloud base did rise to 1,000ft en route, but over Norway was 10/10ths at 6,000ft. Aircraft of both operational phases circled until fuel ran low without seeing *Tirpitz*, although some crews bombed searchlights and the flashes of flak guns.

During the afternoon of 30 March, a PRU Mosquito had been chased by Bf 109s; so a raid was half expected. At 2230 LT the air-raid warning sounded in Trondheim and 30mins later anti-aircraft guns opened up south of *Tirpitz*, which promptly sounded its own alert. During the raid, Trondheim reported between twenty-five and thirty aircraft attacking from all directions except east, with an estimated twenty-five bombs dropped and four aircraft shot down. Four were indeed lost in the Trondheim area, two more crashing into the sea on the return leg. Thus a total of six Halifaxes (two from 10 Squadron, three of 35 and one from 76) were lost, with two 76 Squadron aircraft putting down at Wick and Lossiemouth after running low on fuel. The official verdict read: 'Thick cloud over the target and mist in valleys and fiords made identification of the battleship impossible.'

Winston Churchill remained adamant that *Tirpitz* must be sunk and, so long as she stayed at anchor, air attack seemed the only viable option. On 7 April, Air Chief Marshal Portal (the CAS) raised with AOC-in-C Coastal Command the question of further 'offensive action against enemy forces in Trondheim'. Despite the perceived difficulties and the loss of an aircraft on 4 April, six PRU sorties between 8 and 15 April showed *Tirpitz* in her usual berth. The sortie on 16 April revealed she was once more 'emitting smoke'. However, three flights during the ensuing two days reported no further movement. Then on 24 April, the observation 'almost free from camouflage netting' once more raised qualms about operational preparations, though four more sorties before the afternoon of 28 April saw the netting replaced and additional camouflage rafts in place. Overall, during these weeks, PRU cover and reports from local agents showed that, as the Prime Minister feared, defences around *Tirpitz* had been considerably strengthened. Anti-submarine and torpedo nets were suspended from floats 100yds from the vessel, land-based flak and searchlight positions on concrete bases were both sides of Foetten Fjord, and flak ships close-by. Similar protection surrounded the other warships and the main Trondheim Fjord had its own formidable defences, not least near Trondheim town. Smoke-screen facilities were on board the battleship, on surrounding hills and the prominent Saltoy island.

Another air attack had to be launched, however, and Halifaxes were again chosen. On 11 April, 4 and 5 Groups issued an updated, enhanced version of the 21 March operation order, noting that *Tirpitz*, *Von Scheer* (*sic*) and *Prinz Eugen* were in the same positions. Luftwaffe numbers had altered, however. Twenty-seven bombers, 9 reconnaissance/bombers, 30 Bf 109 fighters and 27 coastal reconnaissance aircraft were in the Trondheim area with 25 more fighters 250–300 miles south between Stavanger and Herdla. No known change had occurred in the radar situation. 'The intention' was for heavy bombers from 4 and 5 Groups to attack *Tirpitz* on 25 April or as soon as possible thereafter; and Gp Capt Graham would again command the operation from Lossiemouth. Including reserves, 4 Group was to send eleven Halifaxes from 10 Squadron to Lossiemouth, eleven from 35 Squadron to Kinloss and twelve from 76 Squadron to Tain. Twelve Lancasters from 5 Group, divided equally between 44 and 97 Squadrons, would go to Lossiemouth. The 5 Group aircraft would carry one 4,000lb RDX-filled HC bomb, 'load to be made up with' 500lb GP bombs with impact fuses. 4 Group squadrons would each put up ten aircraft: 10 and 35 Squadrons were to carry four of the modified

Mark XIX mines (referred to in some documents more accurately as 'depth charges'); 76 Squadron one 'special' light case 4,000lb blast bomb and four 500lb bombs. The routes, radar-avoidance heights, distance, anticipated duration of the operation and air sea rescue arrangements were the same as for the March operation, as were the strict instructions about security. Halifaxes not equipped with No. 6 tank and a total capacity of 1,872 gallons would be fitted with two additional Hampden tanks increasing their fuel load to 1,792 gallons.

The attack would once more be carried out in two phases. The first by 76 Squadron's ten Halifaxes and the twelve Lancasters on *Tirpitz*'s superstructure with the 4,000lb bombs would be from 6,000ft (again west–east or east–west at the captain's discretion), followed by attacks with the 500lb GP bombs on adjacent flak and searchlight positions. This time, instead of clearing the area quickly, first phase aircraft would remain there 'as long as possible during the second phase to act as a diversion'. 10 and 35 squadrons' bombers were to drop their mines from 150ft, not 600ft as before, flying 'from *West to East* [sic]' along the length of the ship from stern to bow and dropping 'their mines close to the stern and between the ship and the shore'. 10 Squadron was to drop its sticks at 100ft intervals, 35 at 200ft intervals. Equipment deemed unnecessary (surprisingly including Gee sets) was to be removed, no second pilot carried, so that the Halifax crews were reduced to six. Rail parties of groundcrew were to reach the advanced bases by the afternoon of 22 April.

Briefing of the designated squadrons commenced on 15 April to allow adequate time for practice. From Linton-on-Ouse, for example, 35 Squadron crews were required to fly set one-way routes at low level, close to selected hills and cliffs. But the unstabilised Course Setting Bomb Sight caused some anxiety, as a target could be lost even after acquisition in the cross-wire. A whimsical entry in the Squadron's ORB for Monday 20 April read: 'Adolf Shickalgruber's [sic] birthday passed in preparation for expected arrival of 76 Squadron.' Three days later, Churchill reminded the House of Commons about *Tirpitz*'s constant threat to the Arctic convoys, as aircraft from the five squadrons converged on the advanced stations. At Tain, 76 Squadron recorded that RAF Regiment personnel manned defences all day due to its arrival. For the third time, too, an aircraft flying up the east coast of England gave naval gunners target practice, its port inner engine's coolant tank being punctured, the fuselage perforated some sixty times.

Graham flew into Lossiemouth on 24 April, and final briefings at Lossiemouth, Kinloss and Tain took place the following day, Saturday 25 April. Somewhat dauntingly, crews were given full details of the size, construction (with emphasis on armoured protection) and armament, including heavy machine-guns and flak capability, of their target plus a comprehensive list of flak positions close-by. 'Known' ones totalled twenty-four heavy guns in the immediate vicinity of *Tirpitz*, fifteen light guns around Vaernes airfield and three light guns north of Lo Fjord. There were a total of forty-two 'unconfirmed' light flak guns ashore, besides several flak ships. No searchlights were reported from 'landsites' (erroneously, as it turned out), 'but the ship and the smaller vessels will no doubt have and use their searchlights for dazzle effect'. The outward leg must be flown below 5,000ft, past Orkney and over Shetland, where the course would change at Herma Ness, the northernmost tip, with a second adjustment at 65 45N 04 00E, 80 miles from Aalesund. Aircraft were to return along the same track, except for flying east of Shetland to make the first landfall at the Outer Skerries. Once more, in Norway the idea was to fly straight up Trondheim Fjord to Saltoy island (1½ miles from *Tirpitz*), where the bombing run would start. After the attack, to leave Foetten Fjord aircraft would turn sharply to port, combat the formidable defences of the warships in Lo Fjord (where *Admiral Hipper* joined *Admiral Scheer* and *Prinz Eugen* on 21 April) and fly along the northern shore of Trondheim Fjord. *Tirpitz* lay where Foetten Fjord was only 330yds wide, about 30ft from the northern bank, with the bows pointing east and stern projecting at an angle towards the centre of the fjord. A double boom protected the starboard (southern) side of the battleship, held approximately 55yds away by floats. Another boom protected the stern. The topography identified from the PRU photo of 23 January was then explained in detail, one high point being 1,900ft near Skalval, 3 miles south-west of *Tirpitz*, another at 1,800ft 12 miles due east. Around Aasen Fjord, the ground was a maximum 750ft. Two long-range Hudsons were to distract the Kristiansand radar station from shortly after 2300, ten others similarly to occupy the radar station at Aalesund from 2350, also taking the opportunity to attack shipping in the harbour. A Coastal Command Catalina from 210 Squadron at Sumburgh would fly along the coast north of the target for the benefit of radar at Stokkoen 'well before T.O.T. for bombers'. Two Beaufighters would attack Lade aerodrome on the outskirts of Trondheim and two others Vaernes, between 2350 and 0000. Four more Beaufighters were to attack Herdla aerodrome to the south at 0100hrs. The plan was both complicated and comprehensive.

The Halifaxes would approach Foetten Fjord at 2,000ft, before descending to '150ft/200ft' beyond Saltoy island, where the mines were to be dropped at 220mph precisely 340yds from the stern of *Tirpitz*, though how this accuracy was to be achieved is not clear. Second phase crews were told that 'one mine directly under the stern will damage propellors and rudders, thus making it necessary to tow the battleship back to a major naval depot for repairs – a battleship in tow would be a set up for our air and naval forces'. Twenty-five per cent of the mines 'down close to the ship between it and the shore would sink it' – an extremely ambitious aim, even in ideal conditions. 4 Group agreed that the task was 'formidable', but optimistically claimed that the first phase bombers would have given the area such a 'shaking' that 'the gun crews are quite liable to be dizzy'. The composer of that particular gem had a distinctly fertile imagination. If the target were obscured by smoke, crews should drop on dead reckoning or in the case of mines, release them on the hillside, so that they could roll down under the keel, an emergency provision which gave rise to a false belief that this was the primary method for releasing the mines. After attacking, bombers were to execute a 180 degree turn to port and retrace their outward track across the North Sea. If, for whatever reason, the bomb-load had not been dropped, this was indeed an hair-raising proposition. *Prinz Eugen*, *Admiral Scheer* and *Admiral Hipper* in nearby Lo Fjord, close to which the returning aircraft must in any case pass, were secondary targets. The positions, specifications and draught of *Admiral Scheer* and *Prinz Eugen* were then given: the former lay 'against the south bank . . . bows pointing approximately north-east', the latter in the south-eastern corner of the fjord with bows pointing north-west. Both ships were protected by booms. No information was offered about *Admiral Hipper*, which had presumably arrived too late for analysis. Each squadron received a time for arriving and leaving the target area, the entire operation at Trondheim theoretically lasting from 0000 until 0140, with neither bombs nor illuminating flares dropped after 0035. Specific instructions were issued about landmarks, with a special warning not to confuse Stjordals with Aasen Fjord. After the final briefing, crews were able to study a model of the target area, prepared by RAF Medmenham, Buckinghamshire.

Air Vice-Marshal Carr and senior naval officers visited Kinloss before the operation to boost morale; Sir Archibald Sinclair (Secretary of State for Air) attended the briefing of 10 Squadron Halifaxes at Lossiemouth; the First World War veteran and former Chief of the Air Staff Marshal of the Royal Air Force Lord Trenchard impressed on 76 Squadron at Tain the importance of the target. Churchill believed that participants would be 'proud to tell your grandchildren . . . [about] this mission'. The King signalled: 'Good Luck. We will be waiting up for your safe return'.

Coastal fog prevented take-off on 25 and 26 April, which led to two nights of riotous parties to relieve tension. A PRU Spitfire found all four warships in their normal berths on the morning of Monday 27 April, and at Vaernes aerodrome were forty aircraft, including Fw 200s and Ju 52s, but no fighters. During the afternoon, Graham ruled that 35 Squadron would carry additional 250lb bombs under the wings to deal with flak, and at 1650 with a favourable met. forecast, decided the operation would go ahead. An armourer looking at a 76 Squadron Halifax, with the bomb-bay doors hand-cranked to rest on the belly of the 4,000lb bomb, ungenerously dubbed it 'a pregnant mayfly'.

It took from 2001 until 2115 DBST on 27 April for the aircraft of five bomber squadrons to take off from the three airfields. At 2020 Wg Cdr J. Marks led 35 Squadron away from Kinloss, in the sparse words of one aircrew member 'under orders to sink a battleship'. 76 Squadron noted the 'splendid take-off' of its eleven aircraft from Tain in 14mins, midnight being the estimated time over target and 0434 back at base, with timed intermediate points along the route to and from Aasen Fjord. A slight variation from the original order saw seven of these Halifaxes carrying one RDX-filled 4,000lb bomb and four 250lb GP bombs with an impact fuse, the other four with a 4,000lb blast bomb and four 250 GP bombs, three having two additional red marker flares. All eleven aircraft had a camera fitted.

Each bomber crew took off individually and navigated alone to the target area. Wg Cdr D. Bennett, OC 10 Squadron, dropped flame floats towards the Norwegian coast for his pilots to follow in ideal conditions: 'the night was calm, the sea dead flat'. Two Lancasters returned early to Lossiemouth with mechanical trouble, one in time for the reserve aircraft (M–Mother) to join the operation. A Halifax piloted by Wg Cdr D.O. Young, OC 76 Squadron, landed back at Tain at 2222 after its starboard inner engine failed. In bright moonlight, with no cloud cover, once the Norwegian coast came into view crews had no difficulty in map reading. By then the diversionary tactics were already in progress elsewhere. Having taken off for an 11½hr flight at 1830, a Catalina flying boat was stooging up and down the coast to occupy enemy radar (especially on the island of Stokken) at the same time as two Hudsons from 608 and

48 squadrons similarly concentrated on Kristiansund North. All of these aircraft saw distant flashes as the raid developed. More aggressively, four Beaufighters attacked Vaernes and Lade airfields, another four went to Herdla (270 miles south of Trondheim) and ten Hudsons concentrated on shipping at Aalesund. Briefed to attack no later than midnight, the Beaufighters detailed for Vaernes arrived late after the main operation had started and found no sign of activity, strangely not even hostile flak in contrast to the reception noted by earlier bombers. Elsewhere, flak was undoubtedly intense, and one Beaufighter was shot down. A Norwegian observer recorded that flak guns on the hills around Trondheim was actually firing down on a Beaufighter flying up the fjord, an experience also reported by several Halifaxes. Of the four Beaufighters sent to Herdla, one aborted and one failed to locate the target, returning to Sumburgh at 0300. At Aalesund, a 250lb bomb apparently hit a small motor vessel, but there was a distinct lack of shipping and most Hudsons looked for secondary targets, like oil tanks.

Meanwhile, the main operation had commenced. The leading Lancaster of 44 Squadron made the designated land-fall at the off-shore island of Smola (70 miles west of Trondheim), climbed to 12,000ft and flew up Strindfjord. Crossing Vaernes airfield, it encountered 'intense accurate predicted heavy flak' without being hit, dived to 7,500ft and at 0006 dropped its 4,000lb bomb on *Tirpitz*, banked to port and released the 500lb bombs on flak positions on the northern peninsula at the head of Foetten Fjord. After using its machine-guns to effect, it turned for home at 0040. Not until 0012 (six minutes after the attack started) did smoke begin to cover the fjord, and later aircraft experienced considerable difficulty in identifying the target. Several dropped on flak flashes, others attacked targets of opportunity like Vaernes airfield. One 76 Squadron Halifax, arriving late, attacked *Prinz Eugen* and *Admiral Scheer* at 0045. First wave aircraft reported dropping their bombs from 6,000–8,000ft, and one was shot down short of *Tirpitz* over Saltoy island. They had thoroughly stirred up the defences.

Second wave Halifaxes of 35 Squadron were scheduled to drop their mines between 0040 and 0100, followed by 10 Squadron. All these low-flying bombers were harassed by flak on Saltoy, their final navigation check before the bombing run. *Tirpitz* was by now completely obscured by smoke and an outcrop of rock above her served as an aiming point. One Halifax was severely damaged short of the target, jettisoned its load and turned for home. Seven did aim at the target, the remaining three failed to locate it. Marks' navigator, Fg Off A. Abels, found the fjord 'full of smoke' and did not even glimpse *Tirpitz*. Plt Off G.M. Dickson, a 10 Squadron navigator, wrote that 'the flak was pretty terrible and gave us hell and we couldn't be sure whether we had bombed the target'.

A number of the attacking aircraft were brought down. K–King of 35 Squadron hit high ground seven miles east of *Tirpitz* near Skielstadmark. Lancaster L–Leather of 97 Squadron exploded in mid-air near Ausetuatnet Lake; and three others went down in the target area. The pilot of 10 Squadron's U–Uncle, Flt Lt G. Miller RAAF, used the landing lights to help him judge height and put down on 'glassy calm and still' water under heavy enemy fire near Malvik. Wg Cdr D. Bennett in B–Baker encountered the smoke-screen at 400ft, flying through a curtain of flak from the ship and surrounding hills. With the starboard wing ablaze, he climbed rapidly, saw the target but felt 'a sitting duck' as the machine was hit again before releasing the mines from 3,000ft. Flying eastwards beyond the fjord, the crew baled out of their stricken aircraft and eventually reached England after crossing the Swedish frontier.

The crew of Halifax S–Sugar, piloted by Plt Off D. MacIntyre RCAF, also ended up in Sweden. As the aircraft climbed away from the target area, the starboard wing burst into flame and MacIntyre realised that he must crash-land. Smoke filled the cockpit and effectively blinded him as from the nose Plt Off I. Hewitt, the navigator, called adjustments to avoid hills and other obstructions. A mere three minutes past *Tirpitz*, which seemed an eternity to the crew, the pilot put down on the frozen Lake Hoklingen.

The machine skidded ½ mile with the wing still blazing. But the entire crew got out safely and escaped over the frontier – in places through 4ft of snow – with the exception of the flight engineer who hurt his ankle and remained behind to be taken prisoner.

Tirpitz had been prepared. At 2308 LT Kristiansund radar, 100 miles south-west, reported four-engined aircraft approaching below the 30,000ft cloud base. Shortly after 2330, the first state of readiness was sounded on the battleship, almost immediately followed by action stations, with the enemy now only 60 miles away. At 2358 her flak guns engaged two bombers, and eight minutes later *Tirpitz* was concealed under its smoke-screen. The last hostile aircraft was heard at 0137, and 20mins later the all-clear sounded. By then, the warship's gunners had fired over 2,000 rounds. One legacy of the attack was countless dead, silver fish floating on the water, victims of the mines.

Sea Hurricanes of 883 Fleet Air Arm Squadron patrolled on the approaches to the Scottish coast, as surviving aircraft landed between 0350 and 0621 DBST. From the five bomber squadrons, forty-four aircraft had taken off (including the reserve Lancaster from Lossiemouth), three were early returns, so forty-one reached the Norwegian coast. Of these, thirty-two reported attacking *Tirpitz* (though very few crews claimed to have seen the target, leaving bomb-aimers effectively to release blind), three attacked other targets and four jettisoned their bomb-loads for different reasons. Four Halifaxes and one Lancaster failed to return. Twenty 4,000lb bombs, twenty 500lb GP, ten 250lb GP and forty-four Mark XIX mines had been dropped. Gallingly, PRU photographs on 28 April showed no damage to the enemy warship, and at noon the crews learnt that they were to repeat the operation that night.

Headquarters 4 Group optimistically hoped that with 'such a large weight of bombs' dropped, underwater damage might emerge later. Meanwhile, the operation had to be remounted on 28–29 April, and for this a major change of timing took place. There had clearly been too long a gap between the phases of the 27–28 April operation, with second wave aircraft approaching the Norwegian coast passing first wave bombers on the way home. Ahead lay defences fully alert. Lancasters of 44 and 97 squadrons were therefore scheduled to take off at 2100, some 40mins later than the three Halifax squadrons. Otherwise the plan was the same: first wave from high level against the defences; second wave low level dropping mines. With the crew all too familiar with the target area, the briefing concentrated on landmarks and hostile positions based on new information from the first raid.

This time, the first wave comprised nine 76 Squadron Halifaxes, of which five (two also with red marker flares) would carry one 4,000lb HC bomb 'with special filling' and four 250lb GP bombs, the other four would take one 4,000lb HC bomb and four 250 GP bombs. The squadron was to set course from Tain at 2030. Twelve Lancasters of 44 and 97 squadrons – eleven with one 4,000lb HC bomb and four 500lb GP bombs, the twelfth carrying ten 500lb and four 250lb GP bombs – would accompany 76 Squadron. These aircraft were to bomb between 0030 and 0040. The fifteen serviceable Halifaxes from 35 and 10 squadrons of the second wave, each carrying five 'depth charges', were briefed to release their weapons between 0041 and 0050.

Now well practised, the Germans quickly deployed the smoke-screen. But before it gathered, bomber crews had time to appreciate the silhouettes of distant mountains in the bright moonlight. The 'excellent visibility' promised by met. forecasters would not last long. First wave aircraft bombed from 6,000ft, though some Lancasters reported targeting the other warships in Lo Fjord as *Tirpitz* could not be seen. Only three of the nine Halifaxes of 76 Squadron in the first wave saw the battleship. After dropping their bombs, many aircraft attacked flak and searchlight positions and, in one instance, Vaernes airfield. Two night fighters were reported by one Halifax, two others separately by two more Halifaxes (quite possibly the same two) – the only enemy aircraft reported in either April operation. These sightings are mysterious, because there were no night fighters close-by. Significantly perhaps, none of the bombers was fired on, so the enemy aircraft may have been simply transiting the area or on reconnaissance. Four Coastal Command Beaufighters of 235 Squadron, deployed in Trondheim Fjord to combat Luftwaffe interference, saw no enemy planes and instead machine-gunned flak positions along the shores. Plt Off Dickson from 10 Squadron again recorded his experiences. With flak guns 'actually firing down on us', the Halifax dropped its mines from 150ft 'into the water near the Tirpitz'. A shell burst close to Dickson as the aircraft climbed sharply to port out of the fjord: 'I was very lucky because it hit my navigation bag and all the bits of shrapnel embedded in that.' Then it became clear that one of the mines had hung up, 'so we flogged all the way over the North Sea with a bomb bay open which added to our drag'. Eventually, the flight engineer managed to lift 'a panel to get at the bomb bay and he hacked away at the supports (with an axe) . . . to dump this damn thing'. However, 'we were pretty mucked about by damage from flak' and the pilot put down at Sumburgh, where the Halifax was declared unserviceable. The crew returned to Lossiemouth in a Harrow to conclude 'an episode that was quite interesting . . . [and] my operations against the Tirpitz'.

Eighteen 4,000lb, twenty-three 500lb GP and one 250lb GP bombs had been dropped, together with forty-eight Mark XIX mines during the attack, which lasted some 75mins. According to *Tirpitz*'s records, the last bomber left the area at 0130 and the closest mine fell during the second wave's attack 70yds away on the starboard beam. Fearing a third successive attack, on the evening of 29 April the battleship moved into the main fjord and sailed along the shore at slow speed until daybreak, when she returned to Foetten Fjord.

However, another raid was not yet on the military calendar: on 29 and 30 April, surviving Halifaxes and Lancasters returned to their home airfields. 76 Squadron ORB recorded: 'All returned in excellent spirits having thoroughly enjoyed two successful operations and also the [unspecified] opportunities for sport and recreation afforded by the Scottish Highlands.' With Bennett in Sweden, 10 Squadron needed to replace its OC. On 7 May, Wg Cdr J.B. Tait was appointed to the post. Two and a half years later, he would lead 617 Squadron Lancasters three times against *Tirpitz* in the space of two months.

4 Group summarised the 28–29 April operation. As one of the second wave failed to take off, nine from 76 and seven each from 35 and 10 squadrons set out across the North Sea. Two of the Halifaxes jettisoned their load and returned early, nineteen reported bombing 'the primary target' and two 35 Squadron aircraft were missing. The weather had been 'again excellent', with 'bright moonlight . . . [providing] considerable help in locating and identifying the target'. The operation had been 'in conjunction' with 5 Group, as well as Hudsons and Beaufighters tasked 'to neutralize the enemy night fighters in the Trondheim area'. 'A great weight of bombs' had been dropped, although the smoke-screen did create difficulty for bomb aimers. As with the first raid, it was hoped that underwater damage would be revealed in due course. That was not to be. None of the mines affected *Tirpitz*, but recovery of some (eight according to enemy records) caught in undergrowth on the slopes above the fjord led the Germans wrongly to decide that the weapon had been designed for use in this way, a false conclusion repeated by later commentators. A post-operational, undated note in the Air Staff files may have unwittingly compounded this error: two attempts were made with a 'roly-poly weapon [1,000lb spherical mine with hydrostatic fuse] . . . to roll mines underneath her [*Tirpitz*] where she lay at Trondheim'. The briefing notes make quite clear that the aim was to drop the mine in the water astern of the battleship, and that releasing over land was an alternative only in poor visibility. Studied closely, the Air Staff note does not contradict this. In retrospect, Bennett dismissed the mines as 'miserable', Ludovic Kennedy as 'useless'. Harsh, but realistic.

Meanwhile, international pressure on Churchill intensified. On 26 April, he admitted that concerns about enemy action were delaying convoys, with an inevitable build-up of merchant ships in port, many of them American vessels carrying cargo from the United States. The following day, Roosevelt greatly feared the political impact if they did not sail 'promptly': 'any word reaching Stalin . . . that our supplies were stopping for any reason would have a most unfortunate effect'. Churchill protested that 'we are at our utmost strain for convoy escorts', which determined that, 'with the best will in the world', the maximum number of convoys could only be three every two months. In turn, Roosevelt emphasised the need to 'break the log jam of ships already loaded or being loaded', or risk 'an impossible and very disquieting impression in Russia'. Churchill pointed out on 2 May the difficulty, given pressing naval commitments elsewhere, in providing a powerful escort, bearing in mind that 'enemy heavy ships and destroyers may at any time strike', and particularly that *Tirpitz* remained undamaged at Trondheim despite 'desperate attacks' by British bombers. 'I beg you not to press us beyond our judgement', he concluded. Reluctantly, next day, Roosevelt agreed 'to acquiesce in your view regarding Russian convoys', but continued to hope that they could sail regularly in the near future. On 6 May, Stalin revealed that he had got wind of the situation, and was not pleased. He understood that 'some ninety steamers loaded with various important war materials for the USSR are bottled up at present in Iceland or in the approaches from America to Iceland', and urged 'all possible measures' be taken to deliver them in May. Churchill reassured Stalin of his commitment to sending 'the maximum amount of war materials', but 'on account of *Tirpitz* and other enemy surface ships at Trondheim the passage of every convoy had become a serious fleet operation'. Faced by advice from the Chiefs of Staff to delay Arctic convoys for six weeks, on 17 May Churchill significantly demurred: 'The Russians are in heavy action, and will expect us to run the risk and pay the price entailed

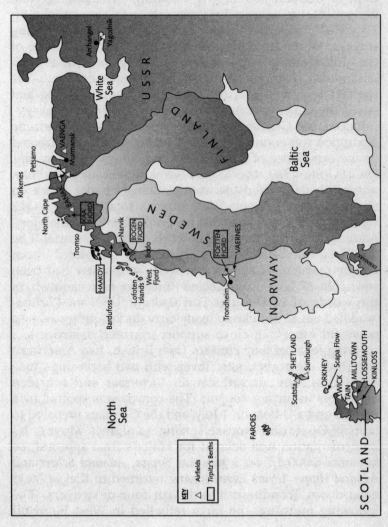

Tirpitz in Norway, 1942–4

by our contribution. The United States ships are queuing up . . . Failure on our part to make the attempt would weaken our influence with both our major Allies.' Pressure from the Alliance partners was transparent.

On 3 May, Air Chief Marshal A.T. Harris (Air Officer Commanding-in-Chief, Bomber Command) signalled Gp Capt S. Graham MC at RAF Leeming: 'The courage and determination shown by your crews in the attacks on Tirpitz was indeed worthy of immediate and outstanding success. Moreover, undismayed by their first experience of the full fury of the defences, they returned with undiminished ardour to the charge'. Undoubtedly true, but the fact remained that the battleship was unharmed and posed the same, potential threat as she had since January.

Indeed, the German warship's capacity to cause maritime disruption was soon to be heavily and tragically underscored by the experience of the USSR-bound convoy PQ17 in July. On 18 June 1942, the British naval attaché in Stockholm warned that the Germans were planning a major attack on the next Arctic convoy. With *Tirpitz*'s foray against PQ12 vividly in mind, the First Sea Lord told C-in-C Home Fleet, Admiral Tovey that he might order the convoy to scatter if he thought it faced annihilation, which Tovey considered 'sheer, bloody murder'. However, the seeds of disaster had been sown. On 27 June, from Iceland thirty-five merchantmen, in the words of Lt Douglas Fairbanks Jr USN on *Wichita*, 'waddled out to sea like so many dirty ducks', protected by a powerful escort: in close-support fourteen destroyers; a covering force of four cruisers (two British, two American) and three destroyers; plus Tovey with two battleships (one American), the aircraft carrier *Victorious* and fourteen destroyers in further support. The convoy was spotted by a Fw 200 and a U-boat on 1 July, and the Germans prepared to launch Operation Roesselsprung (Knight's Move). Its implementation was delayed for Hitler's final approval, so not until 2000 LT on 2 July did *Tirpitz*, *Admiral Scheer* and *Admiral Hipper* (*Prinz Eugen* having returned to Kiel in May) head down Trondheim Fjord with four destroyers. The following morning, the force refuelled in West Fjord off

Narvik and at 0143 on 4 July approached Alten Fjord in the extreme north, at 1010 anchoring off Kaa Fjord. The three warships and a strengthened destroyer escort (despite not having with them three destroyers and the pocket-battleship *Lutzow*, all of which had hit rocks) constituted a powerful, destructive force poised to attack.

In the meantime, apart from the loss of one merchantman to an aerial torpedo, PQ17 was making steady progress in calm weather. Spirits were so high that Rear-Admiral L.H.K. Hamilton, commanding the covering force of cruisers, signalled *Wichita*: 'Independence Day always requires large fireworks. I trust you will not disappoint us.' Little did he know . . .

During the early evening, persistent torpedo bomber attacks were driven off. Then came a carillon of devastating shocks. Ultra interceptions had rightly placed German heavy units in Alten Fjord, and the Admiralty reasoned that they could be in a position to attack PQ17 at about 0200 on 5 July. This was an assumption, no doubt coloured by *Tirpitz*'s March sortie and the intelligence from Sweden on 18 June. Nevertheless, no firm evidence had been received that the battleship or any of the other warships had sailed. What followed was a testimony to the deep-seated unease that the German battleship engendered by her very presence in Norway. In quick succession three incisive orders came from the Admiralty on 4 July: timed at 2111 DBST, 'Secret. Most immediate. Cruiser force withdraw to westwards at high speed'; 2123, 'Secret. Immediate. Owing to threat from surface ships, convoy is to disperse and proceed to Russian ports'; and, finally, at 2136, 'Secret. Most Immediate. Convoy is to scatter' – that is to break up, with each merchantman completely unprotected attempting to make its own way to safety. Capt J. Broome RN, commanding the close escort, concluded that 'this could only mean one thing, that *Tirpitz* was here, she was on the horizon'. None the less, 'going on an opposite course to this scattering convoy, ships we were supposed to be looking after, going the other way, watching them get smaller on the horizon, that was terrible'.

The feared warships were still in port, worried about the position of Tovey and, in particular, *Victorious*. Indeed, at 0937 LT on 4 July, Navy Group North had cancelled the planned operation. Then the British force was discovered at 0655 on 5 July, too far away to pose a threat, and at 1122 under the command of Admiral Otto Schniewind, *Tirpitz*, *Admiral Hipper*, *Admiral Scheer* and seven destroyers weighed anchor. By 1500, they were at sea steering east-north-east, but were soon detected by British and Soviet submarines and aircraft patrolling from Murmansk, whose reports were picked up by German monitoring stations. Afraid that Tovey might make speed to intercept, as he had done in March, at 2100 Grand Admiral Räder ordered the operation to be aborted. By the early hours of 6 July, *Tirpitz* was back in Alten Fjord without firing her guns. At 1030 on 7 July, she sailed again for West Fjord, east of the Lofotens, with *Admiral Scheer* and *Admiral Hipper*, their passage observed by a PRU aircraft at 1045 DBST. *Tirpitz* berthed at Bogenbucht (Narvik) at 0255 on 8 July. Meanwhile, German aircraft and submarines had feasted on PQ17 undisturbed. Only eleven of the thirty-six that 'waddled' away from Iceland reached the Soviet Union. *Tirpitz* had never been in a position to attack PQ17. Tovey sharply concluded that 'the order to scatter the convoy had been premature; its results were disastrous'. Referring to 'this painful episode', Churchill admitted that at the time the German battleship 'riveted our attention'.

The PQ17 disaster had immediate repercussions. An Admiralty summary, dated 6 July, demonstrated clearly how latent fear of *Tirpitz* had, indeed, affected decision-making. 'A move by German heavy units to the North Cape area of Norway, preparatory to an attack on a North Russian convoy, *had previously been anticipated* [emphasis added]. From 2nd July onwards evidence accumulated that the Germans intended such a move, and a PRU [flight] on 4th showed Trondheim empty.' The warships could not be located, and 'break-out patrols' by aircraft and cruisers were mounted north and south of Iceland in case *Tirpitz* were emulating *Bismarck*. The 'most likely' explanation, however, was that the warships were 'on the move in North

Norway, and that an attack on the convoy was *reasonably certain* [emphasis added]'. The following day, Admiralty representatives in Washington observed that, with American merchantmen involved, the operation and success of Arctic convoys deeply concerned politicians and public across the Atlantic. On 10 July, the Defence Committee felt it 'unwise' to send another convoy at present, explaining: 'The threats of course are air attacks, submarines and *Tirpitz*.' That same day, at the Chiefs of Staff meeting, Portal agreed with Pound: 'The major threat to our convoys to North Russia was from enemy surface forces rather than from the air.' Three days later, the Defence Committee formally postponed PQ18 together with convoys planned for August and September, which exposed raw nerve ends in subsequent exchanges between the three Allied leaders. Churchill admitted to Stalin that 'the Germans finally made use of their forces in the manner we have always feared' and he could not risk the Home Fleet east of Bear Island in range of shore-based aircraft. He explained: 'If one or two of our very few powerful ships were to be lost, or even seriously damaged, at the same time as the *Tirpitz* and its accompanying vessels, which are soon to be joined by *Scharnhorst*, remained in action, our whole supremacy in the Atlantic would be forfeited.' Stalin dismissed these arguments for 'discontinuing the transportation of war materials to the northern ports of the USSR as without foundation . . . wholly unconvincing. . . . The Soviet Union is sustaining incomparably graver losses.' In Churchill's graphic words, Stalin then subjected him to 'a cataract of abuse and insult'. Roosevelt acknowledged that Stalin was not always easy to deal with, but with vast tracts of his country in German hands, a 'very dangerous situation . . . confronts him'. He 'must be handled with great care' and, moreover, 'British and American material promises to Russia must be carried out in good faith'. At a meeting with Stalin in Moscow on 13 August 1942, the Soviet leader provocatively remarked: 'This is the first time in history the British Navy had ever turned tail and fled from the battle. You British are afraid of fighting.' Averell

Harriman, Roosevelt's representative and also present, thought Stalin 'really insulting', 'the violence' of his attack 'stunning'. Under such pressure from east and west, Churchill had an unenviable task.

The feasibility of Arctic convoys was unquestionably tied to the latent menace of *Tirpitz*, so starkly illustrated with PQ17. In its wake, writing to Roosevelt Churchill referred mildly to 'frightful difficulties with the Russian convoys', but to the Admiralty he was infinitely more forthright. Aware of Stalin's abrasive irritation at the prospect of any interruption to the programme and acutely conscious that he had promised him on 20 July 1941 to do 'anything sensible and effective that we can do to help . . . [within] limitations imposed upon us by our resources and geographical position', Churchill was loath to stop the convoys. Rather he proposed sailing a convoy protected by two auxiliary carriers in addition to other heavy units to entice the battleship into action 'over two lines of submarines'. Should this tactic fail, he hoped for decisive action by the Fleet Air Arm from the carriers. But the Prime Minister's scheme did not prosper, due to escort commitments such as Operation Pedestal to relieve Malta. Stalin bitterly reflected that 'the British Government refuses to continue the sending of war materials to the Soviet Union via the Northern Route'. PQ18 did eventually sail in September, and significantly perhaps, Rear-Admiral G.J.A. Miles, head of the naval mission in Moscow, raised the question of contingency plans should it be ordered to scatter. In the event, without interference from *Tirpitz*, twenty-seven merchantmen got through, twelve were lost. Significantly, even without an overt threat from *Tirpitz*, seventy-five warships had been needed to escort PQ18. Having informed Stalin that this level of protection could not be provided in the foreseeable future, Churchill wrote to Roosevelt: 'This is a formidable moment in Anglo-American-Soviet relations and you and I must be united in any statement made about convoys.' Interestingly, when Roosevelt agreed to 'give up PQ19 . . . [because] we are short of shipping', he added that there was 'nothing to be gained by notifying Stalin sooner than is necessary'.

Independently, the Royal Navy had been planning a unique operation against *Tirpitz*. In December 1941, Italian frogmen used underwater charges to disable the battleships *Queen Elizabeth* and *Valiant*, having penetrated Alexandria harbour on two-man 'chariots'. From April 1942, the Royal Navy had been developing similar weapons, which were the same size as a 21in torpedo, with a detachable 600lb warhead. The 'charioteers' rode astride their lethal transport, and their target was *Tirpitz*.

After her brief excursion in July, she now lay at anchor in Bogen Fjord, occasionally exercising in West Fjord. PRU photographs showed that enhanced flak defences had been installed on top of *Tirpitz*'s main turrets and the bridge, as well as on land. She remained a formidable target. However, by August 1942, the battleship required a refit, and Hitler refused permission to return to Germany. So, on 23 October, she sailed again for Foetten Fjord. Operation Title, her destruction by charioteers, was planned for 31 October. Towed behind a former fishing vessel, which carried their crews, the two chariots penetrated Trondheim Fjord. However, an unexpected squall caused the tow lines to part fewer than 5 miles from the target, and the imaginative operation had failed. Once more, *Tirpitz* survived.

Another resourceful aerial scheme to sink the battleship, involving 'heavy bombers' operating from the northern Soviet Union, had been raised in Churchill's minute to the First Lord of the Admiralty and Chiefs of Staff Committee on 27 July. Nineteen days earlier, the Chiefs of Staff had noted a proposal to send Hampdens to the Archangel area, and two days later the Defence Committee acknowledged that they might offer a deterrent to *Tirpitz* proceeding outside her own land-based fighter protection. On 12 July, AOC-in-C Coastal Command specifically suggested that 455 Squadron, which was geared for a torpedo role, should be equipped with long-range tanks and despatched on 20 July. In the margin of Air Chief Marshal Sir Philip Joubert de la Ferté's submission, at the Air Ministry ACAS (P), Air Vice-Marshal J.C. Slessor, scribbled 'not a serious proposition' and advised the CAS that 5 Group had tried extra tanks in Hampdens without success. It is therefore reasonable to conclude that on 27 July Churchill was expressing frustration that nothing had come of this scheme, and possibly significant that two days later the Air Ministry warned 30 Mission in Moscow of the likely operation of a Hampden squadron from the Soviet Union to cover PQ18. On 31 July, however, Slessor still expressed doubts about effective use of the Hampdens, though he seemed to see them as 'heavy bombers'. He thought that 'one or two torpedo bomber squadrons' might be made available. In reality, already during June and early July, extensive training had been carried out from RAF Leuchars and RAF Wick in cooperation with 'a battleship, cruiser and destroyers', to convert 144 Squadron to a torpedo role. Night exercises in late July and August followed. On 6 August Slessor admitted that 'practical trials' had proved the Hampdens could fly to the Archangel area, but two days later argued that they should be supplemented by long-range bombers as a 'threat to enemy surface forces'. Such was the momentum now being generated behind this exercise that on 10 August 30 Mission appeared to believe that the 'despatch of 60–80 long-range bombers and 26 torpedo bombers' was imminent.

On 13 August 1942, the American cruiser *Tuscaloosa* and three destroyers sailed for Archangel with groundcrew and equipment for 144 and 455 squadrons. Three weeks later, thirty-two Hampdens followed them. On 2 September, eighteen Hampdens of 144 Squadron led by Wg Cdr J. McLaughlin landed at Sumburgh to refuel and two days later at 2200 DBST took off for Afrikanda, 150 miles south of Murmansk in northern USSR. Nine landed safely; one crashed near the aerodrome; three put down at other Soviet bases; one arrived over the Kola peninsula during a German air-raid and was shot down by Soviet fighters (all but the rear gunner surviving). Another hit a mountain in Sweden, after suffering engine failure, but two crew members lived to be repatriated. The remaining three aircraft simply disappeared. By 5 September, twenty-four Hampdens (twelve from each squadron) had landed safely, together with four PRU Spitfires. Gp Capt F.L. Hopps' force was soon strengthened by arrival of Catalina flying boats from 210 Squadron, scheduled to use nearby lakes. Operating from another Soviet base, Vaenga near Murmansk, on 14 September led McLaughlin eleven Hampdens on an 'operational strike against enemy naval units which were expected to leave Alten Fiord', but a 1¾hr flight proved fruitless. Another later and more lengthy excursion by eleven 144 and twelve 455 aircraft towards Alten Fjord was abandoned, when they were spotted by an enemy machine. The 144 Squadron ORB suggested that their detection in the area may have deterred warships from threatening PQ18. Squadron personnel reached the United Kingdom again by sea on 29 October, disappointed not to have engaged the enemy, but satisfied that 'the main purpose of the detachment was achieved, namely the frustration of enemy naval surface units from attacking convoys between Britain and Murmansk'. They left behind their Hampdens, which after a considerable amount of Service heartburn (though, for political reasons, with Churchill's approval) were given to the Soviets, the Royal Navy having insisted that the torpedoes be brought back to Britain.

The possibility of *Tirpitz* venturing from Narvik was not entirely far-fetched. An intercepted wireless message sent by naval headquarters there on 8 September revealed that repair work had progressed so well that he battleship was at 6hrs readiness to sail at maximum speed. Post-war, captured documents showed, however, that an inspection report of 15 September concluded a major overhaul was necessary, but this was not known to the British at the time. Nor was 'inaccurate and misleading' intelligence information appreciated. Only post-war, for example, was it confirmed that the claim by a Russian submarine to have damaged *Tirpitz* during the PQ17 excursion was 'untrue' and an assertion from the naval attaché in Stockholm on 23 September that boiler tubes had been ordered from Germany 'inaccurate'. Another report from Stockholm that month, alleging that the battleship was lying in

Bogenbucht 'with a heavy list and four holes in her side about 4 metres in diameter', could be discounted in the light of the declared state of readiness on 8 September. On receipt of the inspection report, the Germans decided that *Tirpitz* should sail for Trondheim on 21 October, although in practice she did not do so until two days later because of fears about submarines in the area. She berthed once more in Foetten Fjord late on 24 October. While *Tirpitz* was in Bogenbucht, where the warship was protected by anti-torpedo booms and camouflage, PRU aircraft had again kept a close eye on her. They reported a tanker alongside on 27 August and the battleship underway steaming west at 16 knots on 28 September, though she had returned to her berth with the boom closed on 1 October. Nothing of particular note occurred until 21 October, when she was seen doing 16 knots in company with *Admiral Scheer* and three destroyers: 'training of the main and secondary armament suggest vessels are exercising. No aircraft are visible on the catapult of either ship.'

Once *Tirpitz* had been discovered in Foetten Fjord on 29 October, cover was resumed there. Two days later 'dazzle' camouflage was reported, on 5 November 'camouflage rafts at bow and stern and camouflage netting in position. Low screen erected forward casting a long shadow across the deck.' Twice in December, on 2 and 16, the battleship was seen anchored in Lo Fjord, where *Admiral Scheer* (now back in Germany) had recently been berthed, with the protective boom close and camouflage netting draped between the ship's side and shore. By 5 November, the intention of 'a British commando consisting of six Englishmen and four Norwegians with a special type of torpedo to blow up the *Tirpitz*' – the failed charioteer operation – was known to the Germans. Frequent changes of berth and repeated examination of the hull by divers now took place. The internal repair work outlined in the September report had been completed by 17 December 1942, but the driving motor of her starboard crane was not ready until 8 January 1943.

Apart from the two speculative Hampden operations from Vaenga in September, in 1942 no aerial attack was mounted on *Tirpitz* after 29 April. That is not to say none was planned. On 7 May Harris, while admitting the problems involved, discussed with Lord Cherwell the prospects for another attack. Six days later, from Bomber Command Air Cdre R. Harrison wrote to Air Vice-Marshal W.A. Coryton, AOC 5 Group. Noting that twenty-four CS bombs of the 45in type would be available from 19 May, he wanted a plan prepared for 'the C-in-C's consideration' for a night attack against *Tirpitz* at Trondheim with two flights of Lancasters. Harrison reminded Coryton that from 23 May there was twilight all night 'and no real darkness' in the target area. The 'warning system might be rendered ineffective by flying very low until a landfall is made on the coast of Norway, then climbing to bombing height between that point and the target'. Harrison believed that it was 'customary' to move *Tirpitz* at night, leaving the smoke-screen over her berth, so 'reconnaissance combined with bombing' might therefore be necessary.

Coryton replied swiftly, on 16 May. He understood from the Ministry of Aircraft Production (MAP) that the CS bomb in question would not function 'properly' below 8,000ft, which coincidentally was an ideal height for using the Mark XIV bomb sight and 'above the accurate range of light flak'. However, before the next moon period, he anticipated only seven aircraft being trained with the new bomb sight, which was only just reaching the group. The operation might be 'tactically possible', but he felt that there was insufficient training time 'to give us even a remote chance of success'. The AOC aimed to have 'a dummy ship marked out on a range', but believed it 'essential' that crews obtained 50–70 per cent hits on this before launching the operation. This would take time. If the attack were 'urgent', crews must be taken off main force operations to train. There were 'several [other] important considerations'. Unless a gap in the RDF chain were identified, 'we must accept the certainty of interception by enemy fighters before the target is reached'. Furthermore, there would be ample time to start the smoke-screen. Such a daylight operation he considered 'a perilous undertaking', adding that 'with only 12 shots in the locker, the possibility of a hit appears extremely small'. If the target were so important, then more than twelve aircraft should be involved 'to saturate defences and consequently give a better chance of success'. This particular proposal, therefore, fell on stony ground.

Meanwhile, a plan to deal with the battleship had begun to germinate in 5 Group. On 14 May, Coryton received a comprehensive appreciation from Wg Cdr P.S. Jackson-Taylor of his air intelligence branch. Jackson-Taylor repeated much of the well-known detail concerning the warship's position, adjacent terrain, radar chains and flak defences. But he elaborated them with invaluable, specific additions and recommendations. The depth of water between *Tirpitz* and the shore was under 5 fathoms, though it increased rapidly to 20 fathoms 'a short way out'. From 23 May 1942 there was no twilight, which meant that 'a night bombing attack in the ordinary sense of the word is not possible'; moreover, the enemy could operate his fighters without night fighter control. Two nearby aerodromes – Vaernes (17 miles east of Trondheim) and Lade (2 miles north-east of Trondheim) – were credited with Bf 109Es, and more of these single-engined fighters were at Herdla (270 miles south) and Bodo (200 miles north). An estimated 8mins warning time from the radar would not allow reinforcement from Herdla or Bodo. Vaernes had eight heavy and thirty light flak guns to protect it. Apart from flak in the immediate vicinity of *Tirpitz*, light batteries were both sides of the entrance to Trondheim Fjord; and Trondheim town (south-west of the battleship) had heavy and light flak defences plus between twelve and fifteen searchlights. Off the coast, the islands of Hitterden, Storfosen, Tarva, Froien and Smolen all had flak guns on them.

Lossiemouth to Foetten Fjord was a round 1,435 miles, which in still air represented 7hrs 32mins at 190mph – well within the capability of a Lancaster. Assuming a bomb load of 6,000lb, the operational range at 190mph was 9hrs 45mins. A precision attack with 'a special type of bomb' would require release from 4,000ft and use of the

Stabilised Automatic Bomb Sight. This needed 'a slightly curved approach to the target of approximately 6 miles or 2 minutes in time', which would permit 'no effective evasive action' to combat enemy flak or fighters. Additional difficulties were that any light came from the north, so the enemy warship would 'be in shadow and difficult to locate, and a smoke-screen was likely to be activated to obscure [it]'. Jackson-Taylor recommended attacking out of the sun in box formation at 8,000ft, which was a compromise designed to be above the ceiling of light flak. Diversionary attacks against the fighter airfields should also be considered. However, 'we must be prepared for heavy losses and must accept the fact that material damage to the battleship is a matter of considerable chance particularly in the likely event of a smoke-screen being put up'. The attack would be divided into advance and bombing forces. The former would comprise three sections of three bombers, one flying directly towards Trondheim, the others crossing the coast to north and south of the fjord entrance respectively. This force would reach the coast at Z–45 and make for Vaernes to commit the German fighters. The bombing force would attack *Tirpitz* '15 minutes before twilight, or half an hour after twilight if moonlight conditions are available . . . from different directions', with the bombing height 8,000–9,000ft and sections staggered at 500ft intervals. Each section would bomb on a signal from the formation leader.

Coryton evidently approved Jackson-Taylor's appreciation, for on 1 July its content was refined into a detailed plan. Ten aircraft from each of five squadrons, plus one reserve, were envisaged: from Lossiemouth (97 and 106), Kinloss (207), Tain (61) and Fearn (83), with the AOC personally directing the operation at Lossiemouth. One wave of Lancasters would carry a single 5,500lb CS bomb, the other three 2,000lb AP bombs, which would theoretically allow a margin of approximately two hours of petrol. The attack was to take place on a suitable day between 11 and 18 July.

However, important adjustments had now been made to

Jackson-Taylor's proposal. All the Lancasters would attack *Tirpitz*, Coastal Command Beaufighters taking responsibility for Vaernes and Lade aerodromes at Z–1hr. Three destroyers would be stationed on the route between Lossiemouth and Trondheim, and the object of the operation was 'to inflict the maximum possible damage on the German battleship *Tirpitz*'. That same day Coryton sent the plan to Bomber Command for approval. In his covering letter, he pointed out that a night operation had been ruled out, a midday attack being preferred by fifty Lancasters in formations of three with the sun in the south-west so the bombers could withdraw 'to take evasive action into the sun if attacked by fighters'. He was making arrangements for high-altitude bombing practice on four ranges and the necessary fighter affiliation. Previous operations had been foiled by a smoke-screen 'and in my opinion any hits can only be lucky ones'. Thus small-scale raids were unprofitable: '50 Lancasters gave a chance of success, which we will do our utmost to achieve'.

Two days later a 5 Group conference decided that 106 would be the lead squadron and six Hampdens with Lindholme dinghies would be sent to RAF Sumburgh for additional search duties during the operation. Provisional arrangements for aircrew and groundcrew to converge on the advanced bases were drawn up, and a suggestion made that the squadrons be stepped up at 400–500ft intervals. Eight days later, detailed requirements of bomb-loads, loading facilities, oil and petrol at the advanced stations were produced. Meanwhile, on 4 July, Harris had reacted. In principle, he accepted Coryton's rationale for the operation and the involvement of Coastal Command, suggesting that the Air Ministry should be approached to provide three of the new Stabilised Automatic Bomb Sights per squadron.

Despite the initial support from Bomber Command and the refinement of the 1 July plan in the following fortnight, the operation did not go ahead as scheduled. On 18 July (the end date envisaged for the attack) Air Vice-Marshal R.H.M. Saundby, Harris's SASO at Bomber Command, queried with Coryton the proposed routes to and from the target. The very next day, referring specifically to the correspondence of 1–4 July, 5 Group amended its plan to seven squadrons (97, 106, 207, 61, 83, 44 and 50) each providing nine aircraft with two reserves. Lossiemouth, Kinloss and Tain remained as advanced stations, Peterhead replaced Fearn, Dyce and Wick were added, with a reminder that permission would have to be obtained to use Tain and Dyce, which were Coastal Command's responsibility. Clearly, despite the apparent finality of earlier plans, this operation was still very much in a fluid state. Indeed, the fact that Fearn was declared unsuitable for heavy bombers by the Admiralty as late as 25 July indicates a certain lack of liaison and preparation before the 5 Group plan was drawn up. On 20 July, Coryton indirectly confirmed this. Writing to Harris, he revealed further serious doubts. Following recent experiences over Germany, 'we have reconsidered certain aspects of our plan for the Trondheim party'. It would be 'quite essential' for the whole attack to be completed in 2–5mins, with flights of three attacking at 15,000–18,000ft. Coryton now felt that 'considerable practice' was needed to concentrate squadrons at a predetermined point. 'A Group exercise has therefore been prepared and will be carried out, as soon as weather permits, to practise a good concentration across the country in a loose group formation and the approach to the target with interception and attack by fighter squadrons.' The time of attack had also been varied to 'about mid-day so that the ship should be in full sunlight and still enable us to get a clear run up without the sun on our tails'. For the moment, however, this particular plan must remain on hold. For, after her PQ17 excursion, *Tirpitz* anchored in Bogenbucht, not Trondheim.

Thus, writing to the AOC-in-C on 15 August, Coryton revealed that 'a few days ago' Harris had asked him to examine the feasibility of attacking the battleship at Narvik. AOC 5 Group referred to correspondence in May, when his staff had found proposed use of Hofn aerodrome in Iceland or RAF Sumburgh for an operation against

Narvik 'impracticable'. He then dealt with another variation: 'As regards the proposal to start the Lancasters off from the Lossiemouth area and put in an attack at Narvik whilst en route to Murmansk', the results of preliminary consideration 'were rather depressing'. The Germans radar cover would give 'at least' 50 miles warning and time to put up a smoke-screen, making the chances of 'any hits . . . remote'. Coryton cited a recent German dive-bomber attack on a British cruiser protected by smoke at Malta, which utterly failed. Vaenga was the only suitable Soviet airfield in the Murmansk area, but lay within 25 miles of the front-line, was frequently bombed and might therefore be put out of action at any time. Furthermore, to reach it the Lancasters would risk interception by fifty enemy fighters from Petsamo.

Coryton then cast rather murky light on another planned operation. Knowing that Coastal Command was about to despatch two Hampden squadrons (144 and 455) to the northern USSR , he 'naturally thought they would have some detailed information regarding the facilities available'. On visiting Coastal Command headquarters, he discovered 'to say the least . . . their information is extremely sketchy . . . and apparently it is a complete shot in the dark sending the two Squadrons there'. AOC 5 Group, therefore, concluded that the chances 'of getting a hit would be very small and that without a very considerable pre-arrangement we should only see a very few of the aircraft back'. There was, though, another possibility. The Lancasters could cross Norway and Sweden directly to Kandalashka, some 150 miles south of Murmansk and reputed to be the best Soviet base in the area. *Tirpitz* would then be bombed on the way home with maximum surprise. To confuse the Germans, the press might announce that the aircraft were being sent to reinforce the Soviet Air Force. Nevertheless, Coryton concluded bleakly that without more detailed information about facilities in the Soviet Union, 'to stage an attack against *Tirpitz* at Narvik at the present time would accomplish nothing and would throw away almost all of the aircraft taking part'. However, significantly, the idea of using

RAF heavy bombers to attack the German battleship from a Soviet base had been conceived.

Almost certainly having got wind of Coryton's submission, AOC-in-C, Coastal Command moved swiftly to establish copyright. Writing to Harris on 23 August, and referring to Coryton's visit, Joubert agreed that the prospect of surprising or neutralising the German defences could not be guaranteed in the absence of precise details of the Narvik defences. 'My command' then suggested that an attack from east to west might be more profitable, while pointing out the vulnerability of Vaenga to enemy bombers and favouring Kandalashka 'on the end of the most westerly arm of the White Sea . . . (and) easily identifiable'. He conveyed the impression that Coastal Command had also initiated the idea of a misleading press release, and thus effectively claimed credit for the content of Coryton's letter.

Having captured the high ground in a bureaucratic turf war and implicitly accused Coryton of plagiarism, AOC-in-C, Coastal Command moved on to suggest cooperation with a Lancaster force making its way to the Soviet Union. The Hampden squadrons scheduled to fly to the Soviet Union could go south of Bodo airfield on a course suggesting an attack on *Tirpitz* at Narvik. This would cause the Germans to put up their smoke-screen. Joubert estimated that they would not feel able to discontinue this for 'two or three hours' (at this point an inserted question-mark appeared in the margin of Bomber Command's copy). As a result, the smoke would 'probably be exhausted' by the time that any Lancaster attack actually went in, ideally 3–3½hrs after the Hampdens crossed the coast to disappear 'into the interior where the country is wild and sparsely inhabited and where communications are slow and unreliable'. Confidently, he concluded: 'In my opinion this ruse is more likely to achieve success both of surprise and exhaustion than any other.' The bomber force would go on to land at one of the Soviet airfields. If this plan were to be executed, Joubert would be 'delighted' to send his staff officers to High Wycombe to work out revised routes for the Hampdens. The letter was copied to Coryton, whose reaction has not survived. However, independently, Harris killed it. On 26 August, Saundby reminded the AOC-in-C Bomber Command that an unsuccessful attempt to exhaust the smoke-screen had been tried at Brest, and he was 'very sceptical' of better results in Norway. He believed the Germans were 'good enough organisers to guard against such a happening' and, in any case, 'smoke would tend to hang about in these fjords for many hours unless there is a considerable amount of wind'. Harris's SASO argued that 'a successful attack on the ship in her present position' was unlikely. The AOC-in-C concurred. On 30 August, while thanking Joubert for 'your offer to assist by employing your Hampdens to deceive the enemy into a premature use of his smoke-screen', Harris felt that an attack on *Tirpitz* in her present position 'not a practicable proposition'. He intended 'to defer action until the ship moves closer to the bomber bases, or gives an opportunity by coming back to a German port'. So no Lancaster operation was launched on the battleship at Narvik, and the Hampdens flew to northern USSR in September as originally planned.

Return of *Tirpitz* to Trondheim on 23 October resurrected Jackson-Taylor's draft of 1 July, albeit much-amended following the many subsequent exchanges between 5 Group and Bomber Command. The reason for this revival appears to be a personal minute from the Prime Minister to the First Sea Lord and CAS on 26 October: 'The movement of *Tirpitz* and *Scheer* [*sic*] to Trondheim calls for every effort to strike them while there. Pray let me know in writing, or if you prefer orally, what you have in mind.' Portal replied the following day that Bomber Command was considering 'a mass salvo from about 100 Lancasters' at 20,000ft with 4,000lb bombs. On 30 October, Gp Capt N.W.D. Marwood-Elton wrote to Coryton from High Wycombe wishing 5 Group 'the best of luck in sinking this ship' and enclosing an intelligence appreciation dated that same day. This admitted that no accurate totals of German fighters in Norway could be obtained, and the writer believed 'diversionary attacks by aircraft other than by bombers are extremely unlikely to draw the fighters guarding the *Tirpitz*'.

On the contrary, attention would be drawn to an impending operation against the battleship, which was the only viable target in the area. As Coastal Command had agreed to Beaufighters operating from Sumburgh in association with the 5 Group operation, it was 'strongly recommended' that they either covered the withdrawal or flew with the bombers as escorts. The anonymous intelligence officer concluded: 'I do not consider either of these roles necessary except to hoist the morale of the bombers, which should hardly be necessary with Lancasters.'

So, on 5 November 1942, Gp Capt H. Satterly, SASO 5 Group, drew up Operation Order B.785 with the intention 'to inflict the greatest possible damage on the German battleship *Tirpitz* . . . on the first suitable day'. Bomb-loads would vary between one 5,300lb CS bomb; five 500lb SAP bombs; or one 4,000lb HC bomb and one 500lb SAP. With the diversionary attacks still planned, the operation order followed closely the outline already agreed, except that nine squadrons (9, 44, 49, 50, 57, 61, 97, 106 and 207) would each supply nine Lancasters plus two reserves. This made a minimum attacking force of eighty-one bombers, ninety-nine if the reserve machines were fully committed. 'Secrecy is vital', Satterly emphasised and ordered that detailed information be confined to Station Intelligence and Navigation officers before receipt of the executive signal, which was never sent. The operation remained still-born, possibly because within a month daylight would be severely restricted in Norway, as winter closed in.

Operations by other Allied air forces were briefly considered too. On 21 May 1942, the Joint Services Mission in Washington indicated that President Roosevelt was keen for American heavy bombers to fly in the European theatre. On 12 July, although only eight B-17 Flying Fortresses were then in England, the British Chiefs of Staff noted that after 1 August they would be available for an attack on *Tirpitz* at Trondheim should she return there. The following day, a sceptical Air Staff officer scribbled 'not a serious plan' in the margin of his minutes, and on 27 July Air Vice-Marshal J.C. Slessor, ACAS (P), elaborated his thoughts. Major-General Carl Spaatz, Commanding-General of the 8th Army Air Force, remained 'very interested' in the project. But, for whatever reason, the proposal was not pursued. Nor were suggestions from the Air Ministry in July 1942 that Soviet bombers be deployed against *Tirpitz*.

Hitler remained unconvinced about the performance or the military worth of Germany's capital ships. On 14 November, he quizzed Räder at Berchtesgaden on their inactivity since July, which the C-in-C explained by lack of oil: *Tirpitz*'s brief sortie in search of PQ12 in March, for example, had used up 8,000 tons of precious fuel, the equivalent of an entire month's supply from Rumania. With the navy receiving only one-third of its overall needs, Räder had already described the oil situation as 'very critical'. But Hitler insisted on a viable force at Alten Fjord to threaten the convoys, and *Tirpitz* at Trondheim to deter an Allied invasion of Norway, musing also that Sweden was 'not reliable'. Air cover was an ever-present cause of friction between the German navy and the Luftwaffe, with the navy contending that its needs were never recognised. In December, it complained that only fourteen serviceable Bf 109F fighters were available to defend the whole Trondheim area. Nevertheless, *Tirpitz*'s defences in Foetten Fjord remained truly formidable, and on 28 December, after her refit, the battleship was ready for sea trials. Three days later, *Lutzow*, *Admiral Hipper* and seven destroyers did venture out against convoy JW51B, but broke off the action after the cruiser had been severely damaged.

The Allies did not know that *Tirpitz* had been assigned virtually a reserve role. Her forays so far had caused consternation and, in the case of PQ17, tragedy. She remained a constant danger. During 1942, five major air assaults had been launched on her, none since April, however, and none even close to success. A determined naval operation had been frustrated by the weather, literally within sight of the quarry. In Allied eyes the battleship was as much a dormant threat as ever.

3

BEAST AT BAY, JANUARY 1943–AUGUST 1944

Theoretically, 1943 began well for the Allies. Severe damage to *Admiral Hipper* by the Home Fleet during an abortive operation on 31 December 1942 and complaints from Göring that valuable Luftwaffe resources were being wasted in northern Norway prompted Hitler to harangue Räder on 11 January about the inept performance of his capital ships. Some should be disarmed, their guns put ashore as coastal artillery, others converted to aircraft carriers. The Grand Admiral was ordered to make the necessary arrangements. Instead, on 15 January he submitted a detailed memorandum explaining the theory of 'The Fleet in Being': even in port, warships tied down enemy flotillas that were thus prevented from fighting elsewhere. The naval C-in-C held further that to follow the proposed path 'will be victory for our enemies, gained without any effort on their part'. Hitler remained adamant, and on 30 January Räder resigned.

A fortnight later, Admiral Karl Dönitz, Flag Officer U-boats, formally replaced him. That change did not benefit the Allies. On 26 February Hitler recanted, and furthermore agreed to reinforce Norway with *Scharnhorst*. Meanwhile, *Tirpitz*'s refit had been completed, and off Trondheim her proving trials commenced. On 21 February, Topp was promoted rear-admiral and Capt Hans Meyer took command of the battleship. *Tirpitz*, *Scharnhorst* and *Lutzow*, supported by three cruisers, eight destroyers and eighty U-boats, presented a menacing combination along the North Sea coast; and Dönitz put this entire battle group under Vice-Admiral Oskar Kummetz.

There was ample reason for Churchill to renew demands for air action. On 13 February he furiously minuted the Chief of Combined Operations, the Paymaster-General, First Sea Lord, CAS and C-in-C Bomber Command: 'Have you given up all plans for doing anything to *Tirpitz* while she is in Trondheim? . . . It is a terrible thing that this prize should be waiting and no one be able to think of a way of winning it.' On 30 March, writing to Stalin, he emphasised that in Norway the Germans retained 'a powerful battle fleet' and that the danger to the Arctic convoys remained high. To the First Sea Lord on 5 May, he pugnaciously declaimed: 'I trust all concerned are alive to the importance of sinking this ship, and that it is realised that reasonable losses must be risked in order to do so', querying too whether the use of high-level American bombers was still a viable option. Two months later, on 16 July, the Prime Minister underlined his grave concern to the First Sea Lord, Sir Dudley Pound: 'The destruction of T [*sic*] remained an object of prime and capital importance affecting the whole of the naval war'.

By now, however, an unusual solution to the problem of *Tirpitz* had emerged. The distinguished aeronautical engineer Barnes Neville Wallis, Assistant Chief Designer (Structures) at Vickers-Armstrongs works in Weybridge, Surrey, had drawn up a scheme in 1941 for dropping a 10-ton 'earthquake' bomb at 40,000ft from 'a stratospheric bomber' to destroy a wide variety of targets, including coal mines, dams, oil refineries and lock gates. Significantly, a 'water immersion' variation of the bomb was designed. However, the concept contained in a 117-page, illustrated paper was turned down. Need to destroy dams then became a special focus of attention, and Wallis started to examine ways of projecting a missile dropped from a low-flying aircraft across the surface of a reservoir abutting a dam. This had obvious implications for attacking ships as well. During 1942 he therefore worked on two parallel versions of his so-called 'bouncing bomb' – one to destroy a gravity dam, the other a battleship.

On 14 May, Wallis circulated his thoughts in a persuasive, detailed paper, 'Spherical Bomb – Surface Torpedo'. A spherical bomb, he argued, was 'not susceptible to initial disturbance by the under-belly turbulence of the carrying aircraft at the moment of release'. So a more accurate path than for an 'ordinary bomb' resulted. The pilot would need to make a fast dive, then flatten out to release his load at a height 'not greater than 26ft when travelling at a speed of 470ft/sec in order that the impact angle shall not exceed 5 degrees'. Available data suggested that, given these constraints, a bomb would travel 3,500ft (roughly ¾ mile) in five bounces over water, the fifth just under 4ft high, the first one-half the height of release. Double-casing bridged 'by a series of light timber beams or roughly welded steel girders' would permit any necessary adjustments. 'The charge should sink in close proximity to its target and may be detonated by a hydro-static valve at any pre-determined depth, the rate of sinking being comparatively slow.' In January 1943 a further paper, despite its title 'Air Attack on Dams', included more material specifically relevant to an operation against *Tirpitz*. Figure 9, for example, showed a 'spherical surface torpedo' released 1,000–2,000yds from the target attaining a 'mean velocity of about 150 mph', striking the side of a ship and, with the aid of its back-spin, penetrating the water to explode 'about 15–20ft' below the hull. With the vessel in the illustration anchored close to a steep cliff, the similarity to *Tirpitz* in Foetten Fjord was marked.

But despite strong Admiralty backing, eighteen months of tests and trials at the National Physical Laboratory, Teddington, Chesil Beach and Reculver bombing ranges, on lochs Cairnbawn and Striven in Scotland, the smaller version of the weapon so successfully used to breach the German dams could not be perfected. So, early in September 1943, the Chiefs of Staff decided that, although a cadre would be retained to continue with 'development and operational trials' the bulk of 618 Squadron of Mosquitoes formed to deliver Wallis's weapon (codenamed Highball) would be 'released for other duties'. Effectively, this unique plan of attack on *Tirpitz* had been abandoned.

Soon, however, the urgency of dealing with the German battleship was again demonstrated. But her new refuge presented a formidable challenge to any attacker approaching by land, sea or air. On 24 March 1943, stopping only briefly off Narvik after leaving Trondheim Fjord, *Tirpitz* had anchored in Kaa Fjord, a branch of Alten Fjord in Finnmark close to North Cape, some 200 miles north of Narvik, ready to pounce on the Arctic convoys. Alten Fjord nestled among a collection of sounds and fjords leading off the Loppehavet inlet from the Arctic Ocean, whose entrance was dominated in the north by Hasvik Point and in the south by the defended islands of Loppen and Silden. To reach Alten Fjord, which ran roughly north-west–south-east, a vessel must negotiate Rogn or Stjern sounds which ran either side of Stjern Island with its several habitats and defensive positions. Kaa Fjord was then a cul-de-sac hanging north-east–south-west below Alten Fjord almost at its extremity. Ox Fjord, which ran north–south off Stjern Sound, and Lang Fjord, west–east off Alten Fjord, would also figure prominently in the subsequent story of *Tirpitz*. The hinterland was pitted with ground up to 2,000ft high. West of Kaa Fjord the St Haldde range rose to 1,141ft, and abutting it to the west, east and south undulating terrain approached 1,000ft. Kaa Fjord was approximately 4 miles long, 1¾ miles wide, with a spit of land protruding like a stalagmite from its southern end effectively dividing it into two.

On 6 September, in company with *Scharnhorst* and ten destroyers, *Tirpitz* sailed for the Norwegian archipelago of Spitzbergen, 400 miles north of North Cape, from which meteorological stations were transmitting valuable information to the Allies. Late on 7 September, with *Tirpitz* flying a white ensign as a *ruse de guerre*, the force reached Ice Fjord. Before departing at 1200 LT on 8 September, landing parties had destroyed shore installations in the vicinity and taken prisoners (including one Briton) as the warships bombarded other locations. *Tirpitz*, firing 52 rounds from her 380mm (15in) guns and 82 from her 150mm (5.9in) guns, concentrated on Barentsburg. She anchored in Kaa Fjord once more at 1730 on 9 September. With a touch of hyperbole, the British Ministry of Information declared that 'this action . . . proved to be the swan song of the German navy . . . [as] the German battlefleet retired to bolt holes in the fjords of northern Norway'. More pessimistically, the Admiralty thought 'this raid indicated that the German battleship was likely to become more active'.

In Kaa Fjord, *Tirpitz* thus remained a prime target, and on 22 September Operation Source involving an attack by midget submarines took place. Two of the six X-craft that had been towed across the North Sea behind conventional submarines succeeded in laying time-fused charges beneath the battleship. Publicly, the Germans underplayed the effect of the explosions, but the Admiralty rightly claimed 'considerable damage' in its assessment of 7 December.

Unfortunately, in spite of a most gallant effort, *Tirpitz* had neither been sunk nor permanently immobilised. Highball had failed to materialise and no successful air attack had been launched on the battleship throughout 1943. Several ideas had shown promise, only to wither. Use of American heavy bombers, rejected in 1942 but mentioned again by Churchill in May 1943, was revived during the summer. On 5 June, the US 8th AAF Bomber Command in Britain declared its willingness to 'attack any of the German capital ships with their Fortresses if these ships came within range', and inevitably *Tirpitz* entered the reckoning. Twelve days later, the Air Ministry argued that, in Kaa Fjord off Alten Fjord, the German warship lay beyond the B-17's range, although 'plans had been made to attack her as soon as she came within range (i.e Trondheim)'. On 19 June, the Joint Services Mission (JSM) in Washington suggested that the aircraft could bomb *Tirpitz* and fly on to land in the USSR, bombing her again on the way back. The Air Ministry demurred. The maximum range of a B-17, carrying two 1,600lb bombs, was 1,390 miles 'whereas the distance between the north of Scotland and the nearest suitable landing ground in the Murmansk area via Alten Fjord is 1,430mls'. On 25 June, the JSM came back: the range of a B-17F, 'of which there are available in the United Kingdom sufficient for this operation', was 2,100 miles. It requested that the London Bomber Board re-examine the proposition. Three days afterwards, the Air Ministry admitted that the operation might be 'feasible from the point of view of range', but supported by the British Chiefs of Staff opposed it on the grounds that the 'main' bomber offensive against Germany would be 'seriously' affected; strong fighter opposition could be expected; accurate high-level bombing would be impossible in the anticipated smoke-screen; and the B-17s 'would be subject to heavy air attack whilst waiting in Russia for the return trip'. To say the least, the British were not enthusiastic, and the scheme faded from the planning scene.

The unpalatable conclusion was though that, as 1943 closed, *Tirpitz*'s potential for creating maritime chaos remained very real. During the latter part of the Arctic winter, January–March 1944, while darkness still partially cloaked repair work on *Tirpitz*, Allied planners therefore prepared for a determined aerial assault on the battleship now isolated in Kaa Fjord. *Scharnhorst* had been sunk on 26 December 1943 and *Lutzow* was back in Germany. Assessment of the damage inflicted by the X-craft and estimates of when *Tirpitz* might again become operational were central to this process.

There was no shortage of information about the German battleship from a wide range of sources in addition to Ultra: the Naval Intelligence Division logged sixty-six reports between 1 January and 31 March 1944. Need for vigilant interpretation, though, remained high. An assertion on 6 January that morale on *Tirpitz* was 'bad' due to the X-craft (midget submarine) attack, loss of *Scharnhorst*, 'bombing of Germany . . . [and] long hours of darkness', was at odds with one a week later that crew members were working hard in conjunction with the 750 civilian workmen brought north by the SS *Monte Rosa*. Two separate reports (one based on remarks by a 'German bosun') on 10 January maintained that 'holes filled with cement' (previous repairs) had leaked after 'practice firing'. Three days later, another source contradicted this: the guns had 'rotated . . . but so far no firing'. Despite the anomalies, on 19 January the NID produced an interim summary: 'Temporary repairs are being carried out in north Norway and . . . the repairs will not be completed for another one or two months. She cannot be fully effective for prolonged operations without docking at a German shipyard'. On 30 January, news that her spotter aircraft were at the Bukta seaplane base tacitly confirmed that she was not yet ready for sea. Two days later, a 20-ton crane was erected on a pontoon on the starboard quarter of *Tirpitz*; close-by were five destroyers, a flak ship, the repair craft *Neumark*, a floating power plant and a tanker. The Norwegian High Commission confirmed the presence of these vessels on 9 February and that 'a large iron tank [was] under construction' on a wharf near the German battleship. From clandestine transmitters came information that there were 200 'small smoke generators in Kaa Fjord', but 'no change in pattern of camouflage has been observed. Camouflage from sea consists of three-cornered and fan-shaped fields in three colours. Hull is painted light grey, forward of forward gun turret and aft of the after gun turret to make ship look shorter'. Building of a bridge 'in order that the workmen can go to and from *Monte Rosa* [their depot ship and quarters] shows work will go on for some time.'

During the second half of the month, details of repair activity, surrounding defences and camouflage continued to reach London. On 15 February, a Soviet reconnaissance aircraft photographed the assembled naval and repair craft, with *Tirpitz* 'making smoke'. In the last week of February, crew reinforcements arrived. Still at anchor in Kaa Fjord on 3 March, the battleship's two forward turrets fired salvoes at a floating target. Six days later, civilian 'specialists' working on her reputedly said that she would be ready to leave in March, but a cautious interpreter added that 'ready to leave' should not be taken as 'will be leaving'.

Reviewing the position once more on 4 March, the NID trod carefully. *Tirpitz* could have been towed away after being damaged in September 1943, so the repairs must be designed for her to steam under her own power, and 18 knots could be achieved on one engine. Docking in Germany would certainly make her 'fully effective, but the possibility of her making an operational sortie before that cannot be entirely ruled out'. This conclusion was underlined on 13 March, following a further review of available technical data, with the added warning that local work would not have been carried out 'if the main engines were damaged beyond repair'. *Tirpitz*'s imminent state of readiness was considered on 20 March. She had performed neither sea trials nor exercises since the X-craft attack and would need time to work up to 'full fighting efficiency'. However, she had now done steaming and gunnery trials in Alten Fjord. And it remained uncertain whether she would return to Germany or stay in Norway 'to threaten our Russian convoy route and protect the Norwegian coastline against sea-borne invasion'. Time to deal with her before she became an active menace might, therefore, be short.

A single aerial attack had been mounted by the Soviets over the winter months. During the night of 10/11 February, fifteen aircraft, each with a 2,000lb bomb, set out from their base in good visibility and a full moon, but the weather deteriorated into snow squalls. Only four machines located the target. Norwegian observers reported 'no damage worth mentioning' and the Soviets themselves claimed just one near-miss. The difficulty of hitting *Tirpitz*, let alone disabling her, had once more been starkly demonstrated. In confirming this attack, on 6 April Rear-Admiral F.R. Archer, 'Senior British Naval Officer (SBNO) North Russia', informed the Admiralty that he had been 'pressing Golovko [C-in-C Soviet Northern Fleet] almost daily for the previous two months to bomb *Tirpitz*'.

Meanwhile, British staff officers had been building a comprehensive picture of *Tirpitz*'s defences and the progress of her state of readiness in order to devise and to time the next air attack. On 13 February 1944, the Soviets agreed that three PRU Spitfires could be based at Vaenga, 10 miles north-east of Murmansk. Five days later, the Admiralty asked that they concentrate on establishing the battleship's precise location in view of indications that she had changed anchorage since Operation Source; claims of a significant increase in the number of flak ships in Kaa Fjord should also be investigated. On 28 February, PRU groundcrew personnel and photographic interpreters arrived in Murmansk. The first Catalina flying boat destined to transport photographs back to England arrived at the nearby Kola inlet on 6 March, and the following day the Spitfires landed. Coordination of the RAF and Soviet photo-reconnaissance operations over Alten Fjord was the first hurdle to face; and that proved easier to overcome than the vagaries of meteorology. Low cloud caused cancellation of the scheduled RAF flight on 12 March, though the following day 'Admiral von Tirpitz' (as many Allied sources continued to define her) was seen in her 'usual berth', under high ground on the west of Kaa Fjord. The sortie on 17 March confirmed this, together with possibly four destroyers in nearby Lang Fjord. However, 'poor photographic light' on this occasion and a blizzard three days later frustrated the airborne camera. On 26 March, the Admiralty signalled urgently that *Tirpitz* was 'now known . . . capable of steaming', so daily PR flights should be mounted. But inclement weather allowed only three sorties between 27 March and 2 April.

Ultra decrypts proved infinitely more fruitful. In January, for example, sharp exchanges between *Tirpitz*, Salvage Command and Kiel Arsenal highlighted concern about the non-arrival of promised equipment, and Kiel had to strip oil pumps from the disabled *Gneisenau* to satisfy the battleship's needs, the implication being that every effort was being made to make *Tirpitz* seaworthy. A major setback for the Germans came when a 100-ton crane being transported from Tromso to Alten Fjord suffered damage in heavy seas and had to turn back on 13 January.

Three days later, *Tirpitz* complained that a merchant vessel had arrived without expected supplies for divers: 'The requested materials were urgently required and any further delay in delivery would jeopardize the time of completion.' And on 7 February, an unseemly wrangle erupted with the local U-boat authorities over priority for use of the *Huascaren* repair ship.

Ultra uncovered specific details about defensive priorities and *Tirpitz*'s movements. Clearly, the midget submarine operation thoroughly scared the Germans. On 6 January, Admiral Polar Coast called for 'urgent' protection of Alten Fjord and acceleration of minelaying activities. Arrangements for improving or installing deep anti-submarine nets at Sopnes, Auskarneset and at Lang Fjord, discussed on 4 February, prompted British speculation that *Tirpitz* was about to change her berth or that 'a further heavy unit' was to arrive. Messages about completion of these passive defences continued to pass back and forth during the coming weeks, and on 22 March the work in Lang Fjord remained unfinished. Early in February, it emerged that seaplanes were carrying out regular and frequent anti-submarine patrols along the coast, over Alten and Kaa fjords. On 12 February, *Tirpitz* initiated a false submarine alert, once more demonstrating a generous degree of neurosis.

The threat of aerial attacks figured prominently in enemy thoughts. A smoke-screen exercise on 14 January revealed serious deficiencies, and the Battle Group commander requested 'many additional positions in the hills and the use of 5 additional fishing smacks', the new equipment to be taken from the Bogen and North Cape batteries. On 15 February, sighting of the first PRU aircraft in the area since 23 November 1943 excited special comment and six days later, drawing attention to recent aerial torpedo attacks on minelayers, the Battle Group commander pointed to 'weaknesses of our fighter defences', calling for rapid improvement. On 31 March, reports of two RAF reconnaissance aircraft flying across Kaa Fjord from the east (i.e. the USSR) provoked consternation. The following day, another Spitfire 'certainly covered' warship berths in the Alta area.

From the British standpoint, evidence of *Tirpitz*'s increasing mobility, revealed by the intercepted Enigma transmissions, caused rising concern. On 14 March, the battleship warned senior naval authorities that she intended carrying out trials in Alten Fjord 15/16 March. And the revelation on 16 March that *Tirpitz* and her destroyers would form a separate battle group under the battleship's commander could herald impending offensive operations: 'Significance of new organisation in relation to *Tirpitz*'s future movements cannot be appreciated.' On 17 March, the warship reported the results of her trials: 'Hull, guns and power installation were from a material point of view fully operationally effective.' However, communication facilities were still incomplete and 'unacceptable vibration in midship cruising turbines' meant that machinery had to be flown to Mannerheim for repair. 'Comment. Move of *Tirpitz* south does not appear to be imminent.' A separate intelligence report suggested that she had reached 27 knots during the trials.

On 22 March, *Tirpitz* noted further communication problems: all her teleprinters needed 'immediate' expert technical attention. Within days these snags had been sorted out, and on 31 March the battleship confirmed that she would be settling that day in her usual Kaa Fjord berth within 'Net Cage No. 1' – double anti-submarine and anti-torpedo booms. The battleship announced, too, that speed trials scheduled for 1 April had been postponed until 0530 on 3 April, when she would depart 'for degaussing measurement in Altafjord [*sic*]', followed by high speed trials in Stjernsund and Vargsund, returning to Kaa Fjord at 1800.

Kaa Fjord lay some 80 miles from the main entrance to Alten Fjord, its entrance being protected by a boom, *Tirpitz* herself further protected within the strengthened defences of the new 'cage'. Following the flawed exercise of 14 January, more smoke canisters had been installed on surrounding hills with an estimated twenty fishing smacks in the area similarly equipped and flak guns in eight batteries distributed ashore around the fjord. During the winter, the battleship had indeed occupied two anchorages opposite one another across the narrow western arm of the fjord. It seemed reasonable to assume, though, that the easterly one had been used while the Barbrudalen 'usual' western berth was being strengthened. The light flak armament of *Tirpitz* had been improved with the addition of Flak 38 vierling quadruple-mounted 20mm guns, situated among other places on top of B and C turrets. Theoretically, the battleship could now fire nine single and nine quadruple 20mm flak guns on either beam at approximately 8,500 rounds per minute.

In the third week of March, the Admiralty concluded that *Tirpitz* was unlikely to go to sea against 'a well escorted convoy but might do so if sure she has no big ships or aircraft carriers to contend with'. As the enemy set considerable store by interrupting supplies to the USSR, 'this may influence them to take more than normal risk with *Tirpitz* in her present condition'. It must thus be assumed that '*Tirpitz* may be operationally effective' and that battleship cover for convoy JW58 would be necessary. A stream of reports from Norway during March, based on observations from the shore and merchant vessels in the fjords, bore added witness to the warship's mobility, though in truth no sea trials had yet taken place. Urgent destructive action, nevertheless, seemed necessary.

For some time, preparations had been in hand to attack *Tirpitz* at anchor. On 19 March, the First Sea Lord 'considered we had a very strong force provided we could find *Tirpitz* and time our operations well. A very great deal would therefore depend on the soundness of our reconnaissance and intelligence to enable the C-in-C Home Fleet to judge his time for sailing.' Operation Tungsten was about to be launched.

Ideas about such an operation had begun to circulate among the naval and air staffs in December 1943 and seriously to take shape in the new year under the direction of Vice-Admiral Sir Henry Moore (Second-in-Command of the Home Fleet) with Capt L.D. Mackintosh as his Chief of Staff. On 29 January 1944, the Admiralty forewarned C-in-C Home Fleet: 'In view of the great importance of putting *Tirpitz* out of action, it is requested that you will plan to attack *Tirpitz* in Altenfjord with naval aircraft during the period 7–16 March.' The force should comprise the aircraft carriers *Victorious* (with Fairey Barracuda bombers and Chance-Vought Corsair fighters), *Furious* (one squadron of Barracudas and as many Supermarine Seafire fighters as possible), *Emperor* (Grumman Hellcat fighters), *Pursuer* and *Searcher* (Grumman Wildcat fighters). The Seafires would protect the fleet, the Barracudas carry out a daylight attack on *Tirpitz*, escorted by the 'American-type fighters' with drop tanks. And the Air Ministry was 'examining the possibility of co-operating with a bombing attack' – not enthusiastically, as it turned out.

On 9 February, ACAS (Ops) briefed the CAS. Intelligence sources had convinced the Admiralty that *Tirpitz* would be able to sail from Alten Fjord 'by about the end of March', and a carrier strike was therefore being planned for mid-March with 33 Barracudas (each carrying two 500lb bombs), escorted by 70 or possibly 110 Fleet Air Arm fighters. The First Sea Lord had enquired about the RAF or USAAF mounting associated bombing attacks on *Tirpitz* or diversionary operations. A study had been undertaken, and the Naval Staff agreed that at night Bomber Command had 'no prospect whatsoever of a useful attack'. The Americans believed that 120 of their day bombers attacking *Tirpitz* from a Soviet base would achieve two to three hits with 2,000lb AP bombs from 10,000–20,000ft. However, 'the uncertainty of the weather and the difficulty of coordinating their attacks with that of the Fleet Air Arm would also render their participation in the operation quite impracticable'. Air Vice-Marshal W.A. Coryton concluded that the Royal Navy showed 'undue optimism'. It was unreasonable to expect the anticipated five 500lb SAP hits seriously to damage 'the fire control installation'. There was, Coryton felt, a 'very slender' chance of such success and it was 'questionable whether [Operation] Thrustful [the original designation] is in fact a worthwhile operation'.

Neither RAF nor USAAF bombers did become involved, and if the FAA knew of Coryton's gloomy prediction it had absolutely no impact. On 18 February, an Admiralty minute noted that the five carriers would provide 120 fighters to cope with an estimated German strength of 71 (including 27 flying boats) in the vicinity. In view of this paltry enemy air presence, the First Sea Lord queried whether the number of FAA fighters should not be reduced, the bombing force increased. The views of admirals tend to prevail. On 22 February numbers for Operation Thrustful were adjusted. As a result, 42 (not 33) Barracudas would be escorted by 28 Corsairs, 20 Hellcats and 40 Wildcats. The possibility of adding 24 Avengers from two more escort carriers had been discarded, because the Avenger was deemed less effective as a bomber and seven carriers would require a very larger number of warship escorts. *Victorious* needed dockyard attention, so the operation was postponed 'for approximately two weeks'.

The delay proved unexpectedly beneficial, giving more time for her two Corsair squadrons (1834 and 1836), which joined the carrier respectively on 12 February and 8 March, to work up for the operation. However, in his post-operational report Vice-Admiral Moore considered the docking of *Victorious* actually to be a disadvantage for these 'recently formed units'. Moreover, the two Barracuda squadrons (829 and 831) forming the 8th Torpedo Bomber Reconnaissance (TBR) wing had not yet flown combined exercises. 'A full-scale bombing and air firing range', using a buoyed area to represent *Tirpitz* in Kaa Fjord, 'was constructed at Loch Erriboll near Caithness, and included smoke defences and dummy A.A. batteries and effects'. Some who took part maintain that a convenient island rather than buoys acted as *Tirpitz*, with taped areas on shore representing defensive positions. Aircrew were supplied with target maps to simulate the planned operation. 'Unfavourable weather' was overcome with 'a large number of practices carried out . . . [which] proved to be of inestimable value': 827 Squadron diary recorded intensive dive bombing exercises from 14 March. A full dress rehearsal occurred on 28 March, which Moore pronounced highly successful but some participants thought 'a complete shambles'. Meanwhile, finalisation of operational plans was complicated by use of three different classes of carrier and five different types of aircraft, three of which had seen little operational use with the FAA. Nor had aircrew previously dropped three of the four types of designated bombs. So that enemy submarines and reconnaissance aircraft would be enticed eastwards, the attack would take place on 4 April 1944, as the Murmansk-bound convoy JW58 passed beyond Bear Island.

Detailed plans were refined in February and early March. Lt Cdr F.R.A. Turnbull, 47 Wing commander, later confirmed that he, other wing leaders and staff officers 'attended meetings . . . before and during practice runs' in preparation for 'a most carefully planned and rehearsed operation', which implies that these officers were fully aware of the target at an early stage. Among information that had to be considered in this process that was a signal from the air attaché in Moscow: 'Identification chit in Russian might help but believed high percentage of Soviet Army illiterate. Considerable danger from being mistaken for Germans due to similarity colour of RAF and Luftwaffe uniforms.' He therefore advised that damaged aircraft should make for Sweden, not the USSR. On 4 March, Tungsten replaced Thrustful as the operational codeword, and a sixth carrier, *Fencer*, was added to the original five.

The final plan envisaged the striking force on the two fleet carriers comprising 12 Barracuda dive bombers from 827 Squadron and 9 from 829 Squadron on *Victorious*; 9 from 830 Squadron and 12 from 831 Squadron on *Furious*. Top cover for the attack would be provided by 14 Corsairs each from 1834 and 1836 squadrons on *Victorious*. Fighters to act as close escort to the bombers and to attack enemy gun positions would consist of ten aircraft from each of six squadrons: 800 and 804 (Hellcats) on *Emperor*, 881 and 896 (Wildcats) on *Pursuer*, 882 and 898 (Wildcats) on *Searcher*. Nine Seafires each from 801 and 880 squadrons on *Furious* would protect the fleet by flying Combat Air Patrols. Twelve Swordfish of 842 Squadron and eight more Wildcats would carry out anti-submarine patrols from *Fencer*.

The striking force would be divided into two waves of twenty-one Barracudas carrying a combination of 1,600lb AP (0.08sec delay fuse), 600lb anti-submarine (hydrostatic pistol set at 35ft), 500lb SAP (0.14sec delay) and 500lb MC (instantaneous fuse) bombs. The 1,600lb AP bomb 'could do vital damage if released above 3,500ft', the 500lb SAP bomb 'could do serious between deck damage', the 600lb A/S bomb 'might cause considerable underwater damage by a near miss' and the 500lb MC bomb's 'principal value . . . would be to reduce casualties to our own bombers by detonating above deck and eliminating exposed A.A. gunners'. A proposal to arm Hellcats from *Emperor* with 500lb or 1,000lb bombs in addition to drop tanks was considered 'impracticable', although later attacks on *Tirpitz* would use this tactic. *Victorious* and *Furious* were to exchange 831 and 827 Squadrons prior to the operation. A single TBR wing could then be launched simultaneously from the two carriers. So the first wave would consist of the Barracudas from 827 and 830 Squadrons, ordered to commence their dive at 8,000ft at an angle of 50–60 degrees, releasing 500lb bombs from 2,500ft and 1,600lb AP bombs surprisingly from 3,000ft 'or under'. The bombers would attack 'along the length of the target, one squadron from ahead, one from astern'. The second wave of 829 and 831 squadron Barracudas (52 TBR) would dive from 10,000ft at an angle of 45–55 degrees, attacking in the same manner as the first. For both waves, the 500lb MC bombs would be dropped first. Forty-two fighters were to accompany each wave, using 50 per cent tracer and 50 per cent AP ammunition to strafe flak batteries and the battleship's gun positions.

Victorious sailed from Scapa Flow at noon on 30 March with a powerful Home Fleet force of two battleships accompanied by two cruisers and escorting destroyers under the C-in-C, Admiral Sir Bruce Fraser. The remaining

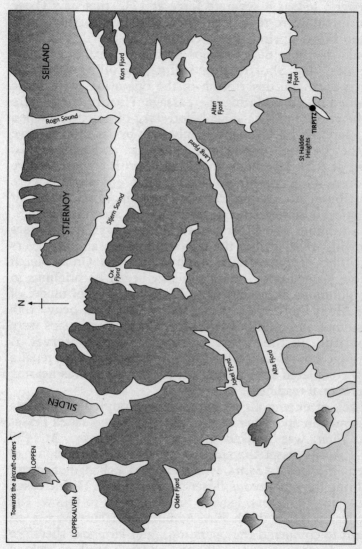

Area of Fleet Air Arm attacks from carriers, April–August 1944

five carriers with cruiser, destroyer and oiler support under Rear-Admiral A.W. La T. Bisset (Rear-Admiral Escort Carriers) left as a separate force at 1715 that day. These two forces were to rendezvous 250 miles north-west of Alten Fjord during the afternoon of 3 April. *Victorious* would then join Bisset's ships for a dawn strike on *Tirpitz* the next day. Shortly after sailing, all pilots would be given a general description of the operation, with more detailed briefings during the passage. Final briefings were to be conducted one hour before take-off, aircraft fuelled and serviced by 1700 and bombed up by 1800 on the eve of the operation. Models of Alten, Kaa and Lang fjords, built at RAF Medmenham, together with comprehensive photos of the target area from different angles, were distributed to each carrier. The commanding officer of *Victorious* admitted later to revealing 'the secret in advance' to a number of officers, with telegraphist air gunners knowing 48hrs before the operation. Pilots and observers had 10hrs of concentrated briefings on board. On 29 March before leaving port *Furious* similarly began its briefings in the gunroom 'fitted out with a large-scale relief model of the Alten Fjord area . . . showing light and heavy flak positions, air-landing strips etc. . . . Photos and maps were plentiful', in the words of one Barracuda observer. A message from C-in-C Home Fleet warned that, with repairs now completed after the X-craft attack, *Tirpitz* was nearing operational readiness.

Lack of enemy air reconnaissance coupled with Ultra information about her forthcoming trials persuaded Fraser that *Tirpitz* was 'unlikely to threaten the convoy'. At 1435 on 1 April, Bisset therefore learnt that the operation had been advanced by 24hrs, which entailed a change of course to bring the rendezvous closer to North Cape. He increased speed to 16.5 knots, leaving his two oilers to follow. The battleship *Anson* (with Vice-Admiral Sir Henry Moore on board to command the operation), and *Victorious* therefore joined Bisset's force at 1600 on Sunday 2 April, as *Duke of York* with her escorts sailed on north-westwards. During a briefing for senior officers at 1715 on *Victorious*, it was found that while the carrier had advanced its time one hour for DBST, *Anson* and *Furious* had omitted to do so. At 1900, Moore set off towards a point 120 miles north-west of Kaa Fjord, the transfer of the squadrons between *Victorious* and *Furious* taking place en route. With him he had his flagship and the two fleet carriers in Force 7; Force 8 under Bisset in the cruiser *Royalist* comprised the four escort carriers. Both forces had further cruiser and destroyer support. To cover Bisset's departure an elaborate bogus wireless network operated from 30 March to 5 April, simulating transmissions from his different vessels, and involved Hatston air station, Loch Erriboll, Scapa Flow, *Kent*, *Rodney* and the depot ship *Tyne*.

Zero hour was 0415 DBST on 3 April. On *Victorious* operational crews were roused at the 'ghastly hour' of 0130 and the final briefing started after breakfast at 0330. Engines were warmed up by maintenance personnel at 0315 with crews settling into their machines 45mins later. Between 0415 and 0423, ten Corsairs took off, followed by twelve Barracudas of 827 Squadron (two with a single 1,600lb AP bomb, eight with three 500lb MC and two with two 600lb A/S bombs) and another Corsair (0424–0430), all the aircraft away in 14mins 9secs. Meanwhile, 0423–0424, two Seafires for fleet defence had been launched from *Furious*, whose nine Barracudas of 830 Squadron (five with a 1,600lb AP bomb, four with three 500lb SAP bombs) took off between 0424 and 0428. Having formed up, led by Lt Cdr R. Baker-Faulkner, the first wave set off for *Tirpitz* at 0436. Rear-Admiral Bisset thought 'it was a grand sight, with the sun just risen, to see this well-balanced striking force departing'; Capt M.M. Denny on *Victorious* said that aircrew 'left the carrier's decks in the greatest heart, and brimful of confidence'. Initially flying at low level to evade radar detection, first wave aircraft climbed to 10,000ft 25 miles from the coast, which they crossed at 0508 LT (coincided with DBST), 37 miles north of *Tirpitz*. With the Baracudas not exceeding 135 knots, Hellcats from the escort carriers above at 190 knots had to weave back and forth to maintain formation.

Three minutes earlier, enemy radar had picked up the incoming machines, but unaccountably the target warship did not receive the information until 0524, when she was in the throes of casting off for her postponed trials. Capt Meyer immediately ordered the flak crews into position and all watertight doors to be closed, though an estimated 20 per cent remained open as the air attacks started. The Barracudas and their escorts crossed Loppen Island at 0515 to fly over Jokel and Lang Fjords towards the target. When the fighters crested the high ridge overlooking Kaa Fjord at 0528, the smoke-screen had not been fully activated. Lt Cdr J. Cooper, OC of 882 Wildcat squadron, wrote later: 'We whistled down over forested hills . . . [and] shot across the fjord in a straggling line abreast shooting into the battleship. . . . Various missiles appeared to be whizzing in all directions. . . . Very exciting.' Clearing the cliff, Cooper lost his underside aerial, and on the way back had time to register ski tracks in the snow before passing over two destroyers in another fjord and giving them 'a short burst'. The Hellcats and Wildcats quickly caused havoc among *Tirpitz*'s gun crews and flak batteries ashore, though by no means all of these positions were silenced. Behind them, the Barracudas had turned to port south of the target and dived to attack along its length from stern to bow at 0529. The bombing phase lasted just one minute, and cost one 830 Squadron Barracuda. The force then withdrew to the north-west. Surviving first wave aircraft began arriving over the fleet again at 0610, landing on *Victorious* 0619–0625 and *Furious* 0618–0638 (less 830/M, shot down); the eleven Corsairs regained *Victorious*, 0632–0642. Denny reported that 'all [his] aircraft returned in flight formation with an unanimous broad grin'. For Barracuda 5G of 830 Squadron, its return to *Furious* warranted more of a collective sigh of relief. Firmly believing that it had released its 1,600lb bomb at 2,700ft over the target, its crew was astounded to be overtaken on the return flight by another Barracuda signalling 'your bomb is still on'. In due course, *Furious* more bluntly advised the pilot to 'go far away and try and shake the damn thing off'. Sub Lt D.E. Rowe RNZN attempted to comply, as his Observer recalled, 'but nothing would rid us of that bloody egg'. The crew was about precariously to ditch in the icy Arctic, when the carrier signalled Rowe to land. 'Then began the nail-biting descent, knowing that we and several of the ship's crew might be blown to smithereens, if we missed *Furious*'s three wires (no crash barriers)'. The pilot, however, 'made a copy-book landing, and we fled the kite as quickly as possible'.

After the first wave attacks caught *Tirpitz* manoeuvring, the battleship lay almost broadside on across Kaa Fjord with her bows close to the western shore. Inspections showed that the engines were unaffected, but critical communication systems had been damaged and flooded starboard compartments were causing a slight list. It was, therefore, decided to abandon the trials and return to the 'cage'. *Tirpitz* was still trying to do this when the second wave appeared to carry out a similar form of attack to that of the first. *Victorious* had flown off ten Corsairs 0515–1520, eleven Barracudas (one of the planned twelve failing to start, four with three 500lb SAP, three with three 500lb MC bombs and four with a single 1,600lb AP bomb) 0520–0534, with nine Barracudas (all with three 500lb SAP bombs) taking off from *Furious*, so that the second wave under Lt Cdr V. Rance departed at 0538, minus another 829 Squadron Barracuda (Q) which crashed shortly after take-off. As the aircraft were on their way to the target, *Furious* rotated the Seafire patrol to ensure that four fighters were always in the air over the fleet. The second wave, like the first, crossed the coast at 10,000ft. As it did so, an expanding smudge of smoke in the distance identified the location of *Tirpitz*, but on closer acquaintance it did not mask her superstructure. Reputedly it also blinded her gunners, whose fire control system had been damaged in the first wave attacks, as an air-raid warning sounded at 0633. Immediately prior to the main attack, Hellcats from 804 Squadron and Wildcats of 896 and 898 squadrons softened up the defences. Lt Cdr S.G. Orr, OC 804 Squadron, noted that the smoke-screen 'came halfway up the mountains on each side', though *Tirpitz*'s stern was just visible. 'I didn't see any point in firing at the ship. So most of my lot decided to have a go at the ack-ack around the cliffs.' Starting their attack at 0636, second wave aircraft had to fly through a predicted box barrage (crews reported two curtains at 8,000ft and 2,000ft). Sub Lt N.H. Bovey described the barrage as 'a substantial umbrella of bursting shells through which we dived . . . [and] because one could no longer see the flashes one felt much better'. Once more a Barracuda (M of 829 Squadron) was shot down over the target area, the TAG baling out to become a prisoner of war.

Victorious put up two Corsairs to enhance combat patrols over the fleet when second wave survivors approached at 0714 and landed her own aircraft 0720–0756, as did *Furious* 0728–0758. With no barriers and a slow lift to the hangars below dictating about three minutes between landings, in the process *Furious* moved so close to the coast that lower deck wits welcomed the impending run ashore. On returning to the task force, one 804 Squadron Hellcat could not lower its arrester hook, the pilot ditched close to the destroyer *Algonquin* and was rescued. Barracuda B–Baker of 831 Squadron failed to release one of its 500lb bombs, but managed to jettison it at sea and land safely. However, a Corsair missed the arrester wire on *Victorious*, 'crashing on its nose about 25 to 30 feet beyond the second barrier' – miraculously without casualties. Reuters also reported the troubled return of an 829 Squadron Barracuda with a bomb hang-up: 'Comdr [Lt Cdr D.] Phillips circled again and glided gently down towards the stern of the carrier to make a perfect landing.' A TAG, who had already landed, eyed an empty flight deck as Phillips appeared, with heads sheepishly poking up once he touched down safely. Phillips himself wrote: 'As I approached I was bound to smile when I saw not a soul in sight except the batsman controlling me with his bats. I smiled even more when the batsman gave me the "cut" sign and immediately jumped into his safety net below the level of the flight deck.' VA2 HF (Moore) signalled the Admiralty: 'Tungsten completed. Admiral von Tirpitz hit by at least one 1,600 bomb and many other bombs. 3 Barracudas one fighter lost. Fighter pilot safe.'

Post-raid reports amplified the raw details. On 5 April, *Victorious* believed the claim of its aircraft 'well founded', the first strike squadrons (827 and 830) obtaining three 1,600lb AP, four 500lb SAP and three 500lb MC hits; one 1,600lb was in the 'vicinity forward superstructure', three 500lb bombs were 'amidships and a number forward of bridge'. Barracudas of 829 and 831 Squadrons secured hits with four 500lb SAP, two 500lb MC and one 600lb A/S bombs: 'one hit starboard side of mainmast which caused large explosion; one about "Y" turret; and three amidships'. No 'substantial damage' occurred, however, from the near misses. '*Tirpitz* was left shrouded in smoke with two fires burning amidships and had ceased fire when the last aircraft dived'. The Commanding Officer of *Victorious* concluded his report to Moore: 'I believe *Tirpitz* now to be useless as a warship', and followed this with a confirmatory signal: 'I have no doubt that *Tirpitz* is out of action and 17 hits I have allowed out of more than 30 claimed is an absolute minimum'. Moore, in his report to the Admiralty, more cautiously believed *Tirpitz* 'seriously damaged'.

Other post-operational reports added detail to the overall summaries. Baker-Faulkner, 8 TBR wing leader, described leaving the fleet at 0436 on a track of 139 degrees, maintained for 9mins to allow the escorting fighters to take up position in 'good' weather – 1/10ths cloud over 10,000ft. At 0457, the strike force began to climb about 25 miles from the coast and at 0459 Loppen Island was identified 'fine on the port bow', which allowed landfall west of the island and the coast to be crossed accurately. The aircraft flew 'close to the westward of the head of Lang Fiord' and eastward down the valley towards Kaa Fjord. No flak was experienced till three miles from the target; then 'heavy but inaccurate' fire commenced. Approximately 10 miles from the battleship, Baker-Faulkner deployed 830 Squadron Barracudas astern of 827, 'shortly afterwards according to wing "synchronised tactics"' redeploying 'starboard half of 827 Squadron'. *Tirpitz* was sighted in the expected position; and Baker-Faulkner ordered the accompanying Wildcats and Hellcats to strafe it and nearby flak sites. As they did so, the Barracudas 'dived to keep hill cover' and flew towards the southern end of Kaa Fjord. Baker-Faulkner explained that he 'pulled up over the top [of a 'mountain'] and dived steeply towards the target itself from a height of approximately 4,000ft', attacking 'from stern to stem . . . [and] releasing bombs at 1,200ft'. Smoke appeared all round the fjord, too late to be effective: 'fighters had shot up target very well and undoubtedly spoilt *Tirpitz*'s gunnery'. Twenty-one aircraft attacked 'in 60secs exactly' before withdrawing north-westwards towards Silden Island roughly parallel to, but to the east of, the incoming track. Despite 'excellent' visibility, Baker-Faulkner enthused that 'a considerable element of surprise was achieved'. No enemy fighters appeared; flak 'spasmodic, erratic and inaccurate'. In the press, he would be quoted more colourfully: 'We caught them with their pants down. Really the attack was a piece of cake.'

Lt Cdr F.R.A. Turnbull, 47 Fighter Wing leader, reinforced and amplified Baker-Faulkner's words. Eleven Corsairs from *Victorious* formed up with the first wave Barracudas 'without difficulty. By the time that height was reached, the sun was well up and on the port bow but cross over as easily given by flying at 11,000ft on the down sun side of the strike.' Although the visibility proved 'excellent', 9/10ths snow cover on the ground made it 'difficult' to see the aircraft below. The slow speed of the bombers meant that there might have been problems in 'identifying friend from foe if enemy fighters had once got into the "beehive"'. After 65mins flying, long-range tanks were jettisoned between Alta and Lang fjords. When the target came into view, the smoke-screen was beginning to gather, and as bombers dived the Corsairs ranged over Lang and Kaa fjords, while the close escort dealt with flak. No activity was observed over an airfield to the south of Kaa Fjord, though two destroyers were getting under way in Lang Fjord and a tanker lay close-by. At 0600, about 30mins after the attack, the

Corsairs set course for the fleet. The longest of their sorties would last 2hrs 30mins.

In his report, Lt Cdr V. Rance, wing leader of 52 TBR, described the second wave action. Nineteen Barracudas took off 0525–0535, formed up at a height of 50–200ft and set off at 0537 (not the official 0538) on a course of 150 degrees magnetic. At such low level, aircraft had difficulty in maintaining line astern, but this eased when they adopted a Vic formation after crossing the coast. Three smoke floats were initially dropped at intervals of one minute to assist the following fighters in 'fine weather, sea slight, swell nil'. Cloud in the target area was less than 1/10ths at 15,000ft, and the bombers closed Kaa Fjord at 10,000ft in a shallow double Vic. Over Norwegian territory, they flew for 12mins at 165 knots true, then slowly reduced height while increasing speed to 195 knots true. When no fighters appeared, Rance ordered the wing into two columns at 210 knots true to aid flak evasion. After *Tirpitz* came into sight to port, the starboard column dropped back 'to keep the leader's column roughly between it and the target'. The final dive commenced at about 7,500ft in the wake of Hellcats attacking shore batteries and Wildcats attacking *Tirpitz*. Rance confirmed a box barrage round *Tirpitz*, 'fire with close range weapons was opened much too early' (due to the fire control problems unknown to Rance) and the entire attack, as with the first wave, lasted just one minute. One Barracuda crashed into a hillside after dropping its bombs. 'A large brown smoke-screen had been laid from generators all round the target area and from the *Tirpitz* itself. . . . It did not interfere with bombing but must have hampered close range weapons considerably', as indeed it did. 'Unquestionably, strafing attacks by fighters and the use of powerful blast bombs by the first few aircraft are of the utmost value in ensuring the safe arrival of the armour-piercing bombs carried by the latter half of the attacking force.' The second wave, Rance concluded, cleared the enemy coast at 355 degrees magnetic.

The leader of 7 Fighter Wing accompanying the second wave similarly explained its part in the operation. After the fighters joined up with 52 TBR, the force departed at 0540 and flew an 'uneventful run . . . according to plan'. The climb commenced 20 miles from the coast, 'an excellent landfall' was made and the coast crossed at 9,000ft. The target was approached by flying west of Lang Fjord on a course of 133 degrees before the aircraft turned east. During the last leg, light flak came up from a position in the valley south of St Haldde. With no fighter opposition, Hellcats diverted to attack flak positions around Kaa Fjord. However, Lt Cdr M.F. Fell noted that as the 'whole of Alten Fjord' was covered in smoke, the target would be difficult to pinpoint. The close escort did dive into the smoke, but only three pilots located and attacked *Tirpitz*, the rest engaged flak positions ashore. Bombing results were 'practically impossible' to assess due to the smoke. The three fighter pilots, who did see the target, recorded that she was lying in the same berth, but broadside on instead of 'up and down the fjord'. The port wing tank of a Barracuda, hit by fire from *Tirpitz* as it pulled out of its dive, burst into flames 30secs later and the aircraft crashed, only one of the crew baling out. The force withdrew at hilltop height in a straight line from the target to Silden Island, with the escorting fighters weaving above the bombers. Again, with no enemy fighters in evidence, many broke off to strafe targets of opportunity and, in particular, two tankers in Lang and Ox fjords. From Silden Island, the aircraft flew uneventfully at sea level. Fell castigated the Barracudas for 'unnecessary and useless chatter' on the air waves, with a 'glaring error' 10 miles after originally leaving the fleet, when somebody broadcast: 'You can see the coast on our starboard bow.' On a more positive note, he said the aircraft camouflage blended well with the landscape and the maps and briefing photographs provided were 'excellent': 'all pilots said that they felt it was like flying over country they already knew and had flown over often before'. Moreover, 'the attack went exactly as arranged' – apart from the poor visibility around the target.

The first wave had undoubtedly caused considerable damage to *Tirpitz*: fire control (a specific target), the bridge telegraph system and hangars particularly suffered. As the aircraft attacked, the battleship was manoeuvring clear of the booms with the aid of tugs, and was therefore not ready fully to defend herself. She was in the process of seeking refuge in the cage once more when a warning came that more enemy aircraft (the second wave) had been sighted. *Tirpitz* was caught unawares as she tried to regain her protected berth. By now, Capt Wolfe Junge, Meyer's second-in-command, had taken charge of the battleship. The second wave also swept the upper deck, and overall 122 were killed, 316 wounded (including civilian workers and supervisors). Several holes had been made in the deck on the port side. Below, the galley was damaged and the ship had listed to starboard, some 875 tons of water having leaked into the bilges. At 0713 LT *Tirpitz* acknowledged several hits by thirty carrier-borne aircraft, which had attacked at 0629 – the first wave. Ultra later learnt that two destroyers had assisted in fighting a fire on the oil tanker *C A Larsen*, which had not been doused until 1649 on 3 April. During that night a hospital ship left Tromso for Kaa Fjord. An intercepted German High Command communiqué of 4 April read: 'British aircraft carriers yesterday attempted an attack on a Norwegian naval base. Our defences broke up the attack, which never came to full engagement. The battleship 'Tirpitz' shot down four enemy aircraft and a patrol vessel shot down two.' Two days later, a strange transmission was sent to the Naval War Staff: ' . . . about eight ratings of *Tirpitz*'s flak had reported that they had definitely observed crosses on aircraft', an assertion not confirmed by officers or wreckage from crashes. This may have been a crude attempt on behalf of the gun crews to deflect criticism of ineffective engagement of attacking aircraft. Non-appearance of enemy fighters has never been satisfactorily explained. However, post-war, Fleet Air Arm officers heard that the Bf 109 squadron allocated for the battleship's defence had apparently been temporarily sent to Germany, its return delayed by bad weather. 'Thank God for that', Lt Cdr Orr reflected.

On board the carriers, aircraft were being loaded with torpedoes for another attack, which Sub Lt N.H. Bovey thought 'hairy' but 'possible'. But success with torpedoes could not have been guaranteed even if *Tirpitz* left her protected anchorage. Moore certainly considered repeating Tungsten the following day, but became convinced that the attacks on 3 April had wrought severe damage. Moreover, he decided, 'the fatigue of the air-crews and their natural reaction after completing a dangerous operation successfully' must be taken into consideration. The weather deteriorated overnight as well. Thus, at 1630 on 6 April the Tungsten 'fleet entered Scapa Flow and aircrews on the decks of the carriers were cheered by the ships' companies'. Lt G.C. Russell-Jackson of 831 Squadron thought it 'a most memorable occasion'. According to 804 Squadron, on the way home the task force had endured 'the usual alarms from "bogey" aircraft and U-boats'.

At Scapa, messages were waiting from King George VI – 'hearty congratulations on your gallant and successful operation' – and Winston Churchill – 'pray congratulate the pilots and air crews concerned on the brilliant feat of arms'. In the wake of an Admiralty press release, newspapers and periodicals enthused about the Fleet Air Arm's success, and indirectly underlined the fear that the German battleship engendered. *The Times* ran the headline 'Tirpitz Crippled by Dawn Raiders' and informed its readers that 'the Tirpitz was set on fire amidships and is now described as "a useless warship"', referring also to 'Germany's only surviving battleship . . . [previously showing] signs of being fit for service'. The *Evening Standard* presented a 'Fighter's Eye View of the *Tirpitz*' with pilots describing their attacks in detail, one concluding: 'When the party was over we got out to sea'. But Fraser was uneasy that the warship had not been sunk. So was Churchill. The Admiralty estimated that in six months repairs would be completed; Junge halved that time.

On 14 April, Fraser sent his formal report to the Admiralty, culled principally from Moore's submission to him. However, by now he was entangled in what Stephen Roskill has termed 'a squabble at the top of the naval hierarchy' with the First Sea Lord, Admiral of the Fleet Sir Andrew Cunningham. According to Cunningham, on

13 April he found Fraser 'in a most truculent and obstinate mood', when he rang him about swiftly re-attacking *Tirpitz*. The First Sea Lord alleged that, with the support of 'his admirals and captains', Fraser refused to consider such an operation. Although Cunningham 'reasoned with him', the C-in-C Home Fleet 'indicated he would haul his flag down if ordered to repeat "Tungsten"'. Cunningham told him to sleep on it and confided in his diary to being baffled by Fraser's 'untenable position'. The following morning at 0945, he phoned Fraser and 'understood him to acquiesce', but subsequently learnt from Admiral Sir Neville Syfret (VCNS) that Fraser refused to carry out the operation and would indeed 'haul down his flag', if ordered to do so. Cunningham could not tolerate this, but delayed the order to give 'wiser councils [*sic*]' more time to prevail, and Fraser did become 'more tractable'.

Fraser recalled the sequence of events differently, denying that he ever mentioned resignation. He argued that the ideal met. conditions of 3 April were unlikely to recur in the near future. Moreover, possibly lulled into a false sense of security by lack of any aerial attack on Kaa Fjord since the battleship arrived in March 1943 (*pace* the minor Soviet affair in February 1944), the Germans would not be so unprepared in future. Fraser felt strongly that success could not be certain and was therefore reluctant to risk heavy losses unnecessarily. He adamantly held that, contrary to Cunningham's assertion, he had not agreed on 14 April to remount the operation. Tacitly, though, he admitted that an unseemly verbal spat (during which C-in-C Home Fleet put the phone down on the First Sea Lord) had taken place between Scapa Flow and Whitehall.

Nevertheless, the process of evaluating the outcome of Operation Tungsten continued. Due to poor weather, PRU flights were possible only on 7 and 24 April and on neither occasion were satisfactory photographs of damage to *Tirpitz* obtained. Immediate visual confirmation therefore rested on the photographs taken by Barracudas on 3 April, detailed in a top secret interpretation report from RAF Medmenham five days afterwards: 'Unmistakable evidence of the success and accuracy of the attack' existed. Two, and possibly four, explosions could be seen for the first strike 'in the vicinity of the control tower, abaft the main mast, on the starboard side of the control tower and in the region of the main after turrets'. 'A high column of smoke emanating from the starboard side of the funnel' during the second strike indicated 'a well established fire' and two other 'intense fires' could be seen further aft on the starboard side. There were 'ripples' on the water, too, from near misses during both strikes.

Lack of post-operational PRU evidence heightened the importance of other information. On 4 April, a Norwegian report dramatically exclaimed: 'You came in the nick of time, she had let go and was under way.' It averred that two of *Tirpitz*'s aircraft had been destroyed, 'foc'sle badly gashed forward of the forward turret, which appears to be pointing below horizontal. All her guns swung to port, but she still has a list to starboard.' Five days later, a similar message claimed 'ambulances driven to and fro for two days', five holes were visible 'in deck on port side' and the list to starboard had not yet been corrected. The officers' mess and galley had suffered a direct hit, but no bombs had affected the magazines. The Germans believed *Tirpitz* would be out of action 'for several months'. The next day, the crew of the ferry boat *Arsvik* reported three hits on the battleship. 'A good German source dated about 15/4' confirmed deck damage, but also asserted that 'the hydrostatic bombs' had caused damage to the hull, which would take eight weeks to repair. The *C A Larsen* merchant vessel had been severely damaged, several smaller ships either sunk or damaged during the attack. On 29 April, came the news that *Tirpitz*'s guns were all 'in order' except one turret for secondary armament, 'masses of scrap' had been brought ashore, special flak exercises had taken place and, crucially, fighter-bombers had arrived – although it was not clear whether the latter meant to participate in the defensive exercises or to be stationed permanently in the area. The warning of the Naval Intelligence Division on 11 April, 'reliable estimates are unlikely on evidence at present available', underlined the perennial headache of all interpreters of source material.

Establishing the number and types of bomb that hit *Tirpitz* was an inescapable prelude to damage assessment. In his report, dated 10 April, Vice-Admiral Moore summarised the bombing performance, based upon operational information available to him. In the first wave, six 1,600lb AP bombs were dropped, two 'classified hits separately identified', another designated a hit 'supported by photographic evidence'; the comparable figures for the second wave 2–1–0. For 500lb SAP bombs, the first wave figures were 27–5–2, the second wave 39–3–2. The first wave dropped 9 500lb MC bombs, 2 were classified hits with a third hit 'supported by photographic evidence'. For the 500lb bombs of the second wave, filled with Torpex explosive, the relevant figures were 9–1–2. Four 600lb A/S were dropped by the first wave, only one being classified a hit; for the second wave, 1 was dropped and designated a hit. Overall, the 'grand total' of attacking aircraft was 40, dropping 97 bombs to claim 16 hits and 8 others supported by photographic evidence. Having had time to examine this and other reports, such as that from Medmenham and intelligence sources, on 3 May the Admiralty decided that 8 'certain' (including three 1,600lb bombs) and 5 'probable' hits occurred, which has somehow translated into 14 confirmed hits with one damaging near miss in some later publications. The disparity was not greatly significant. The battleship had undoubtedly been struck, but apparently the armoured deck had not been penetrated, the engines and boiler rooms were untouched. A year later, Lt I.G.W. Robertson met a German naval captain, apparently 'the executive officer' on *Tirpitz* at this time, who said that a bomb had gone down the funnel and badly affected the ship's fire control system. In his opinion, without a major dockyard overhaul, the battleship could not have fought again. Enemy records, examined post-war, did not specifically mention this, but showed that two bombs penetrated to the armoured deck without going through it, two more ricocheted off the upper deck and a fifth lodged in it. One

1,600lb AP bomb hit the water close to the ship's side and 'penetrated the side plating beneath the armour belt but detonated near the main longitudinal protective bulkhead'. It caused extensive flooding and divers were needed to carry out necessary repairs.

Cdr Eichler, *Tirpitz*'s chief engineer, admitted twelve hits and four near-misses, which he claimed had 'no appreciable effect on the main armament and no large fires were caused'. Interviewed in 1945, Capt Junge acknowledged 'complete surprise'. First reports, when the aircraft were 80km (50 miles) away gave *Tirpitz* minimal time to prepare, and Junge confirmed that flak crews were not fully ready nor all watertight doors closed as the first wave attacked. When he took command, after Meyer had been badly wounded, the narrow fjord had filled with smoke and the battleship was in danger of running aground. He agreed on sixteen hits or near-misses, maintaining that five bombs had reached the armoured deck without penetrating it.

Tirpitz's operational report elaborated on these details. Sea readiness had been ordered for slack water at 0530 LT. The net was accordingly opened, three stern cables cast off and the port anchor weighed at 0635. As the starboard anchor was being raised 'it was observed that a smoke-screen had been started from on shore'. Meanwhile, at 0624 a report had been received that 'more than 32 aircraft were about 43mls north-west' of Kaa Fjord proceeding south. The first machines, 'probably Martlets', were sighted at 0628: eleven 'single and twin-engined planes' to port, between fifteen and eighteen to starboard and more ahead of the ship. With the smoke-screen 'still very thin and only partially . . . [covering] the vessel', the foretop remained exposed as they dived 'simultaneously . . . at about 0630' to strafe the warship. 'The light flak defences, especially as the gun shields requested long before were still not fitted', suffered badly. *Tirpitz* was edging away from her berth at the time, and only 80 per cent of the watertight doors had been closed 'owing to the short notice'. 'The aircraft flying in to port (about 20 in number) flew along the ridge of the mountains, making use of every dip, and so low parallel to the ship that they themselves could only see the foretop, thus making it impossible for the lower lying guns and controls to fire at them. . . . Between 220degs and 240degs from the ship, they suddenly (from a distance of 2,200yd) "hedge-hopped" over the mountain and dived on to the ship, firing with all their guns. The bombs were released from a height of 600–1,000ft.' This was the first wave. *Tirpitz* sustained her first hit at 0631, as 'the thickening smoke made the defence increasingly difficult . . . and some of the crew were still engaged in closing watertight doors'. At 0645, the attackers 'flew off ahead of the ship, flying low and machine-gunning any craft lying in the vicinity'.

With a slight list to starboard, considerable superficial damage, a smoke-filled fjord and fear of more aerial attacks, *Tirpitz*'s trials were abandoned and the battleship began manoeuvring to re-enter the net enclosure. At 0733, a W/T message from the shore warned of more enemy aircraft approaching. As the attack developed, with visibility virtually nil, 'all guns were firing blind through the smoke'. Moreover, 'noise detection was badly hampered by a howling siren that could not be turned off immediately'. Six more hits were incurred, but armour thickness up to 50mm held. After the second wave attack, during which she ceased manoeuvring, *Tirpitz* resumed her return to the sanctuary of the net enclosure. A false report of another, developing air attack led to a brief halt at 0819, during which 'the ship turned again so as to lie broadside to the anticipated course of approach'; this supports the contention that such a movement had been deliberately carried out prior to the second wave's attack. Yet a further false report at 0825, this time of a torpedo track, delayed the battleship still more. The raid officially ended at 0847. By then, 506 105mm, 400 37mm and 8,260 20mm HE rounds had been fired by *Tirpitz*.

Operation Tungsten had been well planned, rehearsed and executed. However, *Tirpitz* had not been disabled. On 16 April, Air Vice-Marshal Coryton, ACAS (Ops) at the Air Ministry, acknowledged that the Admiralty intended 'to repeat Tungsten'. As only one aircraft was currently serviceable there, the PRU flight at Vaenga would need reinforcement. He revealed, also, that a plan for 8th USAAF bombers to attack *Tirpitz* on the same day from the northern USSR had been 'dropped' because use of Soviet airfields would take too long to arrange. Informal discussions had elicited the response, as in February, that the alternative of flying from Scottish airfields would allow an unacceptable margin of just 10–20mins fuel. The Admiralty had, therefore, decided against a formal approach to the Americans, and the Fleet Air Arm would relaunch the operation alone. On 17 April, the SBNO in North Russia was warned that, weather permitting, the operation would take place on 23 or 24 April under the codename Planet. Poor weather then prevented PRU cover, so no new photographs were available for planning or briefing.

Moore sailed again on 21 April, this time without Fraser's second force or the diversion of an Arctic convoy, aiming to strike on 24 April. His carriers were the same, except for the replacement of *Fencer* with *Striker*. Fraser's pessimism proved justified. The fine weather of 3 April was not repeated. Moore waited at the flying-off point hoping for improvement until fuel supplies in the destroyers ran low, and he eventually moved south. In the words of 804 Squadron's diary, the proposed attack on *Tirpitz* 'was washed out owing to the weather'. Six aircraft were subsequently lost in sinking three ships in a convoy near Bodo about 300 miles south of Kaa Fjord, where the harbour and sea lanes had been designated alternative targets. Despite these losses, Operation Planet did re-emphasise the continuing latent fear of *Tirpitz* and Admiralty disbelief that she would never regain her fighting status. The battleship could not be permitted to undergo repair unchallenged.

On 3 May, PRU showed *Tirpitz* in her normal berth, the only reported flight over her for the next twelve days. Three days later, the Admiralty determined that Planet would be carried out again on 15 May under the codename Operation Brawn. More news about *Tirpitz*'s condition had continued to filter through intelligence sources and undoubtedly affected this decision. On 2 May, details of an official German report of 15 April were gleaned, confirming 'deck hits and damage to its A.A. defences in recent air raid [Tungsten]'. Six days later, a 'Norwegian source in Alta' reported that the battleship's engines were undamaged and that 'an attempted journey to Germany is probable' – something not seriously considered by the Germans and mere speculation. More accurately and significantly, a report on 9 May stated that 'smoke generators of barrel type have been erected on top of cliffs on both sides of Alta [*sic*] fjord', *Tirpitz* 'had her engines going' and 200 additional workmen had arrived with still more expected. Repairs were clearly well in hand.

The same day, 9 May, a separate report held that the German Naval Staff had been asked for '130 special wharf labourers to repair damage caused by British air attack on *Tirpitz* by 1.7.44'. A move of the warship to Aalborg had been ruled out as 'too dangerous', given her lack of manoeuvrability and therefore vulnerability during the passage. So repairs, for which 'necessary materials and tools . . . are now lying ready in Oslo', must be completed in Kaa Fjord. Protection during the repair process would be provided by two heavy and four light flak batteries.

Also on 9 May came another interesting postscript to Operation Tungsten, to some extent at odds with other information. 'An A/B from *Tirpitz*' claimed that the battleship 'received nine hits by the funnel and ventilators round about it. All small guns on one side were destroyed. Some internal parts of the ship still blocked. Many of missing crew believed to be imprisoned there.' The arrival of 300 skilled workmen to be quartered on *Tirpitz* was indicated on 13 May and confirmed by a 'good source' the following day. The British naval attaché in Stockholm advised, too, that 'contrary to press reports, ship's company have been confined on board and are not accommodated in barracks ashore'. The implications were that *Tirpitz* had not suffered extensive damage to the mess decks, and uniformed and civilian personnel were labouring hard to get the battleship fighting fit.

On the eve of Operation Brawn, disturbing news arrived. *Tirpitz* had changed her berth with that of the *Monte Rosa* depot ship. She was 'now lying directly opposite where she lay previously . . . under Sakkobadnefjell in Langstroehnesbukta'. This was confirmed by a PRU aircraft at 1515 on 15 May, 95mins before the attacking aircraft took off, with the additional information that a floating crane was beside the battleship.

In the meantime, on 14 May the fleet allocated to execute Operation Brawn approached the taking-off point 120 miles north-west of Kaa Fjord. Its aerial strike force, centred once more on *Victorious* and *Furious*, comprised 27 Barracudas of 8 and 52 TBR wings with 500lb SAP, 500lb MC and 600lb A/S bombs escorted by 28 Corsairs (1834 and 1836 Squadrons), four Seafires and four Wildcats. The aircraft began taking off at 1650 DBST on 15 May, as other fighter patrols protected the fleet. However, with 10/10ths cloud at 1,000ft in the target area, the Barracudas were recalled shortly before reaching the coast; one Barracuda flying ahead was already lost on met. reconnaissance duties. The attack force arrived back at the carriers precisely two hours after take-off, and yet another attempt to sink *Tirpitz* had been aborted.

Within a fortnight, Operation Tiger Claw had been scheduled with *Victorious* and *Furious* again in the van. However, on the operative date (28 May), the weather frustrated the fleet and it therefore sailed south to search for coastal convoys. Three days later, it sank four merchant ships near Aalesund – a meagre consolation prize. Like Planet, Tiger Claw had been called off before the aircraft could be launched. But the Admiralty refused to abandon an effective rerun of Tungsten. On 24 June, the Air Ministry learnt that Tiger Claw would be repeated in mid-July, with PRU cover required from the week commencing 1 July.

With *Tirpitz* having shifted shortly and unexpectedly before the planned attack on 15 May, it was essential to determine not only her state of readiness, but also her accurate position. In this quest, a stream of intelligence reports, which continued to reach the Admiralty, certainly helped. At the end of May, it became clear that *Tirpitz* had been towed to the eastern anchorage (69 57N 23 04E) not moved under her own steam. The shallower berth may have been chosen to assist underwater repairs; her bow was pointing 84E, and she lay 100m from the shore. The repair ship *Neumark* (not *Monte Rosa*) occupied *Tirpitz*'s old anchorage, and new smoke-screen apparatus had been placed on hillsides surrounding Kaa Fjord. An Observation Post had also been deployed at the top of an adjacent cliff to give early warning of approaching aircraft and to direct the ship's flak should problems of control and sighting recur similar to those experienced on 3 April.

An enigmatic message from Stockholm on 5 June read: 'Reported from high naval circles in Berlin: Captain Junge friend of Davidson [naval attaché in Stockholm] now appointed C.O. of "T"': Junge actually assumed command on 21 May. The next day, news came that *Tirpitz*'s hangars and 'other superstructure on after deck' were to undergo extensive structural repairs, the inference being that the battleship could not therefore be operational for some time. On 10 June, though, another source claimed that 'intensive repair work had been carried out on the damaged guns and that the 'German officers maintain ship is now in fighting trim', which non-commissioned ranks 'laugh at'. To add to the confusion, a further message on the same day stated that gunnery personnel from the battleship had arrived at Flensburg and 'been incorporated in coastal artillery'. 'Not believed' was appended to this by an astute intelligence officer. However, this all neatly illustrated once more the need for careful examination of acquired and often contradictory information. A report of 11 June confirmed that repairs to the guns had been completed, and the floating crane had left her side. Critically, too, *Tirpitz* was still lying opposite her usual, western berth with a destroyer close-by, as well as the ex-whaling ship *C A Larsen*.

In mid-June, the naval attaché in Stockholm summarised information recently made available to him: although *Tirpitz*'s 'movement is slow and her draught is abnormal', she was preparing to move south. Since April, 400–600 workmen had been toiling day and night on her, the list having been corrected on 6 April. By 15 June, all external damage had been made good, and according to local naval sources the warship should be ready for sea by 1 July. She had already been seen under way in Alten Fjord. On 25 June, more trials from the eastern berth were reported during the previous week, but 'one does not get the impression that she is preparing for any serious journey'. 'About 21 June . . . an observer on Finsja point (70 04N 22 59E) saw *Tirpitz* moving at slow speed 'escorted by two patrol vessels and one seaplane', and when he arrived in the inner Kaa Fjord at 1845 found her anchored at 69 57N 23 08E. This source estimated that the battleship steamed at 15–20 knots. He also confirmed that the whole main armament could be rotated and superstructure repairs had been finished. A separate transmission put *Tirpitz*'s speed at 20 knots during trials in the first week of July.

Admiral Sir Henry Moore succeeded Fraser as C-in-C Home Fleet on 14 June. The Admiralty was by now convinced that *Tirpitz* could carry out limited operations, and during the next month Operation Mascot came to fruition. Three fleet carriers would be involved. *Indefatigable*, in which Rear Admiral R.R. McGrigor commander of the First Cruiser Squadron flew his flag, had 820 and 826 Squadrons of 9 TBR wing (each with twelve Barracudas), 1770 Squadron with twelve two-seater Fairey Fireflies for escort duty and six Swordfish of 842 Squadron for anti-submarine (A/S) patrols. *Formidable* carried 827 and 830 Squadrons of 8 TBR wing (each with twelve Barracudas) and eighteen Corsairs of 1841 Squadron as escorts. *Furious* on this occasion had no strike bombers, but contained twelve Seafires of 880 Squadron for fleet protection, twenty Hellcats for escort duties and three Swordfish of 842 Squadron for A/S patrols. In the ten days before sailing on the operation, these squadrons practised together 'both from shore bases and from their ships' in accordance with an operational memo from McGrigor dated 4 July and further orders issued eight days later.

A PRU flight on 12 July found *Tirpitz* at the eastern anchorage, with 'no visible signs of damage except that one aircraft crane and a boat to starboard are missing'. All the gun turrets, including flak mountings were 'intact' with a 'mottled' upper deck an apparent attempt at camouflage. Small craft were around the battleship 'among which is a probable diving platform or caisson'. The following day, aircrew learnt that the operation would be during the early hours of 17 July, and from 13 to 16 July a succession of 'very detailed' briefings took place, as maintenance crews strove to get the aircraft serviceable. With the aid of photos and models, 'every opportunity' was taken by aircrew to familiarise themselves with the terrain around *Tirpitz*. There were, too, lectures on 'evasion and escape and escape kits with various accessories were issued'.

The fleet left Scapa at 0830 on Friday 14 July 'in fog and drizzle'. Moore was in the battleship *Duke of York* with the three carriers, four cruisers and twelve destroyers bound for the flying off position (71 15N 19 25E), which was reached without incident or detection after 'entering' the Arctic Circle on 15 July. Fog had been encountered during the passage, but by the evening of 16 July had gone so that a 'light easterly wind and clear conditions prevailed' for the next day.

At 0040 DBST on Monday 17 July, *Furious* began to fly off two Seafires for CAP duties and nine Hellcats, at 0111 despatching eleven more Hellcats (two of which had fuel problems and quickly returned to the carrier). The diary of 1841 Corsair Squadron on *Formidable* recorded: 'At midnight with the sun still shining, we all boarded our cabs and started up for the "big do" at last'. A dozen of the Corsairs carried cameras to photograph the bombing attacks and the other six were to fire on ground targets, provided no enemy fighters appeared. Simultaneously, at 0040, *Indefatigable* started to launch her aircraft into the wind at 30 knots. The aerial armada set off at 0135 after an 'excellent form up', in the words of 826 Squadron's diarist: 18 Hellcats and 12 Fireflies to deal with flak, 18 Corsairs as top cover, 44 Barracudas (one of the scheduled 45 having failed to get airborne) to bomb *Tirpitz* – 8 TBR followed by 9 TBR wing. All the Barracudas, except two carrying three 500lb MC bombs, had a single 1,600lb AP bomb with 0.08sec delay fuse.

The force flew low towards the coast at 50ft and started climbing to 9,000ft 10mins short of Loppen Island at the southern entrance to the Loppehavet inlet and north-west of Kaa Fjord, with the fighter escort weaving above them. The Germans revealed that their approach had been detected by jamming radio transmissions 10 miles from the coast. Once over enemy-held territory, the attacking force deployed in clear visibility. The Firefly leader, Maj V.G.B. Cheesman RM, however, remained unimpressed by the 'cruel looking territory below', over which engine failure would mean 'out harp and halo and hello St Peter'. Cloud began to form and the target area in Kaa Fjord was soon covered in smoke up to 1,000ft, blanketing *Tirpitz* and the surrounding hills. Reaching Kaa Fjord above the Barracudas at 11,000–12,000ft, 1840 Squadron Hellcats had been briefed to strafe shore batteries to the east and flak ships in the fjord, but the targets could only be 'located by the streams of tracer issuing through the smoke-screen. . . . Glimpses were obtained of ships through the smoke and, where possible, the ships were attacked.' Their difficulties were increased by having reached the fjord at its head from north-west and not, as planned, from due west directly over the battleship. Although 'plentiful', targets were 'almost impossible' to find unless they opened fire first. Apart from flak sites, attacks were made inland on an air strip, a camp and 'block houses'. Fireflies of 1770 Squadron silenced two flak positions on land south of *Tirpitz*'s berth, a third on a hillside east of the battleship. These fighters made their 'getaway' by circling from the south of Kaa Fjord, though only one claimed to have seen the primary target. The post-operational rendezvous point was over high ground 5 miles north-west of *Tirpitz*, where the fighters linked up with Barracudas before retiring towards the fleet in small groups.

During the withdrawal, 'a large number of batteries and isolated positions which had been entirely inactive on the inward flight fired on all aircraft passing near them'. The Hellcats shot up many of them, also attacking a tanker in Lang Fjord and motor transport ashore in blast pens near Alteidet (70 03N 22 06E). Three destroyers at the head of Lang Fjord engaged the returning aircraft, and one was bombed by a Barracuda of 8 TBR from *Formidable*. The Barracudas of 9 TBR wing from *Indefatigable* approached the target area from west-south-west above and astern of 8 TBR wing, flying in four columns (three of six and the other of five, with the aircraft stepped up behind one another) from 20 miles short of *Tirpitz*. They found 5/10ths cumulus at 6,000ft in the target area and the battleship obscured by smoke. 'Constant', but 'inaccurate', flak met them, and all except four bombed blindly on flak flashes through the gloom. Of the four that retained their bombs, three jettisoned them in the sea, the fourth with release problems successfully landed back on the carrier still with its bomb-load. One Barracuda ditched ahead of *Indefatigable*, its crew being rescued unharmed. The remaining twenty-one Barracudas from that carrier (including one badly damaged) landed safely between 0305 and 0350. Meanwhile, all eighteen Hellcats returned to *Furious*, five of them damaged. Four were repairable, the fifth had been hit by two 20mm shells while attacking an armed trawler at the entrance to Ox Fjord and had to be written off. Several Barracudas were damaged, too, one ditching beside *Formidable*, from which a 1841 Squadron Corsair was lost in action (its pilot captured). Throughout the operation, Seafire and Swordfish aircraft, from 880 and 842 Squadrons respectively, flew CAP and anti-submarine patrols over the fleet. A second strike, planned to take off at 0800, was cancelled just two minutes before launch when 'fog patches began to appear'. The fleet then returned to Scapa.

Improved German radar cover in Norway had detected the incoming attackers at 0200 LT (hence the earlier radio jamming) and the battleship learnt of this four minutes later. At 0214 smoke generators on the upper deck of *Tirpitz* were taking effect and by 0225 had totally obscured her. Watertight doors were closed at 0217. The battleship's main armament opened fire at 0220, followed shortly afterwards by the secondary armament as the aircraft flew closer. During the attack, which lasted 33mins, *Tirpitz* fired 39 380mm, 359 150mm, 1,973 105mm, 3,967 37mm and 28,550 20mm shells. She was not hit, but estimates of near misses ranged from one to seven. German gunners claimed to have shot down twelve aircraft, whereas in fact only one Corsair crashed in the target area. In the immediate aftermath of the attack, *Tirpitz* reported no damage and only one near miss.

In the post-operational inquest, Moore blamed the posting away of many experienced personnel after Tungsten, and thus use of essentially inexperienced crews on subsequent operations including that on 17 July. He also criticised the strike leader on that occasion for not clearly allocating alternative targets once it became obvious that *Tirpitz* could not be hit accurately. Frustrated by the conditions in which none of its machines 'definitely saw the target', even though all but three of its Barracudas dropped their bombs in the approximate position, 826 Squadron commented on the smooth execution of operational orders but the 'disappointing show'. 880 Squadron simply noted: 'Strike considered unsuccessful, target being obscured by smoke-screen.' The Admiralty, nevertheless, remained committed to sinking *Tirpitz* and a proposal was mooted to mount a series of continuous operations over a 48hr period to wear down the enemy defences and exhaust the smoke generators.

Analysis of crew reports after Operation Mascot enabled the Naval Intelligence Division to build up a comprehensive picture of current defences in and around Kaa Fjord. Flak batteries, with guns of varying calibre – some classified 'heavy' – were encountered on and around Silden Island, along the shores of most fjords south and west of it, especially at the south-western end of Lang Fjord, which appeared to contain a substantial naval anchorage. East of Silden and north-west of Kaa Fjord, the entrance to Ox Fjord, the island of Stjern and Hasvik, at the northern point of Loppehavet, had significant flak concentrations, as had high ground along Alten Fjord. Military barracks were identified at Alteidet on Alten Fjord and at the entrance to Ox Fjord. On the inward flight, a W/T station was attacked on a spit of land due south of Loppen Island. Two destroyers were seen at the entrance to Kors Fjord, an eastern sleeve of Alten Fjord: an 'unidentified vessel' off Hasvik, possibly single destroyers off Loppen and in Older Fjord due south of it, a radar ship off Silden. In the immediate vicinity of *Tirpitz*, apart from the several flak ships and shore batteries, a military camp of tents and huts was seen approximately 2 miles beyond the eastern shore of Kaa Fjord, with blockhouses (perhaps flak towers) at a road junction 3 miles south-east of the eastern berth and 1 mile south of the fjord's extremity. One report placed an Arado 196 flying boat on a lake 2 miles south of Kaa Fjord. Another claimed that a landing strip about 2,000yds x 150yds was under construction, but could not pinpoint its location – either close to the military camp on the eastern shore or due south of Kaa Fjord. The credibility of this observation seemed to be strained by an elaboration that not only had an aircraft been seen in a hangar, but a Fw 190 spotted taking off.

Operation Mascot had, indeed, been disappointing. But *Tirpitz* could not be left untouched. After the operation, the British naval attaché in Stockholm reported: '*Tirpitz* exercises daily in Alten fjord. She generally goes out at 0800 and returns at 1600.' Her speed was approximately 20 knots and her armament 'in full working order'. A similar report from a source in Alta confirmed 'daily trials', her guns 'in order' and an estimated speed of 18 knots. For two days, 31 July and 1 August, the battleship exercised at sea with the 4th destroyer flotilla, and fears rose that she was planning an aggressive sortie. Information reached London, too, that the formidable defences faced during Mascot had been still further strengthened, increasing speculation that Kaa Fjord would become the secure base for future operations. An intelligence summary on 28 July noted that an estimated eight to ten smoke generators were along the shore, not on the hillsides, the nearest being ¾ km from Bosselkop. These had large stocks, but 'impossible to say how long they can last'. Whenever the weather was good at nights since the last attack, a smoke-screen had been laid over the fjord – indicating the Germans' near paranoia about air attacks.

Now partly painted black, *Tirpitz* enjoyed a successful 'trip' on 27 July. A report on 3 August explained that two tankers stored 'the stuff' for the smoke generators, which was ferried by smaller craft. Their present locations were unknown, though possibly in Lang Fjord. Two reports in mid-August suggested that 'on first favourable, moonless night' *Tirpitz* would be towed south via Danish waters 'probably' to Kiel for an extensive refit. But this did not tally with other reliable information that she had exercised in the fjords and at sea under her own steam. On 28 July, SBNO North Russia forwarded more credible details from Soviet aircraft: *Tirpitz* lay in her 'former berth' with three smaller vessels nearby.

Plans were by now well advanced to launch Operation Goodwood, comprising a series of strikes during the third week of August, in pursuit of the Admiralty theory that the defences could be worn down. Once more, preparatory exercises were conducted at Loch Erriboll, with 'splendid scale models of the [Kaa] fjord and its surrounding terrain and excellent photographic cover of the area' being produced for the various pre-operational briefings. This time, the three fleet carriers would be supplemented by two escort carriers, *Trumpeter* and *Nabob*. *Indefatigable* would carry 12 Barracudas of 820 Squadron, as strike aircraft; 1770 (12 Fireflies) and 1840 (12 Hellcats) for escort and attack duties; 887 and 894 squadrons each with 16 Seafires for fleet protection. *Formidable* was to have two strike squadrons (826 and 828) each with 12 Barracudas, plus 1841 and 1842 squadrons respectively with 18 and 12 Corsairs, mainly for top cover escort work, but also able to dive-bomb in an attacking role. *Furious* would carry 12 strike Barracudas of 827 Squadron, 12 Seafires each from 801 and 880 squadrons for fleet protection. The high number of aircraft for fleet protection suggests that the Admiralty was worried about the threat of enemy air attacks, especially if the fleet remained off Norway for some days as successive strikes went in. On *Trumpeter* there would be 8 Avengers of 846 Squadron and 6 Wildcats, on *Nabob* 12 Avengers and 4 Wildcats. Avengers from 852 Squadron on *Nabob* would drop their mines 'fused at varying time delays' beside *Tirpitz* with some set to 'detonate on their way to the bottom', as those from 846 Squadron on *Trumpeter* laid a pattern across the entrance to Kaa Fjord in 'a synchronised attack'. Cdr J.W. Powell, an Observer at the time, recalled: 'It was hoped that the mines dropped alongside would persuade her that the wisest course of action would be to vacate her berth, quickly moving out beyond Kaa Fjord into Alten Fjord – so activating the lay across the narrow neck and attacking *Tirpitz* from below where she had no armour protection'. Both squadrons would attack at 50ft. Briefed on 11 August, the squadron commanders thought this technically 'a very good plan', but privately exchanged doubts about survival chances while 'flying in formation straight and level' in daylight in such a well-defended area. Including this dangerous sub-plot in the wider bombing and strafing operation heavily re-emphasised the perceived acute threat of *Tirpitz*.

Three days after the convoy JW59 left Loch Ewe, during the morning of Friday 18 August, Admiral Sir Henry Moore sailed out of Scapa in *Duke of York* with the three fleet carriers (Rear-Admiral R.R. McGrigor again flying his flag in *Indefatigable*) and two cruisers, followed by the two escort carriers and one cruiser. Off the Faroes, the two groups were joined by destroyers. Detailed briefings took place on board the following day with the operation planned for 21 August, as JW59 passed east of Bear Island. On 20 August, the whole fleet rendezvoused off the Norwegian coast without being detected. Poor flying conditions, however, soon upset the timetable. Operations proved impossible on 21 August, and during that Monday Moore oiled seven destroyers from the escort carriers and cruisers. Principally as 'the fuel situation would not allow of indefinite delay', in spite of 'doubtful weather' at 0530 on 22 August Moore decided to launch

Operation Goodwood I. Take-off would be precisely three hours later, but was then postponed until 1000. Finally the aircraft began taking off at 1100. The Avengers were not launched 'on account of the low cloud conditions' for fear of need to abort. Mines must then be ditched as the aircraft were forbidden to land with them, and insufficient were available on the carriers for another attempt. The main strike force, having formed up, departed at 1150. Fifteen miles short of the coast, as the aircraft started to climb, thick cloud was experienced at 1,500ft and, in accordance with orders, the thirty-one Barracudas and their twenty-four Corsair escorts (commanded by Lt Cdr A.J.L. Temple-West of 9 TBR wing) turned back. Nine Hellcats (1840 Squadron), eleven Fireflies (1770 Squadron) and eight Seafires (887 Squadron) pressed on. The Seafires attacked Banak airfield and Kolvik seaplane base, claiming a He 115 and four Blohm & Voss B v 138 seaplanes destroyed and one hangar set on fire. Flying below the cloud, the Fireflies and Hellcats in the meantime reached Kaa Fjord. At 1249, the Fireflies attacked flak positions, and after climbing 2mins later the Hellcats began to drop 500lb SAP bombs (delayed fuse 0.14sec) on *Tirpitz* (claiming a hit 'abaft bridge') and 'other shipping' through breaks in the cloud. On the way back, two of *Tirpitz*'s Arado 196a seaplanes were destroyed at their anchorage in Bukta and a U-boat damaged at Hammerfest. During the operation, radar and W/T stations at Gaasnes, Kolvik and Ing were reputedly 'severely damaged'. One Hellcat and one Seafire 'did not return', a Barracuda from *Furious* ditched on returning from its abortive flight. At 1710, 887 Squadron accounted for two more Blohm & Voss flying boats as they shadowed the warships. Fifteen minutes later (1725) torpedoes from a U-boat damaged *Nabob* and the frigate *Bickerton* – a timing given in Moore's signal on 26 August.

In his post-operational report Moore in *Duke of York* explained that after Goodwood I he kept with him *Indefatigable* and the seven destroyers refuelled on 21 August, detaching *Formidable, Furious,* two cruisers and the remaining destroyers to meet the fleet oilers. A third flotilla consisting of the two escort carriers, a cruiser and the 5th Escort Group also withdrew westwards to fuel the escorts from its own resources. Unfortunately, this third force 'ran straight over a U-boat, presumably outward bound from Narvik'. *Nabob* and *Bickerton* were torpedoed at '1755 [sic] . . . and the latter sank'. This time, of course, varied from that given immediately after the event, and furthermore 880 Squadron diary noted that *Bickerton* had been 'sunk by own forces'. When the U-boat attacked, Moore was 10 miles away, so he sent *Algonquin* and *Vigilant* to investigate. Eventually, learning that *Nabob* could make steam, he despatched *Trumpeter*, *Algonquin* and the 5th Escort Group to shepherd her back to harbour in the United Kingdom, as *Vigilant* and the cruiser *Kent* rejoined the fleet. With the two escort carriers went the Avenger squadrons, 'some very frustrated aircrews in both ships' and any lingering chance for the ambitious mining plan.

That evening Moore launched Goodwood II, as the start of 'teasing tactics' involving a number of small strikes; it involved just six Hellcats and eight Fireflies from *Indefatigable*. Leaving the fleet at 1830 in 'very good conditions', the Hellcats attacked *Tirpitz* at 1910 with 500lb SAP bombs diving from 8,000ft, claiming two hits, as the Fireflies engaged flak. (Moore later amended these figures to seven Hellcats and seven Fireflies.) Surprise meant that the smoke-screen was ineffective, and on the return flight shipping and other targets of opportunity were attacked. No aircraft were lost.

In reality, *Tirpitz* was hit in neither Goodwood I nor II, but her gun crews were not idle. During the morning and evening attacks her 380mm armament had fired 62 and 13 rounds respectively; 150mm 363 and 124; 105mm some 1,300 and 750; 37mm approximately 1,600 and 1,538; 20mm 15,000 and 15,800. So the sparse operations had caused the battleship's defences no little concern, and the many shore batteries expended significant amounts of ammunition too. The Germans timed the first attacks on *Tirpitz* 1249–1312, acknowledged that Banak had been hit by 'about 10 Spitfires', other shipping had been bombed in Kaa Fjord and the U-boat attacked off Hammerfest. In another raid that evening, 1916–1927, they noted that fifteen carrier-borne aircraft returned to Kaa Fjord without inflicting any damage on shipping. The Germans claimed eight aircraft shot down in the first, four in the second wave. A curious addendum credited two other carrier-borne aircraft with dropping 'a large object in the sea off Loppa (Loppen)' at 1925. The Avengers were not used for mine-laying and by then the escort carriers were on their way back to Scapa.

Although the only carrier then in the area, *Indefatigable* contemplated another strike on 23 August, but fog made weather unsuitable for flying. The following day, at 0700, the other two fleet carriers and accompanying cruisers rejoined her. Goodwood III was, therefore, planned for 24 August, but unsuitable flying weather ruled out operations during that morning. Despite 'pessimistic weather forecasts', at 1430 all three carriers began flying off aircraft 'in very good weather': 33 Barracudas from 820, 826, 827 and 828 Squadrons (each carrying one 1,600lb AP bomb with 0.08sec delay fuse), 24 Corsairs of 1841 and 1842 Squadrons (five with one 1,100lb AP bomb and also 0.08sec delay fuse), 10 Hellcats (each one 500lb AP bomb with 0.14sec delay fuse) and 10 Fireflies (1770 Squadron) bound for Kaa Fjord, eight Seafires to attack Banak airfield once more. Moore noted that 'conditions [were] almost ideal'; and pilots saw the Norwegian coast from 60 miles away. The force was detected a similar distance from *Tirpitz* by enemy radar at 1535. Notified six minutes later, the battleship activated the smoke-screen which had thickened by the time that the Hellcats and Fireflies attacked gun positions at 1600. The attacking force came under fire before Kaa Fjord, however. Sub Lt H.K. Quilter in a 1842 Squadron Corsair flying over the western end of Lang Fjord, almost three minutes short of the target, saw four enemy warships below and a light flash from one of them: 'My first thought was that they must have mistaken us for German aircraft and were asking for a recognition signal.' Then black puffs appeared astern and he realised his error. Later a Barracuda pilot, Sub Lt R.

Fulton, paid tribute to the 'sheer cold-blooded gallantry' of Corsairs, which reportedly traversed the fjord to attack 88mm flak positions.

826 Squadron saw a box barrage over Kaa Fjord as the Barracudas approached, which 'lightened considerably' after the fighter attacks. But it confirmed that the smoke-screen was 'thick and effective' because there was little wind to disperse it. Bombs were released after a 'steep glide' from 10,000–4,000ft, being aimed at the target's anticipated position, as a 828 Squadron Observer recalled: 'The pull out of the dive in the smoke with mountains around us and many other aircraft above was a feature of the occasion which has stuck in the memory.' During the withdrawal, 826 Squadron Barracudas flew over destroyers and a 'cargo motorship' in Lang Fjord, and 4Z was hit by a 20mm shell. Operating from *Furious*, 827 Squadron reinforced this picture: *Tirpitz* 'completely obscured by an effective smoke-screen', bombs dropped blindly and results not observed. According to 1841 Squadron, the light flak 'did not seem nearly as thick as on July 17th, but the heavy stuff was far thicker'. However, the writer of the squadron diary referred to 'any number of flaming onions about', and two Hellcats were lost in this attack, including that of 1840 Squadron's commander, Lt Cdr A.R. Richardson RNZNVR. He was shot down on his third attack while attempting to tear away the aerial of a wireless station with his lowered arrester hook. 'I have never seen anything to equal Richie's courage and determination', declared Maj Cheesman. One Hellcat reported landing a 500lb bomb on B turret.

Five minutes after the fighters, the Barracudas and Corsairs arrived to find *Tirpitz* completely shrouded in smoke and dropped their loads blindly. One 1,600lb bomb hit the battleship to port of the bridge, and a Corsair claimed a possible hit with a 500lb bomb: Moore, though, later referred to 'three possible hits'. In addition to the two Hellcats, three Corsairs were lost and another ditched close to *Formidable* on the return flight. Damage to surviving aircraft was extensive, but on 26 August, after frantic efforts by groundcrew 826 Squadron had eleven serviceable Barracudas. Targets of opportunity were attacked on the way back, including destroyers and flak ships, with claims for damage to a minesweeper and radar station.

At Bukta, another of *Tirpitz*'s seaplanes had been destroyed. When two Fireflies appeared over Kaa Fjord to take photos at 1930, they were greeted by an impenetrable smoke-screen illuminated by colourful sprays of flak. Neither their photos, nor any others taken during the Goodwood operations, revealed anything but smoke. Throughout Goodwood III, Seafires flew continuous patrols over the fleet, and at 2050 880 Squadron transferred two of its aircraft to *Indefatigable* to supplement its fighter strength in anticipation of another attack on *Tirpitz*. Once more, recovery of the aircraft took time and, according to Sub Lt Quilter, *Formidable* looked set 'to steam straight up a fjord . . . [with] the coast well and truly in sight'.

The battleship fired 72 rounds of 380mm ammunition, 510 from the 150mm guns and an average of 30 per cent from the ammunition available for the 105mm, 37mm and 20mm guns. She suffered twenty-one casualties (eight dead) and no major damage, but enjoyed a lucky escape. The Hellcat bomb had scarcely scratched B turret in demolishing a quadruple 20mm flak position on top of it. Potentially more serious was the 1,600lb AP bomb, which pierced the main deck and four others before coming to rest in No. 4 Switch Room without exploding. At 1707 *Tirpitz* sent for a bomb disposal squad from Banak to defuse a 500lb bomb. They found a much larger weapon with a defective fuse and only about half of its intended explosive. At 1948, *Tirpitz* dismissed the attack as 'insignificant'. However, a later more measured summary described Goodwood III as 'undoubtedly the heaviest and most determined so far'. That the large bomb 'did not explode must be considered an exceptional stroke of luck, as the effects of that explosion would have been immeasurable'. The Germans also paid tribute to the 'great skill and dexterity in flying' and admitted 'heavy losses' among flak units ashore. A lucky hit caused the colourful eruption of a naval ammunition dump, too.

After Goodwood III, *Furious* transferred two Seafires and two Barracudas to *Indefatigable* as replacements for losses, and the fleet again temporarily divided at 0300 on 25 August. Under the command of McGrigor, *Indefatigable* and *Formidable*, two cruisers and seven destroyers withdrew westwards to fuel from the fleet oilers, while Moore took *Duke of York*, *Furious*, one cruiser and five destroyers to the Faroes to replenish supplies. During the passage, Moore summarised the arithmetic of destruction during the Goodwood operations to date. Six enemy aircraft had been damaged or destroyed at Banak, where a hangar was also set on fire; three seaplanes (from *Tirpitz*) destroyed or damaged; radar stations at Soroy and Ingoy 'heavily attacked'; one U-boat leaving Hammerfest 'shot up by fighters'; numerous other shipping and shore targets reported strafed 'including destroyer in Langfjord and flakships'. This differed somewhat from reports penned by individual units and was a good deal more conservative.

On reaching the Faroes, Moore detached *Furious* with an escort to Scapa, while he returned to Norway, having requested SBNO North Russia to sail convoy RA 59A on Monday 28 August. At 0300 on 29 August, Moore and McGrigors's forces met at 71 00N 10 00E, after the cruisers *Kent* and *Berwick* had already left for Scapa. Course was now set for the flying off position, as the C-in-C Home Fleet recalled later, 'in spite of almost universal pessimism regarding the weather'. However, conditions unexpectedly improved and 'were found to be suitable'. Officially, at 1430 DBST 'the last combined strike' was flown off from *Indefatigable* and *Formidable*, with seven Seafires carrying out 'a subsidiary attack' on Hammerfest. Some reports state, though, that a further hour's delay occurred due to rain, and the force did not take off until 1530.

Operation Goodwood IV had twenty-six Barracudas each carrying one 1,600lb AP bomb (0.08sec delay fuse), two Corsairs with a 1,000lb AP bomb (also 0.08sec delay fuse), three Hellcats with 500lb MC bombs (instantaneous fuse) in the bombing force. Fifteen Corsairs and ten Fireflies flew as escort to the bombers and to attack flak positions in the target area. An innovation involved four Hellcats flying in the van to mark *Tirpitz* with target indicators. Information from Soviet reconnaissance flights on 29 August, that two flak ships, two 'transport' ships and a repair ship were in Kaa Fjord, three destroyers in Alten Fjord did not arrive before the operation.

German records would later reveal that, aware of increased patrols by FAA aircraft earlier in the day, radar stations had been put on alert. Thus, at 1640 LT a small force of hostile aircraft were located about fifty miles from Kaa Fjord – almost certainly, the Seafires making for Hammerfest. In reality, as well as the delayed departure, an inaccurate wind forecast further disrupted the operation, with landfall being made to the south of, not over, Loppen island. The attacking aircraft, therefore, approached Kaa Fjord from the south-west, not north-west. 826 Squadron noted: 'Rapid form-up and fly off, but unfortunately wrong landfall so roundabout approach to Kaa', which incidentally gave the defences more time to prepare. Due to this unplanned diversion, the smoke-screen had formed before the target indicators could be dropped. When the Barracudas arrived, the whole area was covered in 'thick smoke'. So, despite the novel, good intentions, the bombers still had to attack blindly. At Hammerfest, though, the Seafires achieved 'good results'.

In Kaa Fjord 52 tons of bombs were dropped on and around *Tirpitz*: several near-misses and two hits were claimed, as fighters strafed shore batteries. Yet once more, participants remarked on the surprising absence of enemy fighters. One Firefly and a Corsair were lost over Kaa Fjord, where a 826 Squadron Barracuda was 'nicked by shrapnel in the port wing', one of several attacking aircraft to be damaged. Two 826 Squadron Barracudas also 'cracked up' on landing, one having to be pushed over the side. Sub Lt Quilter in a 1842 Squadron Corsair had a narrow escape. Having survived a severed aileron trim wire, which gave his machine an uncomfortable list to port thereafter, on landing he found that a bullet had penetrated two of his ammunition boxes and come to rest in a third. Fortunately, it had not been an incendiary.

On 26 August, *Tirpitz* learnt that a request from the air force commander in Finland for fighters to defend Alten Fjord had been turned down by the 'Luftwaffe supreme command'. Given the broader picture, with Allied forces advancing from both east and west on the European mainland and Germany being heavily bombed, the decision was not unreasonable. But it explained the lack of opposition in the vicinity of the battleship. Fighters were at a premium in the homeland. At 1700 on 29 August, the Alten Fjord military commander reported an attack by sixty carrier-borne aircraft on Kaa Fjord, claiming 'several' shot down and 'few' casualties among the defenders. Between 1702 and 1725 LT, *Tirpitz* fired 54 rounds from her 380mm guns, 161 from the 150mm and an average of 16 per cent of her 105mm, 37mm and 20mm stocks. Six men were wounded and minor damage caused to a 105mm ammunition hoist. Otherwise, the battleship remained unscathed. A strange postscript occurred on 30 August, however, when Alten Fjord was closed due to suspected sea-mines.

Goodwood (the most costly Fleet Air Arm Operation) now came to a close, with the fleet withdrawing westwards to cover RA 59A. Due to lack of fuel, *Indefatigable* with three destroyers left for Scapa late on 29 August (reaching port on the afternoon of Friday 1 September 'after an uneventful passage'), *Formidable* with two destroyers twenty-four hours later. *Duke of York* with six destroyers did not sail for Scapa until 1100 on 1 September, once the convoy was considered safe. The attack on 29 August would be the final attempt by the Fleet Air Arm to sink *Tirpitz*, but this was not known at the time. Post-operational analyses assumed that another operation would be launched soon. The press published details of 'the greatest Fleet Air Arm operation of the war' in colourful, enthusiastic columns crowned by headlines like 'They Struck from the Sea' . . . 'Six Times Attacked' . . . 'How We Hit the Tirpitz'. Readers learnt that the German battleship had been hit during four strikes, between 23 and 29 August, though they may have overlooked the low-key addendum: 'Some hits were claimed, but owing to smoke-screens put up by the enemy it was not possible to observe the results'.

Rear-Admiral R.R. McGrigor, commanding the First Cruiser Squadron and in tactical charge of Goodwood, reviewed the operations on 1 October. Met. forecasts had proved 'quite unreliable', as 'weather conditions in the target area seldom approximate to those prevailing at sea locally round the fleet'. McGrigor believed that 'the best method appears to be to close until the cloud conditions over the hills can be observed'. He had strong reservations about the planned approach over Loppen Island, preferring the one accidentally followed on 29 August. 'The best departure point for the strike' was west of 22 00E (i.e. south of Loppen) and along Kvaenangen Fjord, behind St Haldde high ground to reach the target from the south, or more precisely between south-east and south-west 'according to the direction of the sun'. This would entail dealing with 'the minimum number of flak positions' short of *Tirpitz*. The withdrawal should be north-west towards Loppen or Silden islands avoiding flak positions between the target and the seaward end of Alten Fjord. McGrigor favoured using target marking aircraft.

He then summarised the achievements of Goodwood: 'possible' hits by a Corsair (one 1,000lb AP bomb) and Hellcat (a 500lb MC bomb) on *Tirpitz* – a considerable reduction in the original claims. The naval W/T station at Loppen was 'again damaged'; a U-boat depot ship attacked in Helle Fjord; three destroyers in Leir Botn shot up (two 'silenced') and a small ship off Bosenop 'left smoking'; a tanker in Sjern sound 'set on fire'; a 'small merchantman' in Hammerfest and one boom vessel in Kaa Fjord 'damaged'; three small vessels at Silden, Auskarnetset and Bukta 'attacked'; and oil tanks at Lervik 'left burning'. In conclusion, McGrigor maintained that the Barracudas were 'too slow' and since Operation Tungsten had 'never reached Kaa Fjord before *Tirpitz* disappeared under smoke'.

Air Marshal A.T. Harris, who as a group captain pre-war became convinced that bombers would sink battleships. (Imperial War Museum –IWM)

September 1941. *Tirpitz* berthed in Kiel at the entrance to the Inner Dockyard Basin (IWM)

Tirpitz firing her two stern turrets during working-up trials. (IWM)

February 1942. *Tirpitz* in Foetten Fjord, near Trondheim, with camouflage rafts at bow and stern. (IWM)

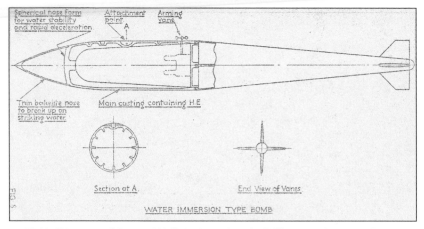

1941. Diagram of Barnes Wallis' 10 ton bomb. Tallboy used against *Tirpitz* three years later was a scaled-down version. (Author)

Barnes Neville Wallis (left) with A.D. Grant, his administrative assistant at Vickers-Armstrong, who took part in Highball and Tallboy development trials. (Vickers)

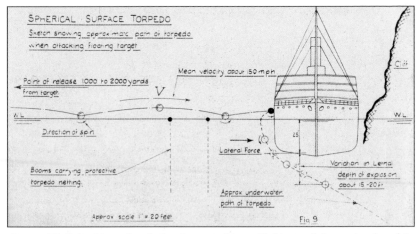

Barnes Wallis' scheme for destroying warships with his small 'bouncing bomb', codenamed Highball, 1942. (Author)

July 1942. After causing mayhem in Arctic convoy PQ-17 simply by threatening to attack, *Tirpitz* is seen here inside protective nets at Bogen Fjord, near Narvik. (IWM)

Kaa Fjord, north Norway. Photograph taken by a soviet aircraft, May 1943. (IWM)

Hellcat fighter pilots on the escort carrier *Emperor* study a model of Kaa Fjord before the Fleet Air Arm's Operation Tungsten, April 1944. (IWM)

Lt Cdr J. Cooper, OC 882 Squadron FAA of Wildcat fighters during Operation Tungsten, photographed when he was serving in 881 Squadron. (Bovey)

Lt Cdr S.G. Orr, OC 804 Squadron FAA on the escort carrier *Emperor* preparing for Operation Tungsten, 3 April 1944. (Orr)

804 Squadron FAA Hellcats on the escort carrier *Emperor* waiting to take off for Operation Tungsten, 3 April 1944. (Orr)

Fleet Air Arm bomber crews being briefed by Cdr S.T.C. Harrison for Operation Tungsten, April 1944. (IWM)

A present for *Tirpitz* from the Fleet Air Arm to be delivered during Operation Tungsten, April 1944. (IWM)

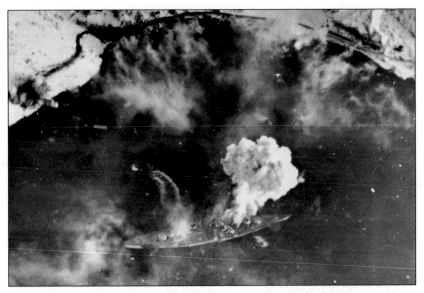

Operation Tungsten. Bombs from Fleet Air Arm Barracudas hit *Tirpitz* in Kaa Fjord, 3 April 1944. (IWM)

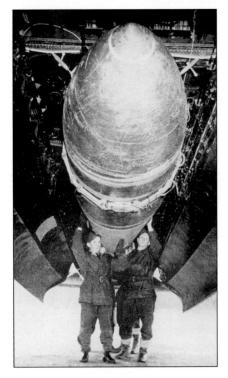

Tallboy, 12,000lb bomb, in the bomb-bay of a Lancaster. (Bennett)

Roy Chadwick (left), designer of the Lancaster bomber, was closely involved with its modification for carrying Tallboy. He is seen here with Wg Cdr G.P. Gibson, who led 617 Squadron to the German dams with Barnes Wallis' 'bouncing bomb'. (Wallis)

Air Vice-Marshal the Hon R.A. Cochrane, AOC 5 (Bomber) Group RAF, whose staff drew up the plans for 9 and 617 Squadrons to attack *Tirpitz* with Tallboy bombs. (IWM)

Crew of Lancaster KC-D of 617 Squadron at Woodhall Spa after attacking *Tirpitz* from Yagodnik near Archangel, 17 September 1944. The pilot, Wg Cdr J.B. Tait, is fourth from right. Unknown passengers are second left and far right. (Reed)

Steamer moored on Dvina river close to Yagodnik air base near Archangel in September 1944. This was the permanent home of man-eating bugs an temporary abode for RAF personnel involved in Operation Paravane. (Bennett)

Crew of Lancaster KC-D of 617 Squadron after returning from Yagodnik, 22 September 1944. The pilot, Flt Lt R.E. Knights, is third from left. The bomb-bay doors had been fitted on the Soviet base after the originals were damaged in unloading Tallboy. (Knights)

Tirpitz anchored off Haakoy, near Tromso, her final berth, November 1944. note protective anti-torpedo booms. (IWM)

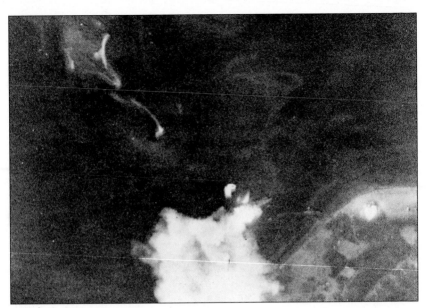

Tirpitz engulfed in smoke following bomb strikes, 12 November 1944. Note the flash of a stray Tallboy on the adjacent island. (IWM)

An American at Woodhall Spa. The crew of Fg Off J.H. Leavitt (centre), one of two American pilots to bomb *Tirpitz* in Norway with No 617 Squadron RAF. Sgt Daley (far right), the mid-upper gunner, did not fly on this operation. (Cole)

The 9 Squadron Lancaster crew of Fg Off R.J. Harris (third left), excluding the mid-upper gunner (left), which attacked *Tirpitz* during Operation Obviate, 29 October 1944. (Harris)

YEAR 1944		AIRCRAFT		PILOT, OR 1ST PILOT	2ND PILOT, PUPIL OR PASSENGER	DUTY (INCLUDING RESULTS AND REMARKS)
MONTH	DATE	Type	No.			
—	—	—	—	—	—	— TOTALS BROUGHT FORWARD
Oct.	3	Lancaster	O. 715 LM	Self.	Crew.	Practice Bombing.
Oct.	7	Lancaster	W.	Self	Crew F/Lt Cook	Operations: Flushing
Oct.	26	Lancaster	W.	Self	Crew.	Air Test.
Oct.	27	Lancaster	W.	Self.	Crew.	Bombing
Oct.	28	Lancaster	W.	Self	Crew	Base – Kinloss (1X 12,000lb)
Oct.	29	Lancaster	W.	Self.	Crew	Operations: "Tirpitz". Tromso. Norway. 12000 lb
Oct.	30	Lancaster	W	Self.	Crew	Kinloss — Base.
	elroe	S/LDR		Summary for October.. 1944 1.		
	O.C. B FLT.			Unit .9. Sqdn.. Aircraft.		2. Lancaster. I
J.R. Bazen - W/cmo				Date .30. 10. 44. Types.		3.
O.C 9 Sqdn.				Signature R.Harris F/O.		4.

Extract from the log book of Fg Off R.J. Harris, No 9 Squadron RAF, showing Operation Obviate against *Tirpitz*, 29 October 1944.

'Sic transit gloria mundi'. *Tirpitz*'s final resting place off Haakoy, near Tromso.
(IWM)

Midshipman Alfred Zuba, on duty in *Tirpitz*'s Gunnery Fire Control Section during Operation Catechism on 12 November 1944, was rescued through a hole cut in the upturned hull. (Bennett)

617 Squadron Aircrew Association

Tirpitz Commemoration Dinner

Petwood Hotel Woodhall Spa, Lincs

13th November 1999

13 November 1999. Menu card of the 55th commemoration dinner at which seven of the pilots on Operation Catechism were present. (Author)

Sgt J.C. Pinning, flight engineer of 9 Squadron's WS-T, which was attacked by two German fighters near Tromso on 12 November 1944, post-war beside a Tallboy crater on Haakoy. (Pinning)

Fighter-bombers, like Hellcats and Corsairs, could get to the target before the smoke-screen became fully active, but the size and number of bombs carried by them made their attacks 'of limited value'. 'Special intensive bombing training' must be given to crews 'to obtain results from the fleeting opportunities that may occur'. He concluded that any future carrier attacks on *Tirpitz* should be carried out either by 'Mosquitoes . . . or as many Hellcats and Corsairs as possible with suitable anti-flak support provided these can be adapted to carry 1,600lb bombs'.

In his final report on 3 November, Moore reinforced McGrigor's point about the slowness of Barracudas in attacking targets 'as far inland as Kaa Fjord', which allowed ample time for a smoke-screen to form. Naval fighters, he felt, might 'just beat the smoke but are not normally trained or fitted to carry bombs'. Like the rear-admiral commanding the First Cruiser Squadron, he believed that even 'experts with local knowledge' were likely to provide 'inaccurate' weather forecasts. 'The best policy is to proceed to the flying off position and see what the conditions are', which differed from McGrigor's contention that the decision should be taken with the force in the air. Of 'a Teasing Policy' – a series of minor strikes to wear down the defences – he was highly critical: 'The weather only gives periodical and fleeting chances; [and] periods of darkness give respite to the defences. . . . It is thus impracticable to maintain a continuous series of attacks and the object of the teasing tactics is therefore not achieved.'

Evidently unknown to Moore and McGrigor, while the Goodwood operations were in progress the idea of using Mosquitoes from carriers, rejected in 1943, had been revived. On 2 August, the CAS (Portal) favoured such an attack on *Tirpitz* 'if we think that the chances of success are commensurate with the losses likely to be incurred'. But 'adequate training' must be provided. He could not see why General D.D. Eisenhower, Supreme Commander Allied Expeditionary Force (SCAEF), should become involved as the 'Highball squadron' (618) – not committed to Eisenhower – could be used.

None the less, the matter was referred to Eisenhower, and on 14 August, while appreciating 'that the infliction of further damage to the *Tirpitz* would have important effects on future naval plans', he would not agree to the withdrawal of a Mosquito squadron from operations over Germany. Five days later, the First Sea Lord submitted a memorandum to the Chiefs of Staff Committee: 'Owing to the important effect which the elimination of *Tirpitz* would have on world-wide dispositions of Battleships and Fleet carriers and on the early strengthening of the Eastern Fleet, the Admiralty had sought every means of attacking this ship'. It was now prepared to bomb the battleship with Mosquitoes. Referring to Eisenhower's rejection of the proposal, Cunningham held that the Supreme Commander was not 'in a position to gauge the world-wide implications of an attack resulting in the elimination of *Tirpitz*. This must be a matter of decision at the highest level'. The First Sea Lord was playing for high political stakes, particularly when he added that this issue raised the wider question of Eisenhower's control over air operations post-Overlord.

On 23 August, the inter-Service Joint Planning Staff produced a report following instructions from the Chiefs of Staff, and therefore drafted before any of the Goodwood operations. It opened by referring to 'recent attacks by Fleet Air Arm aircraft . . . [being] unsuccessful because of the low speed of the Barracuda', which gave time for 'an effective smoke-screen' to form. The JPS therefore proposed 'that an attack should be delivered by a force of 8 to 15 [*sic*] Mosquito aircraft taking off from one or two carriers, and landing back in North Russia'. The Air Staff thought that there was 'a reasonable chance' of the Mosquitoes reaching *Tirpitz* before the smoke-screen thickened. A month would be necessary to modify and test the designated aircraft for carrying a 2,000lb AP bomb or 4,000lb capital ship (CS) bomb; for fitting a Mark XIV bomb sight; and to train the crews. 'Given good training, no fighter interference and minimum avoiding action for flak', fifteen Mosquitoes (each with one 2,000lb bomb, though two might be possible) 'should have a good chance of obtaining two effective hits', which if they penetrated 'under the main armour' should put the battleship out of action 'for at least four months'. 'The chance of sinking, or inflicting major damage depends so much on the position of the strikes that certainly can only be achieved by obtaining a large number of hits'. But the Air Staff insisted on no less than one month's training.

The JPS paper, 'Attack on the *Tirpitz*', then examined the rationale for mounting yet another operation. In so doing, it clearly demonstrated how much the Allies still viewed her as a menace. 'Although not fully effective, the *Tirpitz* is at present capable of carrying out limited operations, or of returning to Germany. A period of a few months in a German dockyard would, we think, fully restore her fighting efficiency'. The paper went on to emphasise the need for 'eliminating' *Tirpitz*. Firstly, 'so long as she remains in being, she is a serious potential threat to our sea communications'. This had, since the outbreak of war, been a fundamental strategic argument. 'One successful sortie, *even in her present state* [emphasis added], might take a heavy toll of our Russian and possibly Atlantic convoys, including reinforcements for France' – the spectre of a rerun of *Bismarck*'s foray, now with dire implications for the United States. The JPS elaborated this point: 'The Home Fleet and our air forces cannot guarantee that the *Tirpitz*, even in her present state, will not break out, particularly if she is prepared to risk everything in a final effort.' Alternatively, if the battleship were allowed to slip back to Germany for a refit, 'the potential threat at a later date would be increased'. She must be attacked forthwith. The paper's second line of argument centred on the concentration of warships retained with the Home Fleet to guard her: 'at least one fast battleship and one fleet carrier, which would otherwise form an important part of our Far East Fleet'. This was not novel reasoning, but again it showed that the Allied perception of *Tirpitz* had not altered since 1939: she must be sunk. At the very least, disabling her for four months might put her out of action for the remainder of the European war, which could be over by Christmas.

The JPS, apparently unaware of Portal's suggestion of using 618 Squadron, acknowledged that a Mosquito attack on *Tirpitz* would entail the diversion for 'approximately six weeks' of one of the six squadrons currently controlled by Eisenhower for bombing operations over Germany. This would mean the reduction of 'some 500 tons of bombs', which ' we consider . . . is unlikely to have an appreciable effect on the progress of operations in Europe'. If the Soviets agreed to the Mosquitoes landing in the northern USSR, 'the operation proposed by the Admiralty is just feasible'. However, 'to have a reasonable chance of immobilising the Tirpitz for at least four months . . . at least 15 Mosquitoes' must be withdrawn from Germany for six weeks; '. . . the advantages which may be gained by undertaking this attack are such as to justify' this.

Attractive though the concept might be, and accompanied as it was by a certain amount of sabre-rattling from the Chiefs of Staff that Eisenhower could be 'overruled . . . on the grounds of the security of this country', the small print of operational planning had now to be addressed. Referring to the JPS document, on 24 August the DCAS studied the proposal in the light of 'a practicable operation'. He agreed that the withdrawal of one Mosquito squadron for six weeks would not be disastrous. For the *Tirpitz* operation, each Mosquito should carry two 2,000lb AP bombs. These were preferable to a 4,000lb CS bomb, which had to strike the deck almost vertically from a minimum of 6,000ft. Parochial interests could also be advanced: 'If the operation should prove successful, it will enhance the prestige of the Royal Air Force in the eyes of the Royal Navy.' Fortunately, more professional considerations prevailed. On 26 August, Sir Douglas Evill informed the Chiefs of Staff Committee that 'some doubt about the tactical feasibility of the proposed [Mosquito] attack' existed in the Air Ministry. The smoke-screen over Kaa Fjord became effective in 10–15mins (unknown to Evill the Germans had reduced the response time to 7mins) and the Mosquitoes would 'certainly' be detected 8 or 9mins from the target, so the margin for error was 'very narrow'. He concluded that 'the probability of obtaining a hit was in any case comparatively small'. Detailed planning for the operation never got underway, and the difficulty of operating Mosquitoes from a carrier identified in the past may well have been another critical stumbling block.

Attacks on *Tirpitz* from carrier-based aircraft were now at an end. RAF Bomber Command was about to reoccupy centre stage.

4

RUSSIAN VENTURE, SEPTEMBER 1944

With the demise of the latest Mosquito project, Air Chief Marshal Sir Arthur Harris took primary responsibility for dealing with *Tirpitz* before the onset of winter darkness. He had just over three months to do so.

At the end of August, a report from Norway noted that after Goodwood IV *Tirpitz* had been observed on trials in Alten Fjord; information independently supported by the British naval attaché in Stockholm on 2 September. She had clearly not been badly damaged. Using this and other available information, on 13 September the Naval Intelligence Division concluded that necessary repairs following 'the midget submarine of the 22nd September 1943 and the F.A.A. attack of 3rd April 1944 . . . [had] probably been completed'. *Tirpitz* could steam at only reduced speed, but her armament was 'probably effective'. Docking facilities were not available outside of Germany, so a passage south might be attempted 'in the near future'. However, much more seriously, 'the possibility of her carrying out a limited operation cannot . . . be excluded'. This had been the rationale for the proposed Mosquito operation and, indeed, the Goodwood operations. In the Admiralty's eyes, the warship still posed a very real threat, and further reports suggested that she would undertake sea trials on 16 September.

The task of dealing with *Tirpitz* now devolved on 5 Group, though there was a belief among some aircrew that the AOC, Air Vice-Marshal the Hon. R.A. Cochrane, lobbied Harris for the privilege. One major consideration was to find a bomb able to pierce the battleship's armoured decks and wreak destruction in vital areas below. In the immediate aftermath of the destruction of the Moehne and Eder dams during the celebrated Dambusters Raid of May 1943, Cochrane had focused attention on Barnes Wallis's earlier proposal for a 10 ton bomb that would burrow itself beneath a target, explode underground and create a destructive camouflet literally to undermine a target. AOC 5 Group's operational interest centred on canal and river targets in Germany, which had so far eluded bombers, and a meeting in the Air Ministry on 8 June 1943 agreed that Wallis should reinvestigate the feasibility of his proposed weapon to attack them.

At this meeting, Wallis undertook to produce a report on the estimated effect of dropping his earthquake bomb not from the projected 40,000ft, but from 20,000ft – within the capacity of the Lancaster. On 26 June, his amended proposals reached DB Ops at the Air Ministry: an interim weapon of 12,000lb was suggested. At this stage, the 10 ton (22,400lb) weapon, the basis of his *Note* in 1941 and later codenamed Grand Slam, remained in the background as Tallboy (L). A smaller 4,000lb version appeared as Tallboy (S), the 12,000lb bomb was officially Tallboy (M), though it would soon be universally referred to simply as 'Tallboy', reputedly after its inventor who was 6ft 1in.

In the wake of Wallis's report, rapid development took place. During August, scaled-down calibration tests were carried out and on 12 September 1943 the prototype bomb was ready. By the close of 1943 325 Tallboys were on order, 125 under licence in the USA. An exhaustive series of tests and trials had been necessary to perfect not only the size, shape and content (5,000lb explosive or *c.* 42 per cent gross weight), but its fusing (three separate pistols were installed near the tail to counteract malfunction), loading system and release mechanism. Not all problems were quickly solved. On 9 January 1944, a meeting in Wallis's temporary office at Burhill Golf Club, attended by Cochrane, discussed 'Tallboy Installation and Development Trials'. Wallis described experiments at the Road Research Laboratory at Harmondsworth (an establishment closely involved with pre-Dambusters Raid experiments) to determine the best method of attacking E-boat and U-boat pens with their formidable protective structures. Contrary to the *Note*'s idea of dropping such a weapon alongside a target to burrow underneath it, 'the largest charges we could lay alongside were scarcely sufficient to do any material damage'. Attacking the roof became the only viable option. 'I estimate the penetration into solid reinforced concrete of Tallboy "M" at about 8ft', Wallis said. Unwittingly, he had pointed the way to using Tallboy on *Tirpitz*: for concrete roofs, read armoured decks. Range trials with specially-modified Lancasters were conducted at the Aeroplane and Armament Experimental Establishment (A&AEE), Boscombe Down, in February 1944.

Another progress meeting at the Air Ministry on 22 March looked in detail at the 'future employment of "Tallboy" (medium) weapon'. DB Ops, who chaired the meeting, opened by saying that the aim would be to discuss 'the development and supply' of Tallboy. Wallis explained that the latest test with models had estimated that, dropped from 20,000ft 'into favourable soil', Tallboy would penetrate about 60ft. A camouflet effect could not be achieved from this height, but in clay a crater 100–110ft wide and 45ft deep would be created. Professor Solly Zuckerman queried the effect of Tallboy on coastal artillery emplacements given the imminence of Operation Overlord. Wallis considered that a near miss would probably not destroy the concrete structures, but 'a 40-yard miss would result in a tilt of about 1 degree', which would render the guns unusable. He 'hoped' that, with a direct hit, Tallboy would 'penetrate concrete to a depth of five feet' (not the eight predicted in January). 'In the absence of comprehensive trials', breaking up on striking the ground could not be wholly discounted.

Tests conducted at the Ashley Walk bombing range near Fordingbridge in the New Forest, Hampshire, during March did confirm doubts about ability of the proposed casing to withstand impact with the ground. It was therefore strengthened and a dropping trial carried out at the Crichel Down range in Dorset from 16,000ft by a Lancaster travelling east to west at 1300 BST on Monday 27 March. On completion of the trial, a 38ft deep shaft was gradually excavated followed by a 21ft lateral tunnel by RAF bomb disposal personnel from Broadclyst, near Exeter, and Middle Wallop on Salisbury Plain under Sgt B.C. Westbrook. The aim was to recover the inert-filled weapon, which had burrowed deep into the chalk as expected. Westbrook later recalled: 'We hit the nose of the bomb first. It had turned completely over at the end of its flight.' But on their arrival, Wallis and Gp Capt Winterbotham were 'highly elated . . . [because] two of the three fuses at the rear of the bomb had operated correctly'. Westbrook was given '£2 to take all crew members into Christchurch for a celebratory drink'. More trials at Ashley Walk on 24 and 25 April confirmed the effectiveness of subsequent modifications to the casing.

The following month a report after a different series of experiments at Orfordness Research Station in East Anglia, conducted under the auspices of the MAP, dealt with other problems. 'Dropping trials of the original model of Tallboy displayed considerable oscillation after the bomb had fallen approximately 15,000ft. A modified tail, with the fins set at 5degs to the axis, has been tested with promising results.' Faced with the problem of oscillation, Wallis devised this method of counteracting the spinning tendency and tested his solution in a wind tunnel. Essentially, Tallboy now rotated around its longitudinal axis, gathering speed until the bomb stabilised like a gyroscope. Wallis later explained that Tallboy had 'perfect aerodynamic shape' and with its 'increasingly rapid spin' broke the sound barrier during its descent. Adjustments had also to be made after two hang-ups in the bomb-bay before five inert-filled Tallboys were successfully dropped from 18,000ft at a true airspeed of 190mph. The modified weapon achieved a terminal velocity of 3,300ft/sec, 'is very consistent' in flight and reached a striking velocity of 1,080 ft/sec. However, all the Tallboys dropped had drifted an average 90ft to port. On 27 May 1944, the MAP decided that this was due to the spin, for which the more accurate bomb sight (SABS Mk IIA) would compensate.

Within a year of the Air Ministry meeting in 1943, on 8–9 June 1944 617 Squadron used Tallboy operationally against the Saumur railway tunnel in France, 125 miles south of the Normandy beachhead. Successful employment against other targets, such as V-weapon sites, underlined the worth of Wallis's latest bomb and led to the order for it being increased to 2,000 (half to be manufactured in the USA). On 25 June 1944, HQ 5 Group analysed the operational attacks carried out with Tallboy that month. No drift to port had been identified, but release failures were worrying. A minor delay in functioning produced 'slight overshoot in range and if the delay is more than momentary, random errors'. An addendum to a Photographic Interpretation Report of 27 July, based mainly on operations against V-weapon sites, considered use of Tallboy against shipping at anchor. It concluded that small craft might be capsized if one were dropped in the water close-by, the 'plates below water level' of larger vessels damaged. The relevance to *Tirpitz* would later become apparent.

In the autumn of 1944, despite the general use of simply 'Tallboy', the official designation of the bomb remained 'Bomb, HE, Aircraft, MC, 12,000lb', reflecting the bureaucratic argument that with a delay fuse sometimes shortened to 0.025secs it could not be a deep-penetration weapon. Ergo, it was a medium capacity (MC) bomb. Nevertheless, with its proven ability to penetrate reinforced concrete and potential to inflict underwater damage on a large ship at anchor, Tallboy became a prime candidate with which to attack *Tirpitz*. Fg Off D.A.L. Bell, a 617 Squadron navigator, described Tallboy as 'sharp as a pin at the nose,

followed by five feet of hardened nickel steel. . . . with a
fluted tail, was designed to fly like an arrow and was a
precision weapon'. Another squadron navigator, Flt Lt T.
Bennett, noted that Wallis strove for 10yds accuracy.
Separate commentators more colourfully thought it 'shining,
blue and black steel, slim and perfectly streamlined' or
'beautiful, like a midget submarine'. In its final operational
form, Tallboy (M) had an overall length of 21ft, 38in
diameter at its widest, with a pointed nose and long tail, the
four off-set fins resting just short of the apex. The thickness
of casing in the centre section containing the 5,200lb of
Torpex explosive was 4.1in, for the tail 1.25in. Tallboy had
been primarily developed for land targets, not warships,
although Wallis had not conceived it exclusively for this use.

Tallboy was not the only new potential destroyer of *Tirpitz*.
In July 1942, the MAP called for a weapon capable of
damaging the underside of a capital ship at anchor, and the
JW (Johnny Walker) air-dropped mine was born. Early
experiments were carried out with a 24in long and 8in wide,
scaled-down practice weapon, with drops later made from a
Hampden or Beaufort at Porton Down and Gare Loch in
Scotland. A report from the Marine Aircraft Experimental
Establishment at RAF Helensburgh on 16 January 1943
emphasised need 'to ensure that the parachutes are able
reliably to control the flight of the bomb and keep it stable'.
For, unlike Tallboy, the JW mine was not streamlined and an
attached parachute (discarded when the mine hit the water)
not only ensured stability but also slowed the speed of
descent. The Air Ministry advised Bomber Command on
29 January 1943: 'Owing to employment of a high pressure
hydrogen bottle, bombs should be jettisoned by aircraft
exposed to fighter attack or flak.' In the margin opposite this
sentence, Harris scribbled dismissively: 'Just makes the
whole thing nonsense.' He had a point.

On 17 February 1943, Air Chief Marshal Sir Charles
Portal (CAS) sent a personal note to Air Marshal F.J.
Linnell (CRD at the MAP) emphasising that the JW mine,
though not yet perfected, was urgently required. Portal
believed, wrongly, that 'it has been specially designed for

operations in the Norwegian fjords' and revealed that the Prime Minister wanted a meeting 'in the very near future' to discuss progress. Linnell replied the following day: 'The flight in air and entry are now satisfactory, but there has so far been no reliable run of correct operation after entering the water.' On 2 March, the CRD elaborated. Twelve mines had been dropped in the first series of Scottish trials. After adjustments and corrections, four more were released from 3,000ft at 120 knots – still unsatisfactorily. More trials were scheduled from RAF Helensburgh on 5 March. Evidently, these tests and others that month did make progress for, on 3 April, aiming instructions were laid down: the mine should be released upwind of the 'intended point of impact by an amount equivalent to 2yds for each mile per hour of wind and for each thousand feet of height'. In still water, 'probable errors' ranged from 66yds at 2,000ft to 1,130yds at 15,000ft. These were, in truth, ideal figures, not taking into account operational factors. By now, the restrictions castigated by Harris had apparently been abandoned. Nevertheless, Kaa Fjord would offer an infinitely more challenging environment than Gare Loch. On 1 July 1943, Gp Capt N.W.D. Marwood-Elton at the Air Ministry prophetically wrote: 'The J.W. bomb when available for operational use will probably be allotted to No 617 Squadron'.

Officially the JW mine Mark I weighed 'about 400lb' and contained 'about 90lb of Torpex in the form of a shaped charge with a heavy cone', which 'is at least as effective as a solid charge of 120lb weight'. Some later sources maintain that the relevant figures were 500lb and 100lb of Torpex, and an Air Ministry post-operational document gave the figure '350lbs'. The differences are not significant. With a 72in length and maximum 20in diameter, it was roughly rectangular in shape and 'almost the same density as sea water'. The charge was inserted into the central section, and in the tail was 'a small buoyancy chamber which is alternately flooded and blown at intervals of about one minute by means of a compressed gas system'. The special fuse contained two additional devices. It would activate on impact if the mine hit a solid surface (like a ship or land) instead of water, and a self-destructive mechanism would explode the bomb when all the gas was expended. In theory, the latter would prevent it being recovered and defused if washed ashore. Attached to the tail was the special parachute, opened by a static cord as the JW mine left the aircraft, and at the same time the weapon was armed by withdrawal of a safety pin from the fuse. When the mine hit the water, the parachute would automatically fall away and, critically, the striker in the impact valve would start the gas flowing. At about 20ft below the surface, a hydrostatic valve closed off the gas supply to the buoyancy chamber and at 60ft the mine stopped descending. Rising again towards the surface, it should strike the target ship, if accurately dropped. If not, it would sink once more, hop (or 'walk', hence the name) laterally for 30ft and repeat the process, if necessary more than once. This characteristic led Bell to dub them 'wandering mines'. More pointedly, Flt Lt T.C. Iveson, who three times bombed *Tirpitz* with 617 Squadron, on being told that 'they would jump around and strike the underside of the ship', thought it 'a crazy idea'. One immediate drawback was that the mine required a minimum depth of 50ft in which to operate, which ruled out dockyards like Kiel and Gydnia. *Tirpitz* in Kaa Fjord presented a more attractive proposition.

Thus, in September 1944, Bomber Command had two special weapons with which to attack *Tirpitz*: Tallboy to pierce her decks and possibly with a near-miss cause underwater damage; the JW mine directly to strike her hull from below. However, Air Cdre C.N.H. Bilney informed Harris that he disagreed with Cochrane's view of 'J.W. as an effective weapon against the Tirpitz. This bomb is practically unaimable as it has a T.V. [terminal velocity] of only 160ft/sec and the chances of dropping bombs within the torpedo nets are therefore low. There is a release height limit of 12,000ft.' Bilney pointed out that 'in its final form', there had only been ten practice releases of the mine from

5,000ft at 120 knots, two of which had failed to function – one 'undoubtedly' through being dropped in shallow water. Depressingly, he concluded: 'As the direction of "walk" of these bombs is entirely fortuitous, and once commenced does not necessarily continue in the same direction, the chances of hitting a confined target such as the Tirpitz would appear to be small.'

Initially, 617 Squadron at Woodhall Spa was the only squadron equipped to carry Tallboy. After its inaugural pinpoint attack on the west German dams, which earned it the nickname of 'Dambusters', the squadron had carried out a wide variety of precision raids and, under Wg Cdr G.L. Cheshire, pioneered low-level marking for the main bombing force. In September 1944, it was commanded by Wg Cdr J.B. 'Willy' Tait DSO & 2 Bars DFC & Bar, who had been decorated after a daylight raid on Kiel in 1941 and on 7 May 1942 taken over 10 Squadron when its OC (Wg Cdr D. Bennett) was shot down during one of the Halifax operations against Tirpitz. Early in September, Tait was warned in absolute secrecy by Cochrane that he was to attack Tirpitz. Legend has it that the AOC started with the brusque statement: 'Tait you're going to sink the Tirpitz.' Shortly afterwards, Tait briefed the squadron in general terms, telling them it was 'an unusual operation, no more than that, and night flying in formation would be required'. So they began night gaggle practices with lights on, which were soon abandoned as infinitely dangerous. Iveson reacted with relief: 'Thank Christ for that. Who wants to roam around over the North Sea on a cold night, when we could be in a pub?' The gaggle was an operational formation of four or five aircraft a maximum 2,500ft deep that presented a wide front to fighters. Nor did it offer a compact target to flak gunners. It also gave mutual fire protection in the air and was sufficiently close to achieve a concentration of bombs. Realising that the forthcoming operation would be long distance and over water, Tirpitz was mentioned by 'one or two', but not generally.

By now, 9 Squadron at Bardney, Lincolnshire, had been trained to use Tallboy as well. On 31 August, its ORB recorded that the weapon had been 'introduced to No 9 Squadron and one specimen was drop-tested'. The next day, the armament officer went to Woodhall Spa's armoury 'to collect Tallboy equipment'. For the past two months in preparation for this new weapon, attacks had been undertaken 'against very small targets', such as the E-boat pens at Ijmuiden. As a result, technical steps had been taken to improve accuracy. The Mark XIV bomb sight was specially 'tuned'; 'investigations of the use of the A.P.I. Wind Finding Attachment were also made in order to determine the best method of its operational use'.

HQ 5 Group was instructed 'at the end of August . . . to explore the possibilities of an attack on the German battleship Tirpitz and should such an attack prove feasible to prepare a plan'. Staff officers identified four main problems in order of difficulty: weather, smoke-screen, weapons and range. Examination of available information, coupled with 'first hand evidence' from Sqn Ldr D.R.M. Furniss who had flown 'many' PRU sorties in the area, concluded that only three days in September were likely to have less than 3/10ths cloud over Alten Fjord. Well-known met. details were repeated: prevailing northerly and westerly winds crossing the warm Gulf Stream 'invariably' caused stratus on the coast; 'clear skies could only be expected as a result of winds with a land fetch blowing from the south-east or south'.

The efficiency of Kaa Fjord's smoke-screen 'had been proved on numerous occasions' during FAA attacks. Operational photos (especially those from the Goodwood operations in August provided by the Fleet Air Arm) showed that 'not only the Tirpitz herself but also the whole of Kaa Fiord could be covered in dense smoke some hundreds of feet thick'. The wind direction did not matter, and Tirpitz 'could be covered completely within approximately ten minutes of the smoke being turned on'. Understandably, therefore, HQ 5 Group pointed out that surprise was 'essential and the enemy's warning of the approach of an attacking force had to be reduced to the absolute minimum'. An efficient radar system was known to cover the seaward approaches, so 'the only hope of achieving a sufficient measure of surprise' lay in approaching from south or south-east 'at as high a speed as possible' to reduce the warning time to a maximum eight minutes.

In response to the third problem identified by staff officers, 'a study of the constructional details of the Tirpitz showed that none but the heaviest and strongest type of bomb could penetrate her horizontal armour and burst within the ship'. A hit from a Tallboy 'would cause tremendous damage, incomparably greater than could ever be caused by any other bomb in existence'. 'Even though the ship was obscured' by smoke, use of the available 150 JW mines 'provided a chance of obtaining a hit'. Photographs revealed that, when the fjord was covered with smoke, the tops of hills either side of *Tirpitz* remained clear. 'To guard against the possibility of an attack wholly abortive', JW mines were to be 'aimed at a readily distinguishable lake on the top of the north side of the fiord' usually unaffected by smoke. By using 'false bomb sight settings . . . and by selecting suitable stick spacing', it was hoped 'to produce a pattern of [JW] bombs approximately 750yds square centred over the target'.

This left only range, curiously ranked fourth in order of difficulty. Under orders from Cochrane, Tait sent selected 617 Squadron Lancasters on long flights of varying distances with different fuel and bomb-loads, conclusively to prove that the battleship was out of range from Scotland. Scatsta, north-west of Lerwick in the Shetlands, was considered as a staging airfield, even though it 'lies in hill country', its 'approaches [were] generally poor' and it had no night flying facilities. Then old files were retrieved from dusty cupboards, and the idea of using a Soviet airfield was rekindled. Two possibles were located at the port of Murmansk. After consulting the Soviet government, 30 Mission in Moscow advised the Air Ministry that Vaenga II on the Kola inlet 14 miles north-east of Murmansk, with two runways (1,500yds and 1,200yds long), 'good' surface and approach, 355 miles from *Tirpitz* and previously used by the RAF, was available. Independently, on 30 August the Air Ministry drew attention to Vaenga I with three runways (2,000, 1,750 and 1,350yds long) and only 9¾ miles from Murmansk. 151 Wing had used it in 1941 and it appeared capable of handling 180 aircraft, but it did have its drawbacks: 'Sand slight bumps – no grass; very dusty; absorbent, but some difficulty caused by splashes in dips; sand filters advised for aircraft.' Furthermore, the main road to Murmansk, which ran alongside the airfield, had poor quality cobbles. Nevertheless, on 31 August Bomber Command asked the Air Ministry to make sure that supplies of 100 octane fuel, oil and glycol sufficient for thirty Lancasters were ready at Vaenga I from 7 September.

Then, on 1 September, Bomber Command revealed tepid support from PRU personnel for both Vaenga bases, which prompted Harris to declare them 'probably . . . unsuitable'. There were other operational considerations – 'the proximity of a considerable German fighter force' and 'the almost complete absence of accommodation and service facilities'. So Yagodnik, 15 miles south-east of Archangel, also with 'good' approaches but a single 1,600yds 'arctic turf, sand-based' runway and 680 miles from *Tirpitz* was preferred; Vaenga was quietly shelved. 'The track mileage' from Lossiemouth to Yagodnik via Kaa Fjord was 2,100 miles and 'considered feasible for a Lancaster carrying normal full tanks of fuel'. A provisional operational plan was drawn up taking the Lancasters from Lossiemouth north to the Shetlands, then to 65 00N 06 00E, a point off the Norwegian coast north-west of Trondheim. From there the aircraft would fly east-north-east to 65 60N 16 30E and thence north-north-east to Kaa Fjord. After the attack, the squadrons would turn south-east over Lapland and the White Sea to Yagodnik. Interestingly, the updated 1872 map used to plot the route lacked political boundaries, so there was no clear indication of whether or not Swedish air space were to be entered on this leg. Once refuelled and, if necessary repaired, the aircraft would fly due west over Finland, the Gulf of Bothnia, Sweden and Norway to the turning point near Trondheim, the Shetlands and Lossiemouth.

On 6 September, the Air Ministry acknowledged that Yagodnik would be the Soviet airfield, adding to 5 Group: 'Flight plan would be appreciated as Soviet Naval Air Force keen to fly on simultaneous strike on German Air Force fighter airfields'. 5 Group replied later that day, 'for onward transmission to 30 Mission', that twenty-four Lancasters would land at Yagodnik at approximately 0730 GMT after attacking *Tirpitz*. 'The operation will take place on first day when weather suitable, but not before September 10th.' Two Liberators, carrying maintenance personnel, spare equipment and the officer commanding the operation, would fly from 65 00N 06 47E direct to Yagodnik, arriving on the day of the operation some three hours before the bombers. The signal ended: 'Much appreciate offer to strike against GAF airfields but to guard against possible operation of smoke-screen in Kaa fjord hope no Soviet aircraft will fly west of 28deg E until after 0430 GMT.' The following day, 5 Group informed Bomber Command and the Admiralty of its proposed routes to and from Yagodnik, requesting that destroyers be stationed along the return route at 63 00N 02 00E and 64 30N 05 30E, with a third on stand-by at Sullum Voe. Meanwhile, on 6 September, Tait had gone to Bardney to liaise with 9 Squadron. Having told his Squadron Navigation Leader (Flt Lt T. Bennett) about the target, Tait had already despatched him to RAF Northholt to draw maps of northern Norway and, as a cover, North Africa and eastern Europe as well. On his return, Bennett urged his OC to take others into his confidence, to which Tait sharply replied 'certainly not'. Security was paramount. However, long-distance cross-country runs and exercises over water provided fertile ground for speculation in the ale houses of Lincoln. Pictures of *Tirpitz* in the national press and the RAF's intelligence digest, *Evidence in Camera*, with details of recent steaming trials scarcely dampened rumours of an operation against the German battleship. Sqn Ldr G.E. Fawke and his crew from 617 Squadron were sent to confirm the suitability of RAF Scatsta as an emergency field and were alarmed to learn that they must radio in advance to ensure that sheep were driven off the landing area. Back at base, all pilots were instructed to practise 'very short landings', no doubt in preparation for an unscheduled visit to Scatsta.

5 Group Operation Order B. 393, issued on 7 September, opened by stating that 'numerous attacks' on *Tirpitz* in Kaa Fjord had damaged her 'particularly by the midget submarines and later to a lesser extent by aircraft of the Fleet Air Arm', but not decisively. 'She is now repaired and in a fit condition to go to sea.' The narrow nature of the fjord and 'extensive protective booms' made torpedo attacks 'impracticable'. Carrier-based aircraft could not take 'bombs of sufficient weight' to be effective, and it had, therefore, been decided 'that a force of heavy bombers is to attack the *Tirpitz* using special weapons suitable for the purpose'. 'Extensive precautions' taken by the Germans 'to preserve the safety of the *Tirpitz*' included anchoring her 'well inland close under the steep sides of the narrow fiord'. In addition to *Tirpitz*'s own 16 heavy and 16 light flak guns, they had placed 'approximately 38 heavy and 22 light' flak guns around the sides of the fjord. There was also 'an efficient chain of R.D.F. (radar) stations' – though there was 'good reason to believe that air forces approaching from the landward are unlikely to be detected until about a quarter of an hour before reaching Kaa fjord. . . . A highly efficient smoke-screen system' became fully effective in 'about 10 minutes. . . . From the bitter experience of the Fleet Air Arm, it is known that the whole Fjord can be quickly filled with deep thick smoke. . . . Surprise was, therefore, vital to the success of the enterprise.'

The Op. Order went on: 'The battleship's main armour was designed to give her maximum protection from bombing attack or plunging fire, and her horizontal armour consisted of two layers, the upper 2ins armour plate, and the lower 20ft below, of 3.2ins. The thickness of the lower layer is increased over the gun turrets and magazines.' However, 'the bottom of the ship is unprotected, consisting of two skins, each approximately one inch thickness'. This meant that while 'only the heaviest weapon can be really effective from above, a comparatively small weapon would suffice if it could be placed under the ship's bottom'. To perform these tasks, 'two weapons are available for use by heavy aircraft of Bomber Command': Tallboy and the JW mine.

A Lancaster could not fly to and from Kaa Fjord with Tallboy, full tanks and an all-up weight exceeding 67,000lb. Extra fuel tanks would unacceptably increase this weight, so an advanced base in the Archangel area was 'essential'. On the other hand, Lancasters with JW mines had an all-up weight of less than 62,000lb, could therefore carry additional fuel and return to Scotland. Mid-upper turrets were to be removed 'from all aircraft taking part in this operation'. In retrospect, some participants dispute that this was done, and the fact that from both squadrons almost all of the Lancasters flew with seven crew members is inconclusive. That some crews took one gunner may be more significant, and Flt Lt T. Bennett (617 Squadron Navigation Leader) is certain that the mid-upper turrets were removed.

It was intended that 48hrs would be allowed for a 'thorough' briefing of all crews at Woodhall with the aid of a large model, but the sequence of the briefings is unclear. Without doubt, some crew members from Bardney did travel to Woodhall for a combined briefing, at which one pilot recalls Sir Archibald Sinclair being present. The Secretary of State for Air announced that a former OC of 617 Squadron, Wg Cdr G.L. Cheshire, had been awarded the VC, and this was made public on 9 September. Therefore it seems likely, as maintained by two other pilots, that the combined briefing took place on 8 September, the day after the Op. Order and two days before the earliest date of the operation. This would have permitted the designated time for further study of the briefing material. Those present learnt that when met. conditions in the target area were 'likely to become suitable' aircraft would proceed 'fully bombed up' to Lossiemouth, Kinloss and Milltown, where they would be topped up with fuel and await further orders. However, some aircrew insisted later that only one briefing occurred and did not recall ever being prepared to fly via Lossiemouth to bomb on the way to Yagodnik. The fact that three pilots placed the combined briefing on 8 September may be important, for it could have been restricted to certain personnel and not been a general one. Nevertheless, all aircrew were certainly briefed on their individual stations about the new plan to fly directly to Yagodnik during the morning of 11 September.

The aim laid down in B.393 was 'to sink the *Tirpitz*'. For the operation, the Lancasters would be divided into Force A (twelve each with Tallboy from 617 and 9 Squadrons), which would bomb *Tirpitz* and fly on to Yagodnik, covering an estimated 1,845 miles. Force B (six from each squadron with JW mines) would return to their Scottish advanced base after bombing, refuelling if necessary at Scatsta in the Shetlands and cover approximately 2,283 miles. Should any of Force B have fewer than 1,000 gallons of fuel in the target area or be experiencing engine trouble, they would proceed to Yagodnik with Force A. Vaenga airfield, reached via 68 50N 28 00E to avoid enemy fighters at Kirkenes, was the alternative to Yagodnik. A film unit Lancaster would go with Force B, have no bombs, carry 2,954 gallons of petrol and proceed directly to Northholt after the attack. Each Force A aircraft would take one Tallboy (time delay fuse 0.07secs), 'full inner, centre and outer tanks [2,154 gallons]'; Force B aircraft each carry twelve JW mines, full tanks as for Force A, plus '250galls in special overload tanks' – one Wellington long-range tank in the fuselage and a Mosquito drop tank, though these were never actually fitted for this operation.

From the advanced bases, the aircraft would climb slowly to 2,000ft towards 63 00N 02 00E, where they would rapidly lost height to 1,000ft to 65 40N 16 40N via 65 00N 02 00E, where ' a gradual climb' would take place to cross the Norwegian-Swedish frontier between 6,000 and 7,000ft. After crossing the high mountains, an altitude of 4,000–5,000ft would be maintained until the rendezvous point (67 26N 19 10E), which would be reached in daylight. The rendezvous point would be marked by smoke bombs under the direction of the force leader. Early arrivals would orbit left-handed at 5,000ft until all aircraft assembled to be led off to the target in pre-arranged formation, climbing to bombing height as they did so. Four Force B aircraft would fly five minutes ahead to establish wind speed and direction. Force A would be 'allotted bombing heights evenly distributed between 13,000 and 17,000ft'; Force B similarly 10,000–12,000ft. Should cloud cause problems, a minimum attacking height would be 8,000ft. From the target, Force A would fly to Yagodnik at 1,000ft, Force B a maximum of 5,000ft to the United Kingdom. If the target were clear, Tallboy aircraft should bomb visually. If not, they were 'to cross the target and to take photographs of the smoke-screen with the object of identifying the position of the smoke generators for subsequent use as aiming points'. They would then take their unreleased bombs to Yagodnik. Force B would bomb even if the target were obscured, provided that the indirect aiming point could be identified. Watches were to be synchronised to GMT; radio silence maintained, though W/Ops were to keep a listening watch on specified wavelengths. Pilots were 'to start bombing runs so that they make good the ground track for which they are briefed at TAS [True Air Speed] 200 mph'. *Tirpitz* was believed to be anchored in the eastern berth (shown as Point A on briefing papers). But her former, western berth appeared as Point B and crews were warned that she might be at either. H-hour would vary according to the day of attack, but 'be approximately one and a half hours after morning civil twilight at the target'. Detailed arrangements followed for the movement of equipment and sixty-nine maintenance personnel plus the aircrew and operational headquarters staff to Milltown, Kinloss and Lossiemouth. For the purposes of load calculation, administrators were reminded that 'the average weight of a man fully clothed is 200lbs'.

Throughout 10 September a succession of cypher messages passed between the SBNO at Archangel, the Air

Ministry and 5 Group concerning detailed arrangements for the reception of Force A at Yagodnik. For example, the aircraft were to pass north of Archangel to Lake Ijmozeru, then fly at 1,000ft to Yagodnik; the Soviet R/T equipment had a maximum 100km (62.5 miles) range; various call signs and codenames were exchanged. As one Lancaster would painfully confirm, the SBNO expressed doubt about the accuracy of aircraft recognition among enthusiastic gunners in 'some frontier posts'. Unaccountably, however, not until the evening of 11 September did the Air Ministry signal 30 Mission in Moscow, the SBNOs at Archangel and Murmansk: 'Weather conditions in the target area at present varying too rapidly to offer prospect of success at the end of a long haul from UK base.' The whole bombing force would fly directly to Yagodnik and mount the operation from there. Forty-one aircraft (thirty-eight Lancasters, two Liberators and one Mosquito – a figure not including the film unit Lancaster), with a total 290 personnel would begin to land at Yagodnik at 0239 GMT on 12 September. They would fly from Lincoln to North Unst over the North Sea at low level, across high ground in Scandinavia and reach the Russo-Finnish border at 65 00N 29 40E at 6,000ft at approximately 0115 GMT. The Air Ministry asked 30 Mission to express regret to the Soviet authorities 'at the short notice given, but if opportunity of favourable weather en route is not taken immediately operation may not be possible'. It was, indeed, 'short notice', for the timing of this signal meant that the aircraft would be airborne before the Soviets knew that they were on their way.

A flurry of signals was also despatched on 11 September to the Admiralty and Home Fleet, among other addressees, announcing the late change of plan. 5 Group ORB recorded: 'On the morning of September 11th, there still appeared no prospect of S.E. winds over the target, and it was impossible to forecast breaks in the cloud sufficiently far ahead and accurately to enable the force first to fly to Lossiemouth and then, after refuelling, to set off for the target.' The scheme 'as originally conceived' required aircraft to cross the Norwegian coast in darkness and bomb one to two hours after dawn. 'A quick decision was therefore made on this morning to dispatch force forthwith to Yagodnik, where they should refuel and refit, and be prepared to seize the first opportunity of suitable weather conditions.' The aim now was for the aircraft to take off 'at approximately 1700hrs GMT . . . and arrive at Archangel in daylight the following morning'.

5 Group noted that on 10 September, aircrew of 617 and 9 Squadrons destined for 'secret operations' and groundcrew due to accompany them were grounded by indifferent weather. Then came the change of plan on 11 September. So that evening, between 1859 and 1926 DBST eighteen Lancasters of 9 Squadron led by Wg Cdr J.M. Bazin took off for Yagodnik, 'the intention being to operate from there against the German battleship "T", then lying in Kaa Fiord, an inlet in the south-west extremity of Alten fiord, Norway'. They were accompanied by a Lancaster of 463 Squadron carrying a film unit. Two Transport Command Liberators of 511 Squadron from RAF Lyneham, Wiltshire, left Bardney 'slightly before' the operational aircraft. A 540 Squadron Mosquito, destined for photographic and reconnaissance duties, did not leave Bardney until 12 September, aiming to cross the Soviet-Finnish border at 20,000ft at 1026 GMT and land at Yagodnik at 1140 GMT (in the event, arriving only 20mins late). Meanwhile, at Woodhall Spa on 11 September, a newly arrived American pilot serving in the RAF, Fg Off J.H. Leavitt, had been told by Sqn Ldr G.E. Fawke, 'John, you're in charge of the flight. I'm off to Russia.' Leavitt, like another recent arrival Fg Off A.W. Joplin RNZAF, had been briefed for the operation but not detailed for it. Between 1856 and 1915 DBST nineteen 617 Squadron Lancasters took off; a twentieth (Flt Lt G. Stout) left at 1937. Precisely half of the 617 aircraft were Lancaster I, the other ten Lancaster III with Merlin engines built under licence by the Packard Motor Company in Detroit. According to 5 Group, all the operational aircraft departed 'without incident . . . in clear weather'.

None of the operational Lancasters put down in Scotland as originally intended, but flew up the east coast of England to pick up the briefed Op. Order route at the northern tip of the Shetlands. One 9 Squadron Lancaster (R, piloted by Fg Off R.C. Lake) had to jettison its bomb in the North Sea, after the Tallboy worked loose in the bomb-bay, and returned early. So thirty-seven Lancasters, two Liberators and the film unit Lancaster flew towards the Soviet Union through the night of 11/12 September. None were lost to enemy action, but several crews had hair-raising stories to tell.

The men on the Liberators, piloted by Flt Lt G.H. Capsey and Flt Lt Adams, were no exception. Normally 511 Squadron flew Yorks, but Liberators were chosen for this operation because Yagodnik was believed to have spares for this type of aircraft. Used to operating flights to the Middle East and Far East, the crews packed tropical kit and proceeded to Bardney on 7 September. As senior officer, Capsey was fully briefed but sworn to secrecy. Realising that the weight of essential Lancaster spares to be taken in the Liberators had not been addressed, he gained permission to summon an experienced NCO from Lyneham. Once a Merlin engine, Lancaster undercarriage leg and wheel, radio spares, other maintenance and repair equipment plus several cases of tinned food had been duly loaded, each aircraft had capacity for fourteen passenger seats. Into these, Gp Capt C.C. McMullen, administrative staff of the operational HQ to be set up at Yagodnik and groundcrew personnel settled. Concerned about fuel for their heavy loads with the change of plan, the Liberator pilots secured permission to put down at Lossiemouth to top up.

Nearing the Scottish base, Capsey and Adams were perturbed to see Beaufighters nosing suspiciously towards them. 'As our sole armament was a very pistol, we kept our fingers crossed' that they had been advised. Fortunately they had, and after leaving Lossiemouth the Liberators proceeded at 400ft below enemy radar to 65 00N before climbing to 8,000ft over the Norwegian mountains in a cloudless sky. Accurate map reading proved possible until the weather closed in over Finland and, maintaining the required radio silence, the two aircraft lost contact with one another. Capsey's Liberator relied on its Bendix radio compass and tuned to the Archangel frequency, which to the crew's relief flickered into life at approximately 0700 LT (0400 GMT). Guided by the signal, the pilot set course for Solomabla, then turned south along the Dvina river. Suddenly the buildings of Archangel were below as the Liberator's port wing narrowly missed the masts of the radio station. Almost disaster with safety in sight. As Capsey crossed the city, a searchlight guided him to a 'horrible little field . . . bounded on three sides by hangars and on the fourth by the river bed'. The airfield bore no resemblance to the briefed destination. But several Lancasters, including one that had crashed on its belly, were already there. With considerable trepidation Capsey joined them. His qualms were justified. This was Kegostrov, an island close to Archangel, and not Yagodnik, which was some 12 miles upstream. Later that morning, 12 September, Capsey took off for Yagodnik where he found Adams. The HQ and maintenance crews for Operation Paravane were all now at the advanced base.

Prior to Capsey's arrival Kegostrov had witnessed an extraordinary incident. Plt Off R.J. Harris of 9 Squadron (WS-E) followed Sqn Ldr D.R. Wyness of 617 Squadron in to land, only to see a horse career across the airfield as KC-Y was about to touch down. Taking violent evasive action, Wyness effectively wrote off his machine when the undercarriage collapsed. In the general confusion, Harris incongruously pitched the nose of his Lancaster into a potato patch and damaged the aircraft so badly that it was not ready for the forthcoming operation. His bomb-aimer, Plt Off H.F.C. Parsons, explained further: the aircraft was circling Archangel with the cloud base 'about 700ft' when Parsons saw an airfield with another Lancaster about to land. As Harris followed it in, a rainbow of very lights shot up. This was thought to be a warning that they were coming in down wind, but, on later reflection, perhaps more of an indication that this was not the right spot.

Parsons saw figures scatter as the aircraft scraped a perimeter parapet. When the machine found its unorthodox resting place, it lodged in a ditch with its tail high in the air. Trapped in virtual darkness as earth enclosed his compartment and unable to use his escape hatch, Parsons crawled up into the main cockpit to discover that the remainder of the crew had gone out via the pilot's overhead exit. Anxiously, he scrambled after them on to the wing to conclude 'a terrifying experience'.

Two other crews recorded unscheduled landings in strange circumstances, too. Fg Off D.A.L. Bell, navigator in the 617 Lancaster piloted by Lt H.C. 'Nick' Knilans USAAF who had enlisted in the RCAF, subsequently joined the USAAF and was on his last operation with the RAF, recalled seeing 'the blazing sunset as it hung over the Orkney island only to sink slowly into the north Atlantic', after which he had to navigate in utter darkness and radio silence. Not until the Gulf of Bothnia, where the lights of neutral Sweden could be seen clearly, was he able to obtain reliable visual checks. As morning broke, drizzle and low cloud over Finland forced Knilans down to 50ft with mist-covered forests a constant hazard and the promised radio assistance from the Soviets conspicuously absent. It later emerged that the attacking aircraft had been given the wrong call sign (8BP instead of 8VP) and possibly even the wrong frequency. A forecast of a 1,500ft cloud base with six miles visibility in the Archangel area turned out to be 10/10ths cloud at 150–300ft and visibility of about 600yd. The 5 Group post-operational intelligence report described weather conditions at Yagodnik as 'very bad' with the cloud 'base varying from nil to 100 feet, and heavy rain'. Glimpsing water below, Knilans' crew realised that they had flown too far east and turned back. After almost scraping the masts of two coastal vessels, Knilans put down on a narrow piece of soft ground just inland. The Lancaster had been in the air for 12½hrs and two of its engines cut out as it landed. Knilans rolled to a halt perilously close to a belt of trees. His account of the unscheduled landing was even more colourful. Having completed his reciprocal course, he circled over a small fishing village and spotted a nearby hay field. Flying over it, he saw 'five barefoot boys about 10yrs old . . . [making] vigorous motions with their heads and hands. I gathered that they were signalling that we would be OK to land there.' Approaching the downward sloping ground downwind via a convenient gully, Knilans scraped over a surrounding wire fence, which brushed the protruding rear guns, 'plopped down' into mud, which affected the brakes, and managed to ease round a haystack without damaging the oleo legs or wheels. Understandably, he gave a thumbs-up of relief/triumph to the five grinning boys.

Incredibly, Knilans was not the first 617 pilot to seek refuge that day on this waterlogged turf. Fl Lt T.C. Iveson had already arrived at 0715 GMT (1015 LT). Like Knilans' wireless operator, Fg Off A. Tittle had not been able to raise the Soviets on air. With fuel running low, Iveson saw the field, but was concerned (wrongly, as it transpired) about the safety of landing with his load of JW mines, so jettisoned them in a lake. After Knilans touched down, both captains decided to remain in their aircraft, and soon afterwards a Jeep cautiously circled them out of range. Once their identity had been established, 'out came an open truck with Russian soldiers in it, some wearing German greatcoats and most unshaven'. Fourteen RAF personnel piled in with them for a journey over rough tracks to the nearby garrison town, where they were off-loaded at the end of a muddy, untarmaced main street resembling a Wild West film set. The crews were led along the raised wooden sidewalk, where broken and missing boards threatened to deposit the unwary into oozing slime beneath. They were then effectively confined to a room with sentries posted outside and served a meal of fish ('raw' in some memories, 'salmon' in others) and black bread. Accompanying this fare were pitchers of water – or so it seemed until thirsty airmen gulped it greedily. Vodka was not normally consumed – and certainly not in large quantities – in RAF messes. The results were predictable and uncomfortable. The local commandant was astounded when Iveson showed him on a wall map that they had flown from Lincolnshire and were bound for Yagodnik. Contact was made with that airfield and Tait materialised in a decrepit biplane to guide Iveson there later that afternoon.

Knilans was less fortunate. His aircraft's lack of petrol dictated an overnight stay. In the morning, according to Bell, the aircraft had been turned round for departure in the rain-soaked conditions by 'manskies' (the quaint term used by the interpreter for manual labour). Take-off proved anything but trouble free. In his log, Knilans recorded 'caught in down draft' but Bell claimed that the flight engineer misheard 'flaps up' for 'wheels up'. For whatever reason, the Lancaster hit the trees losing the pitot head, bomb-sight and bomb-bay doors and damaging both elevators. Tallboy remained secure, but the cockpit windscreen had been perforated by a 3ft x 2½in branch, which continued its path over the main spar and into the fuselage. Later it was mounted on the wall of the officers' mess at Woodhall Spa (the Petwood Hotel) with a caption: 'Believe it or not.' Meanwhile, Knilans had to use one hand to shield his face from the wind and cope with an overheating starboard outer engine peppered with foliage and pine needles. At Yagodnik, repairs were carried out with parts from other crashed and unserviceable aircraft, but to replace the bomb-bay doors the Tallboy had to be lowered to the ground. In the absence of the appropriate hoisting gear, reputedly 'manskies' were again summoned to perform.

Although he had an untroubled short flight from Onega to Yagodnik, Iveson did not escape entirely scot-free. On 13 September, he took off for Kegostrov with six Soviet groundcrew aboard to help take worthwhile equipment from Sqn Ldr Wyness's crashed aircraft. Unable to establish airspeed, he discovered that the protective cover for the pitot head had not been removed. Sgt J.D. Phillips managed to dislodge it by using the heater and KC-F went on to collect Wyness (who would go with Iveson on the operation as second pilot) and return to Yagodnik, where the JW mines from Fg Off Carey's damaged aircraft were transferred to its bomb-bay.

Even before his wobbly excursion to Onega City, Wg Cdr

Tait had, like other aircraft, experienced what RAF Bardney described as 'appalling weather conditions' over the final stage of the route. Similarly, 5 Group later referred to 'considerable low cloud and rain . . . almost 150mls from Archangel. . . . Aircraft flew just above tree tops over the most desolate country imaginable – lakes, forests and swamps. Map reading was impossible, weather conditions alone made this too difficult, and in addition it was found that maps of the area were inaccurate – many villages and even railway lines being omitted.' Over Finland and the USSR, Tait went as low as 300ft. His W/Op (Fg Off A.J. Ward) tried to raise Yagodnik in vain, believing in retrospect that the wrong frequency had been given to him. Then the bomb aimer (Fg Off W.A. Daniel RCAF) saw a river – the Dvina in which Yagodnik lay on an island. Tait went even lower, found the airfield and landed safely at 0809 LT. Only twenty-three other operational Lancasters, twelve from 617 and eleven from 9 Squadrons, joined him. That of Fg Off R.F. Adams (9/W) had survived a particularly nasty flight. Approaching the Norwegian coast, when he could still have legitimately turned back, Adams feathered his starboard outer engine with a coolant leak, and pressed on. Like others pilots, he ran into bad weather and for two hours flew at 300ft, refusing to jettison the Tallboy, until he managed to put down safely at Yagodnik – the island was roughly 3 miles long, 1 mile wide with a 6,000ft north-east–south-west grass landing strip for the Soviet Naval Air Station. Unfortunately, such was the pressure on groundcrew technicians that an engine change could not be made before the operation.

For Sqn Ldr Fawke's flight engineer, F/Sgt A.W. Cherrington, as ETA got nearer 'the fuel problem raised its head and I had to sort out the engines'. That was not the only problem. In common with so many navigators beyond the Gulf of Bothnia, Flt Lt Bennett looked down 'on a scene from a Hollywood horror movie: tips of pines sticking up through a sea of mist'. He recalled the briefing by an Air Ministry met. officer: 'Cloud below 1,500ft is unknown in this area at this time of the year'. As he did so, a voice over the intercom echoed his thoughts – 'wish he was bloody well here'. But Bennett found the mouth of the Dvina and followed it straight to Yagodnik. Seeing a Soviet batsman flourishing red and green flags with aplomb, Fawke set down as another Lancaster did so dangerously from the opposite direction. KC-J, to Cherrington's consternation, 'almost finished up in the watch tower'. However, as part of the 'great welcome . . . we had a typical Russian meal of black bread, strong coffee, reindeer meat, some veg, but I don't know what, pancakes and loads of vodka'.

Fg Off F.H.A. Watts in 617 Squadron's KC-N found the 'Marconi homer' invaluable, when map-reading became impossible in 'featureless country'. 'Upon switching on', he recalled, 'the needles on the pilot's panel erected themselves and although only 40 per cent efficient managed to keep re-erecting long enough for me to apply necessary directional corrections and the device enabled us to pick up the River Dvina and Yagodnik. "Oh ye of little faith", my wireless operator breathed'.

At Bardney Flt Lt J.D. Melrose, flying WS-J on its 100th operation with 9 Squadron, had been acutely aware of the unusual all-up weight. Taxiing towards the end of the runway 'using as many feet as I could we trundled along with everybody starting to sweat a bit, then I lifted her just over the fence. I tucked up the undercarriage as soon as I could and got the flaps up. Ted [Sgt E. Selfe] and I were working like beavers to get her up to 1,000ft before we settled down'. Like other crews, after crossing Norway and being warned away from urban centres by Swedish ack ack, Melrose hit the bad weather, went down low and admitted to getting through forty Player cigarettes before his navigator map read them successfully to Yagodnik.

Several aircraft reported 'isolated instances of ineffective flak from positions in Sweden and Finland', but KC-E of 617 Squadron (Fg Off D.W. Carey RAAF) was the only one to be damaged. At 0422 GMT, Carey broke cloud at about 1,000ft at 64 42N 33 32E and was engaged by two light flak guns. Both ailerons were hit and the elevator control damaged; the fuselage and extra fuel tanks were holed, and an aerial was shot away. The rear gunner (Fg Off C.A. Witherick) responded (disturbing the occupant of a distinctive, small building, who emerged hastily adjusting his trousers) as the Lancaster regained the cloud to make 'a good landing' at Yagodnik.

By 0800 GMT (1100 LT) on 12 September, when their fuel must have been expended, thirteen Lancasters were unaccounted for at Yagodnik. News gradually filtered through of landings and crashes in outlying areas: five at Kegostrov (64 33N 40 26E), two near Vaskova (64 16N 40 48E and 64 30N 40 00E), two at Onega City (approx. 63 50N 38 00E), one each at Chubalo-Navolsk (64 30N 40 14E), Belomorsk (63 32N 32 00E recorded, but approx 64 30N 35 00E), Molotovsk (64 30N 40 00E) and in the Talagi area (approximately 64 45N 40 45E). About this phase of the operation, 9 Squadron was caustic. Weather forecasts issued in the United Kingdom for 'the arrival at Archangel were "good"' with radio assistance from Murmansk and Archangel promised. In the event, from the Russo-Finnish border, cloud was 10/10ths down to 300–500ft, then heavy rain gave a maximum two miles visibility for the final 200–300 miles of the flight. 'Moreover, the beam stations were of no assistance as these worked on an entirely different system and required a code which was not known' – yet another reason offered for failure of W/T communications. Acidly, the Squadron report added that the Soviet forecast accurately predicting the met. conditions had been available twenty-four hours in advance: 'It was unfortunate that this forecast was not available in England before take-off.' Referring to the late notification to 30 Mission of the change of plans on 11 September, it went on: 'It was also unfortunate that the signal informing Archangel of the departure did not arrive until a few hours before the aircraft arrived'. Only 'superb airmanship in saving their aircraft and bomb loads' had averted 'a complete disaster'. Similarly, the pilot of the film crew Lancaster was both complimentary and scathing: 'Navigational skill in appalling weather conditions was responsible for the greater percentage of aircraft landing at Yagodnik. There were absolutely no facilities as the beacon was U/S . . . Apart from this, maps were inaccurate and pin points were of no value.' Flt Lt B.A. Buckham RAAF clearly did not enjoy the experience.

Under the extraordinary circumstances, though, 5 Group acknowledged that the Soviet authorities 'performed wonders in giving all available help', even dropping in the remote Talagi location a parachutist, who regrettably proceeded to lose himself and the crew he was leading to safety. Fortunately, no aircrew were injured, but Lancasters M, D, Q and H from 9 Squadron were 'severely damaged' and 'subsequently abandoned'; B and Y from 617 were also written off. The five accessible wrecks (less that at Talagi) were cannabalised for spare parts to make less damaged machines serviceable. Thirty-one bombers were eventually 'collected at Yagodnik where accommodation and re-fuelling facilities existed', though not all could be made ready to attack *Tirpitz* in time. The availability of only small petrol bowsers was an added complication and refuelling of the serviceable machines took 18hrs. Furthermore, even with the assistance of Soviet technicians, the repairs were laborious and lengthy: extensive work on Knilans' aircraft was not completed until the night of 14/15 September, which allowed the crew to attack *Tirpitz*. The official conclusion on the crashes was that each of the aircraft had 'either landed with its undercarriage retracted or had struck some obstacle which removed one or both legs of the undercarriage'. The report decided that the 'primary cause of the crashes was the adverse weather . . . The secondary cause was shortage of fuel. Each captain did all possible to save his aircraft, and it is considered that disciplinary action is not required. In fact, many of them deserve congratulations for their determined efforts to find an airfield and for their excellent airmanship in landing without injury to any of their crews.'

On the morning of 14 September, twenty Tallboy and six JW Lancasters plus the film unit machine were ready to fly. The PRU Mosquito duly took off for *Tirpitz* at 0210 DBST (0310 LT), as a prelude to the crews leaving at 0800 and carrying out the attack four hours later. At 0645, the

Mosquito reappeared to report poor weather, and the attack was postponed. Entertainment was, therefore, laid on by the Soviet hosts. This did not prevent Tait parading 617 Squadron personnel on the airfield and directing them in 'organised P.T.' during the morning. An official lunch, punctuated and succeeded by copious toasts in vodka, was followed by an afternoon football match 'in which', according to the British MO, 'a well-trained and smartly turned out S.N.A.F. [Soviet Naval Air Force] team beat a scratch RAF team'. Other spectators commented on the endless supply of substitutes fielded by the opposition, among them the station commander, who duly scored the ritual senior officer's goal – according to one account luckily off his knee, to another from the penalty spot. Each goal by the home side was greeted with a fanfare from the attendant military band that to untutored ears sounded suspiciously like the 'See the Conquering Hero Comes' from Handel's oratorio, *Judas Maccabeus*. The Soviets undoubtedly won the encounter, but the score varied between 4–0 and 7–0 depending on individual memory and, perhaps, the extent of lunchtime liquid refreshment. One spectator even optimistically registered a goal for the RAF in a 16–1 scoreline. Flt Lt T. Bennett remains convinced that the Soviet team's goalkeeper played for Moscow Dynamos in their post-war games against Arsenal and Chelsea during a goodwill tour to Britain. That evening, a prolonged war epic (without sub-titles) was shown in the camp cinema. Other entertainment was also laid on as a correspondent in *'V' Group News* explained: 'On one occasion, a lecture on a Russian composer which started 55 minutes late, lasted for 75 minutes, was a complete mystery from start to finish to the British members of the audience.' Squarish partners, clad in baggy uniforms with stiff collars, during a dance did not meet with universal approval either. Ungraciously a would-be RAF beau recalled after fifty years that they were 'big and hefty and very heavy footed'. If true, it did not deter certain visiting airmen from other athletic fraternisation. Despite the language barrier, 'a bit of Allied nuzzling and mutually satisfying frolic in the tundra' reputedly took place. Less contentious activity involved an exhibition of the hokey-cokey by 617 Squadron on the dance floor under the direction of their intrepid OC.

Trips to Archangel proved eventful, too. One day-long excursion entailed lunch at the Intourist hotel, a concert of operatic arias and consumption of the local brew (vodka) in generous quantities. As a result, one hardy soul attempted to swim back to Yagodnik. During a second expedition, two pilots contrived to evade the set programme and also sampled copious glasses of potent clear liquid. They did not attempt to emulate Johnny Weismuller, but did incur the wrath of their OC by keeping the return boat waiting. An economic postscript followed. On 25 October, 30 Mission forwarded to the Air Ministry a bill for 9,239 roubles 'being expenses incurred by personnel at Archangel for entertainment of RAF and Russian personnel concerned in Operation Paravane'. The Mission believed the programme 'well worth while' and that the amount should be met from an RAF fund and not passed on to the officers and men involved. No charge was levied, however, for the enamelled red star, embossed with a yellow hammer and sickle, that was solemnly presented to all those who attacked *Tirpitz*. Subsequently, the Air Ministry enforced regulations forbidding the wearing of such unauthorised decorations on Service uniforms.

The RAF MO, Flt Lt R.M.S. Matthews, paid tribute to the Soviet catering organisation and the interpreter, 'who were untiring in their efforts to please'. 5 Group pointed out, too, that the Soviets had expected 'some 250 guests but last minute alterations had increased this to 325' – Force B in addition to Force A. One officer succumbed to a 'moderately severe clinical dysentery', and 'a quantity of disinfectant was not able to mitigate the unpleasantness of the latrines for him' in the sick quarters. Matthews remarked that 'an outburst of similarly severe dysentery on an epidemic scale would have produced great difficulties in nursing'. He did not mention the plague of mosquitoes and bed bugs that afflicted aircrew. Along the northern edge of the airfield, permanent and semi-permanent wooden buildings contained administrative offices and the Soviet barracks. To the west were a number of dug-outs, half-submerged in the ground with their roofs covered in earth. To these most non-commissioned ranks were consigned. Officers and senior NCOs had the apparent luxury of a boat moored on the Dvina. About the miseries of these various billets, one sufferer afterwards wrote: 'The accommodation consisted of a paddle steamer, which was moored to the river bank, and several underground huts. These huts provide warmth in winter but the absence of any kind of ventilation and the fact that a large brick fireplace forms a major part of the accommodation leads to a degree of stuffiness difficult to bear, and appears to form a breeding ground for various forms of life. The first few nights produced a large number of bug eaten victims' until murderous counter-measures were pursued. Unobtrusively to avoid offence to their hosts, the MO was summoned to fumigate the blankets – unfortunately, not with 100 per cent success. Flt Lt Iveson separately described life afloat. After an uncomfortable first night, he donned socks and flying jersey over his pyjamas, scarf, gloves and balaclava – not with total success, as bite marks in the morning showed. Only one officer (Wg Cdr Tait) needed no such protection, escaping completely the attention of the rampant insects, which prompted Fg Off Witherick to declare that 'clearly even Commie bugs' respected rank. An embarrassing postscript to the whole sorry saga of irritation occurred back in England, when Flt Lt J.D. Melrose and his 9 Squadron crew were affected with a simultaneous urge to scratch furiously in a London hostelry. The agitation and dismay of other customers and the management prompted them swiftly to seek relief in the RAF Medical Centre, Great Portland Street.

In spite of the various discomforts and distractions, feverish preparations to attack *Tirpitz* continued; and the fetid subterranean cinema, gloomily illuminated by oil lamps during the day, became the venue for the final briefing. Amendments to Operation Order B. 393 were dictated by the reduced availability of aircraft and the new operational base. The two squadrons were to attack at the same time: Force A (Tallboy aircraft) would bomb at between 14,000 and 18,000ft in four waves ('gaggles') of five Lancasters in line abreast, with 'a few hundred yards' between each wave, and individual waves occupying 1,000ft in height. The aircraft would attack from the south along the fore and aft axis of *Tirpitz*, 'the five aircraft in each wave having slightly converging headings owing to their distance apart in line abreast'. Lancasters carrying Tallboy were ordered to bomb visually, and if this proved impossible to return to the advanced base with their weapon. Force B (JW mines) would fly in two lines abreast, one 'immediately behind' the other (flying south-east to north-west) and bomb from between 10,000 and 12,000ft. They would do so 'indirectly on a small lake just north of the position where the ship was reported to be lying. In view of the difficulty of aiming a store with a T.V. [terminal velocity] of 160ft per sec, it was decided to produce a pattern approximately 750yds by 750yds and centre this over the target'. Allowance for wind having been made, range distribution relied on setting a stick length of approximately 750yd, line distribution on the aircraft attacking at prescribed intervals between 340 degrees and 005 degrees. After take-off, the whole air armada would fly below 1,000ft to the Finnish border, then Force A would climb to bombing height plus 2,000ft, Force B to 16,000ft. Three 9 Squadron aircraft would go ahead to establish wind speed and direction in the target area. Approximately 60 miles from *Tirpitz* ('considered the limit of surprise'), the wind finders would 'fall in behind Force A . . . in the last wave at the lowest bombing height' as Force B began to diverge ultimately to fly a course 10 degrees to starboard for its south-east–north-west run across Kaa Fjord. At the same time, both forces would start to descend to bombing height and increase speed. Fg Off J.A. Sanders admitted to being 'somewhat alarmed', when he got to his aircraft. 'The sergeant armourer was just descending from the bomb-bay with a small wooden ladder'. He greeted the pilot: 'Please

TIRPITZ

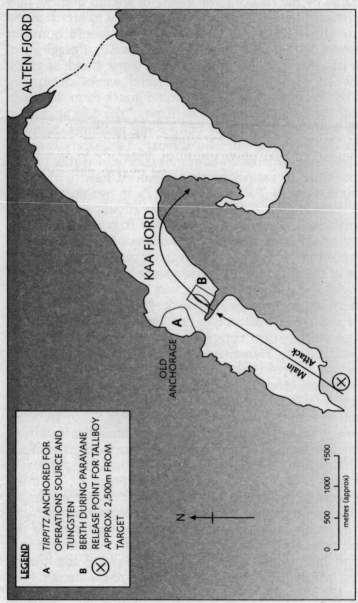

ALTEN FJORD

KAA FJORD

OLD ANCHORAGE

A

B

Main Attack

⊗

LEGEND

A *TIRPITZ* ANCHORED FOR OPERATIONS SOURCE AND TUNGSTEN

B BERTH DURING PARAVANE

⊗ RELEASE POINT FOR TALLBOY APPROX. 2,500m FROM TARGET

N

0   500   1000   1500
metres (approx)

Operation Paravane flown from UYagodnik, near Archangel, by RAF Bomber Command, 15 September 1944 do not bring any of the (JW mines) back, they are set to self-destruct in 15hrs.' 'I sincerely hoped that the boffins had got it right', Sanders recalled.

At 1423 LT on 15 September, through the SBNO at Archangel, Gp Capt McMullen signalled to Air Vice-Marshal Cochrane that Operation Paravane was in progress. The PRU Mosquito had returned at 0400 GMT (0700 LT) to report: 'Target area cloudless and no cloud 80mls SSW of target. No bad weather between Yagodnik and target. Visibility excellent.' McMullen continued: 'Considered that opportunity of attacking in favourable weather conditions should not be missed particularly as we had doubts about the good weather existing.' He confirmed that the operation had followed Cochrane's 'recommendation' of 13 September, which suggested flying at 1,000ft until 25 00E to avoid detection by the radar chain centred on Kirkenes and approaching the target via 68 00N 22 00E. A more detailed route avoiding 'urban concentrations' was sent to Grantham from the Air Ministry on 14 September, and at 1235 DBST on 15 September 5 Group did advise McMullen not to route his force closer than 50 miles south of the radar station at 68 10N 27 10E. It was, of course, too late, like the addendum: 'Weather not cast iron but may be fit.'

According to a 5 Group intelligence summary on 21 September, Knilans' having been repaired overnight, Force A aircraft, Force B aircraft and one film unit aircraft began taking off from Yagodnik at 0830 DBST, setting course at 0900 at 1,000ft, all the aircraft having become airborne in 23mins. Of the seventeen 617 Squadron Lancasters, thirteen carried Tallboy, four JW mines; 9 Squadron put up eight Tallboy and two 'special bombs' aircraft. The final turning point north towards Kaa Fjord, reached by Tait at 1106 and where pilots began their climb to bombing height, had partly been dictated by Cochrane's information about radar stations, partly by a route designed to suggest an attack on Narvik.

A major feature of post-operational reports would be different, and sometimes contradictory, detail. One such report referred to 10/10ths cloud at 1,000–1,500ft on the way to the target and, according to 9 Squadron, at one stage the Tallboy aircraft 'got several miles west (of) track and had to make an alteration of course'. 617 Squadron held, though, that 'the journey to the target went according to plan', while acknowledging that 'ineffective' flak at Lulea, Abo and Gotteborg had possibly been fired 'as a warning'. Lt Knilans' navigator, Bell, recalled that his Lancaster flew over a deserted airfield with its runway lights on, and feared that enemy fighters were aloft waiting. But none appeared. Another vivid account held that the low-flying bombers stampeded a herd of reindeer. Whether or not a course deviation did occur, both squadrons agreed that the attacking force reached the target on time at 1255 DBST. Looking from a distance at *Tirpitz* nestling under a cliff, one pilot thought she looked just like the briefing model at Woodhall; and a navigator likened her to a 'black matchstick'.

On 16 September, McMullen despatched his initial report from Yagodnik. The attack had taken place at 1100 GMT on the previous day, in 'excellent' conditions of 2/10ths strato cumulus over Kaa Fjord. 'Surprise was definitely achieved and a smoke-screen was put into operation some 8–10mins before first bombing'. Those bombing early saw *Tirpitz* 'in the usual position on the east [*sic*] side of the fjord and crews were reasonably sure of identification'. Due to the smoke-screen, later crews 'saw only about ⅓ of the ship or saw the superstructure only'. Three Force A (Tallboy) machines did not bomb and two had a hang-up in the bomb bay. 'Generally crews report that Tallboy bombing was accurate, and it is considered by several that one hit was obtained but this cannot be confirmed.' 'Some' bombs fell on the shore; no JW mines were observed in the water near the target, though 'some' did fall on land east of the target. 'Flak was moderate but very inaccurate', though three Lancasters suffered 'minor damage'. No fighters were seen. The PRU Mosquito had flown over Kaa Fjord 2hrs 20mins after the attack, but only spotted *Tirpitz* through a 'small gap' in the 9/10ths cloud from 9,000ft. The battleship 'was floating but could not determine whether any damage had been done'.

The following day, 17 September, McMullen re-affirmed that 'one explosion with red flame and black smoke 'had been seen in target area, but cautioned that the 'very effective' smoke-screen made its precise location difficult to assess. The 'explosion may well have been from the Tirpitz or from the Neumark or on the shore'. No films had been processed at Yagodnik, but 'allum maps' would be sent back with the first returning aircraft. McMullen revealed that he had thought about another attack, but could only muster two Tallboys and one load of JW mines. The weather was doubtful (on 16 September the Mosquito encountered 10/10ths cloud), there were 'numerous . . . small troubles' and no operation could be mounted until 17 September at the earliest. 'With considerable reluctance' McMullen, therefore, abandoned ideas of another attack on *Tirpitz*. Drily, he added: 'We appear to have lost the fight with the Tirpitz and will have been defeated by the local insects which thrive on Keatings.'

Debriefing of the operational crews at Yagodnik and back in England fleshed out the various post-raid signals and summaries. In 617, Fg Off D.W. Carey confirmed that his Lancaster (E) was so badly damaged that it could not fly to *Tirpitz*, its JW mines being transferred to Iveson's KC-F. Two immediate write-offs (Category E) were the Lancasters of Sqn Ldr D.R. Wyness (Y), which crashed-landed at Kestrogov at 0540 GMT on 12 September with JW mines, and Fg Off I.S. Ross RAAF (B) with a Tallboy. On 15 September, from 617 Squadron thirteen (H, J, M, O, D, A, G, Q, R, S, W, U, Z) carried Tallboy. In addition, H, J, D took a 120lb smoke bomb and a marker marine Mark 2, with D (Tait) also carrying a red target indicator, none of which were used. Four 617 Squadron Lancasters (K, N, F, V) had JW mines.

Five aircraft – Flt Lt G.S. Stout (R) from 14,200ft, Flt Lt H.J. Pryor (U) from 14,400ft, Wg Cdr J.B. Tait (D) from 15,000ft, Flt Lt C.J.G. Howard (M) from 16,000ft and Fg Off A.E. Kell RAAF from 17,400ft, all in the first gaggle –

dropped their Tallboy at 1256 DBST. Stout reported 'explosions seen in neighbourhood of ship but results obscured by smoke. After bombing was over there was a column of black smoke rising above the smoke-screen.' Pryor said it was 'impossible to assess owing to smoke-screen'. Tait reported 'no results observed because of smoke-screen. One explosion seen but this could not be placed.' Howard said 'run commenced on ship, which soon became obscured by smoke from screen. Bombed on flashes from ship's guns. Five bombs seen to explode in area of ship.' Kell reported 'the target in the graticule on the commencement of the run up, but before release, the vessel was obscured by the smoke-screen. Impossible to assess result of bombing.' At 1256½ Flt Lt D.J. Oram (Z) released his Tallboy from 15,400ft: 'No results observed but bombs seen to be bursting around position of the ship. Damaged by flak'; Lt H.C. Knilans USAAF (W) followed at 1300 from 15,000ft, 'bomb bursts seen through smoke but no actual results seen'; and Sqn Ldr G.E. Fawke (J) at 1305 from 15,600ft 'bombed estimated position of ship and concentration of flak bursts. Only one [bomb] burst seen which gave large explosion and cloud of smoke. Other flames seen but results obscured by smoke-screen.' Fawke's flight engineer (Cherrington) remarked that 'by the time we arrived the target was partly covered', and Bennett recalled that WC-J made a number of attempts before attacking from a different direction (virtually due east). Fg Off J. Castagnola (S) 'made two bombing runs. Hung up first run. The target was already partially obscured when we bombed. We estimate we overshot about 20/30 yards. Several bombs fell near, but assessment impossible owing to smoke-screen.' He reported dropping Tallboy from 17,500ft at 1358 DBST, which seems to be wrong. If he did two runs after an initial hang up, *Tirpitz* would have been blanketed by this time, not 'partially obscured'. On the other hand, '1258' would not have allowed time for two runs; so the precise time that Castagnola dropped the ninth Tallboy is unclear. Flt Lt R.E. Knights (O) did three abortive runs while trying to locate the target and took his Tallboy back to Yagodnik; so did Fg Off J. Gingles (A) and Sqn Ldr J.V. Cockshott (H), who 'ran over the target at 1357 local time' (1257 DBST) though did not release his bomb as *Tirpitz* was 'completely obscured'. Flt Lt M.D. Hamilton (G) also tried three runs, but could not free his hung-up Tallboy which was finally released four miles south of the target from 15,000ft at 1415. He reported 'one big explosion about 20/30 yards to port of the target, but no direct hit seen'.

From Force B aircraft of 617 Squadron, two released their JW mines at 1304: Fg Off F.H.A. Watts (N) from 12,000ft, 'smoke-screen preventing assessment of attack'; Fg Off J.A. Sanders (K) from 11,350ft, 'aiming in sights. Assessment of bombing impossible owing to smoke-screen.' Flt Lt T.C. Iveson (F) did so at 1304½ from 11,800ft, 'target completely obscured by smoke-screen'; but as Fg Off F. Levy (V) was lost on the way back to England, the time and height at which the fourth load of JW mines were dropped is not known, though probably not after 1305. The times at which the 617 Squadron aircraft landed at Yagodnik are not shown in surviving documents, but the spread of the bombing and the difficulties experienced by at least some on the way back appears to rule out the reported orderly flight and landing of the whole force in 30mins.

The ten 9 Squadron Lancasters took off between 0946 and 1012 Soviet LT, one hour ahead of DBST used in other papers. Curiously and confusingly, however, the times of attack were given in GMT, so Fg Off W.D. Tweddle apparently took off at 1007 and bombed at 1056. Flt Lt J.D. Melrose officially dropped his Tallboy at 1055 (1255 DBST, one minute before Tait) from 14,900ft, reporting 'stern of ship seen in sights. Five "Tallboys" seen to burst between ship and boom.' However, Tait is adamant that no other aircraft was in front of him when he bombed. This is not impossible. Melrose recalled that Tait was closing on his starboard beam, on a slightly different bearing and, despite the official timing, bombed 'fractionally' before him. 'I never orbited the target after the bomb was gone. No use. Got straight out. Always did and always would do', he added. Tweddle reported bombing at 1056 (1256 DBST, when the five Lancasters of Tait's gaggle dropped their Tallboys) from 15,800ft: 'Outline of ship seen on run-up and bomb dropped on its estimated position. Effective smoke-screen prevented observation of results other than a large column of brown smoke rising from the target.' Sqn Ldr H.R. Pooley followed at 1057 (1257 DBST) from 14,000ft, 'three bursts seen. One looked as if it might be a possible hit, but smoke-screen precluded accurate observation'; and Fg Off B. Taylor released his bomb also at 1057 from 18,000ft – 'outline of ship seen through the smoke-screen. Two "Tallboys" seen to explode, one of which seemed to be close to the ship.' Fg Off A.F. Jones RAAF bombed at 1100 (1300 DBST) from 12,500ft, 'flashes of ship's guns seen. Results of bombing not seen. One plume of smoke seen at estimated position of ship'; and Wg Cdr J.M. Bazin dropped the sixth 9 Squadron Tallboy at 1104 (1304 DBST) from 15,000ft, 'identified by intense light flak from position of ship. Smoke-screen started at 1055 hours. On first run ship believed visible but made second run to make sure; smoke-screen however prevented accurate observation, and no results of bombing seen'. The Tallboy of Fg Off J.J. Dunne RAAF 'hung up owing to technical failure' and he took it back to Yagodnik; similarly Fg Off M. Scott made four runs over the target trying to release Tallboy, which 'eventually fell off through bomb doors', presumably on the way back. At 1104 (1304 DBST) Fg Off D. Macintosh dropped his JW mines from 10,800ft, 'fjord completely covered by smoke. Some JW bombs seen to fall in water and some on east side of fjord'; Fg Off J.E. Stowell also dropped his mines from 10,800ft at 1107 (1307 DBST): 'Smoke-screen obscured ship. About twenty JW bombs fell in the fjord. Own bombs believed in correct area'. The time that 9 Squadron pilots reported dropping Tallboy indicates that they did so individually and not in line abreast. Aircraft of both squadrons with JW mines also appear to have bombed individually. The plan for the

9 Squadron wind finders to fall in behind 617 to join the last gaggle does not appear to have been adhered to, and may therefore have been verbally altered at briefing.

The film unit Lancaster from 463 Squadron reported taking off at 0848 DBST with a full crew, two camera operators, 'BBC and press representatives'. 'All aircraft set course behind the leader [Tait] dead on time.' The met. forecast proved 'very accurate', but 'a battery of medium flak' opened up at 69 30N 22 10E, and 'first impressions' were that this enemy unit alerted *Tirpitz*, because the smoke-screen began to appear five minutes short of Kaa Fjord. The battleship was 'ascertained visually' as the Lancasters approached, which Tait confirmed by R/T. 'The bombing of the leader and the next two aircraft appeared to be very accurate and an explosion followed some seconds after', which was 'backed up by black smoke which later was inclined to billow'. When the JW aircraft attacked, the smoke was thick, but the pilot of the film unit Lancaster, Flt Lt Buckham, saw the mines fall 'in the centre of the smoke-screen'. The flak from 'defence positions and cruisers and destroyers was moderate but inaccurate'. No aircraft were seen to be damaged and, after the bombing ceased, Buckham set course for 71 00N 17 00E, descending to sea level once the coast had been cleared, in 'very poor' weather. Landfall was made 'in the vicinity of Aberdeen' and the film unit machine landed at Waddington at 2255 DBST.

The crews at Yagodnik had to wait a little longer to get home, those of the Liberators until 28 September. Quite apart from those made unserviceable by crashes, some aircrew did not return in the Lancaster that took them to the USSR. Flt Lt L.W. Curtis (Knilans' W/Op) flew back with Flt Lt G.S. Stout; Fg Off R.J. Harris (9 Squadron) took back WS-N to Lossiemouth 19/20 September and on to Bardney on 22 September, but had piloted WS-E out. Flying overnight, the bulk of 617 Squadron aircraft left between 16 and 19 September. Tait in KC-D set course from Yagodnik at 1834 LT (1534 GMT) on 16 September with fifteen other Lancasters (J, S, H, K, F, U, R, A & V of 617; B, U, J, T, Z & O from 9 Squadron, though 9/Z had to return to Yagodnik with engine trouble). The 617 OC landed at Woodhall at 0333 BST on 17 September. For most of the returning aircraft, the trip was 'mainly uneventful except for ineffective flak encountered over Sweden and Denmark', though Iveson's log-book shows that KC-F was fired on over Finland too. The course adopted was more southerly and direct than the outward leg to Yagodnik, going via southern Finland, Sweden north of Stockholm, between the Jutland peninsula and the Norwegian mainland, over the Danish islands and North Sea to the Wash. During the flight, 617/V (Fg Off F. Levy) with members of Sqn Ldr Wyness's crew aboard was lost. Levy's W/Op acknowledged a signal from RAF Dyce at 0221 DBST on 17 September, then there was silence. The RAF later learnt that Levy had been off-course south of Trondheim, flying at 3,500ft in stormy weather, and had hit high ground at Syningen near Nesbyen in Norway during the early hours of 17 September. Local sources suggest that he tried to illuminate the terrain by throwing out flares and broke radio silence to report engine trouble. Eleven bodies were found in the wreckage and interred in a mass grave. Post-war they were reburied and every year on the anniversary of the crash flowers are laid on the graves by schoolchildren during a commemorative ceremony.

Five more 617 (G, M, N, Q, W) and four 9 Squadron (L, P, Z, C) Lancasters left Yagodnik at 1615 GMT on 17 September; but not before Knilans had made a somewhat hair-raising double trip in a single-engined, two-seater Yak fighter, with a flight engineer perched precariously on his lap. The Soviet pilot took them to 'a wooden runway 10mls away', from which Knilans and the flight engineer were expected to fly off a Lancaster grounded there since 12 September. Knilans was willing to attempt the feat, in spite of a short runway and a tree-covered hill 'directly in the flight path'. His RAF companion proved less enthusiastic, so an uncomfortable return flight in the Yak followed.

In this group of crews, Watts in KC-N hit 'a huge occluded frontal system' over Sweden, lost his pitot head and 'all indicated air speed', then discovered that fog had closed in over Woodhall causing him to divert to Lossiemouth. Three 9 (N flown by Harris with a JW bomb load, W & V) and two 617 (E & Z) Squadron Lancasters left on 18 September. Flying in Knilans' KC-W on 17 September, Bell the navigator recalled that 'our aircraft had a bent frame, was difficult to control, and the starboard outer engine needed a major overhaul'. He failed to mention three extra passengers from a crashed aircraft. Off course near Stockholm, the Lancaster attracted the hostile attention of Swedish anti-aircraft guns. ('Hell, I thought these guys were supposed to be neutral', hollered Knilans.) Like Watts, they found Woodhall fog-bound and diverted to Lossiemouth. On 19 September, Knilans finally returned to Woodhall and KC-W was unceremoniously hauled off to be scrapped. The last two Lancasters (9/E and 617/O) followed at 1545 GMT on 21 September. Both machines had been repaired in the Soviet Union. WS-E, which Harris had damaged in landing at Kegostrov, left its Tallboy behind and was flown home by another pilot. KC-O (Flt Lt Knight's Lancaster) underwent an engine change supervised by the flight engineer (Fg Off E. Twells). Removing the Tallboy brought back from Kaa Fjord, local technicians damaged the bomb-bay doors so extensively that they had to be replaced as well.

After flak damage incurred over *Tirpitz* had been repaired, the PRU Mosquito took off for home on 24 September, but turned back with 'starboard engine trouble'. It finally departed for Lossiemouth at 0010 GMT (0310 LT) on 26 September. Delayed by a leaking auxiliary tank in one of them, which allowed more sight-seeing in Archangel, the Liberators were the last to take off for Bardney, officially departing at 1955 GMT (though Capsey recorded 2055 LT, 1755 GMT) on 27 September, with a signal to Cochrane from McMullen: 'request customs be notified as a formality'. The Group Captain was credited with a keen sense of humour, which his AOC reputedly did not share. However, McMullen had already despatched a sharp missive to 5 Group commander, which decidedly lacked humour: 'Request enquiry to be initiated to determine which captains indulged in dangerous low flying in departure from Yagodnik on 18 September. I briefed each captain that low flying was not to be done yet one blatantly disobeyed orders. Two verey [*sic*] cartridges were fired from the aircraft from about 50 feet and one fell in a forest and may have caused a serious fire. The Russians do not admire such lack of discipline and it causes considerable embarrassment for those of us remaining. I shall submit a report on the incident on return and am now trying to gather evidence to determine which aircraft was concerned.' After the tortuous six-week paper-chase of an official enquiry, two 617 Squadron offenders (not one), seeking to prevent 9 Squadron Lancasters taking off – a legacy of 'horseplay' between the two squadrons – were identified. By then, one offender was in Sweden after crashing during another attack on *Tirpitz*, so his fellow reprobate did penance for both in the Station Commander's office at Bardney. Several crews had an unpleasant shock of a different nature on landing. The Lancasters flew back using Soviet aviation fuel, decidedly short of the required 100 octane quality and in an advanced stage of melting the spark plugs.

More immediately, on 18 September, McMullen had asked Cochrane for permission to hand over the four 9 Squadron and two 617 Squadron Lancasters beyond repair at Yagodnik: 'Will remove all possible easily portable equipment from those aircraft which are accessible' – the crash in the Talagi area being too remote to reach. Two days later, he explained to Cochrane that it would be 'exceedingly difficult' to pack six unused Tallboys and two damaged engines (one Merlin 24 and one Merlin 38) for transportation by sea and suggested that they be handed over to the Soviets.

Evidence of damage to *Tirpitz* was by now gathering. Analysis of photographs taken by attacking aircraft on 15 September showed that the 'effective smoke-screen obscured usual berth of *Tirpitz* but a faint outline of part of a large ship is visible on some photos. Bursts from 12,000lb bombs indicate near misses or possibly a direct hit, at least four bursts being within the boom enclosed area.' To say the least, this was inconclusive. A Norwegian intelligence report on 20 September claimed that 'on Friday 15th September 17 Russian aircraft [a natural error given the direction of approach] attacked Von Tirpitz [*sic*]. One hit on foredeck was registered and three small ships were sunk. From land it can be seen that Von Tirpitz is damaged. Since this attack Kaa Fiord has been continuously covered with smoke.' That smoke prevented the PRU Mosquito securing any photos until 0930 GMT on 20 September, and even then the 'photographs [were] too hazy to make a detailed statement'. Nevertheless, it could be seen that *Tirpitz* lay in her 'usual berth but the ship has swung slightly. Large area of discolouration on upper deck forward of "A" turret suggests damage in this region. No list apparent but may be slightly down by the bows.' At 1325 GMT that same day, a 'single vertical photograph' from a Soviet reconnaissance aircraft, confirmed the battleship's position and the fact that 'there appears to be a raised structure on the upper deck forward of "A" turret about 25ft x 30ft'. Also on 20 September, a Norwegian ashore reported *Tirpitz* at anchor 'under Sakkobadne cliff' surrounded by destroyers, smaller naval vessels and a depot ship. Two separate reports on 22 September repeated rumours that the battleship had been hit in the bows and another that 'the forward part of the ship is under water, while a little of the after part is above water'. On 30 September, the Naval Intelligence Division concluded : '*Tirpitz* received, almost certainly, one hit forward by a 12,000lb bomb. She may also have been damaged by near misses.' It went on to speculate that damage might be 'considerable' and temporary repairs in Alten Fjord necessary 'before she is fit again to move'.

The next day, 'a solid and reliable' Norwegian, who saw *Tirpitz* regularly, observed: 'She got a direct hit on starboard side which made a hole from the bow towards the stern 17m long. The hole is both above and below the waterline and is so large that motors boats [*sic*] could go in.' He said that neither the turrets nor the forward part of the warship was, nor ever had been, under water, but just after the attack the bows had been low in the water and the ship had a list, now corrected. *Tirpitz* was 'still down by the head'. A more extreme report sent on 1 October alleged: '"T" received a direct hit by a heavy bomb on her bow, which is sunk low in the water', adding imaginatively: 'I believe she rests on the bottom.' On 2 October more eyewitness evidence arrived. Two small Dutch ships alongside *Tirpitz* 'were blown into small pieces. Our source believes that these . . . shielded "T" from the full force of the explosions.' During the attack a tank was destroyed ashore, 'probably used as a sort of diving bell during the repair of the propeller damage from submarine attack. A new tank built in Kaa Fjord and taken into use just before latest attack was also destroyed.' Cloud frustrated Soviet reconnaissance sorties on 9, 10 and 11 October, but the next day a successful photo showed *Tirpitz* still in position.

In summarising 617 Squadron's part in the operation, the station commander at Woodhall Spa noted that the aircraft had each flown some 4,905 miles, including the attack on *Tirpitz*. 'Unfortunately, the smoke-screen completely obscured the target but probably one hit and two near misses were obtained. Subsequent reports tended to confirm a hit forward with the ship down at the bows.' Quaintly, he referred to 'the German Battlecruiser "Von Tirpitz"'. He admitted that 'the maps and charts available to give coverage for the route to the Advanced Base were found in certain instances to be inaccurate and owing to the fact that the wireless operators were furnished with a faulty method of working Russian Stations no use could be made of loop bearings or homings. Good use was made of all navigational aids and astro-navigation and drifts were used quite extensively', which seems at odds with Bell who found his artificial aids largely useless. The Station Commander concluded that 'the new Radio Altimeter SCR 718A was found to be very useful and was used in calculation of the true QFE for the Advance Base. This proved to be extremely valuable in view of the very low cloud base which was encountered.' On 25 September,

Woodhall Spa reported to 54 Base Commander that eleven Lancaster IIIs and nine Lancaster Is from 617 Squadron had bombed *Tirpitz* between 1256 and 1305 at 11,800–17,000ft: 'Moderate scattered H/F [heavy flak] for short bursts, bursting to 16,000ft. Intense L/F [light flak] over Tirpitz – ceiling 8,000ft.' The following day, using evidence from Bardney 53 Base Commander informed 5 Group that ten (9 Squadron) Lancasters had attacked between 1055 and 1105 GMT: 'Inaccurate heavy flak from about 16 guns on land and five guns on flak ship approximately 1ml north of Tirpitz.' 9 Squadron concluded that the raid had been 'highly successful', with the battleship hit 'by at least one Tallboy'. Reflecting on the operation from which 'the bods returned with all manner of insignia – red stars, hammers and sickles, a red flag etc', one 617 pilot mused that the consensus of opinion was 'a damn interesting trip, but I wouldn't want to do it again'. The Liberator crews from Lyneham were not called upon to do so, but they too brought back an unauthorised memento. The banner 'Welcome to the Glorious Flyers of the Royal Air Force', suspended over the living quarters at Yagodnik, reappeared at 511 Squadron's New Year's Party.

An unidentified and undated report (possibly from 617 Squadron) stated that thirty Lancasters, including the film unit aircraft, took off for Kaa Fjord and five aborted. But McMullen informed AOC 5 Group on 15 September that, excluding the BCFU machine, twenty-seven (twenty-one with Tallboys, six with JW mines) had done so, and these details were repeated in the 5 Group intelligence summary six days later. In his report of 1 October, Air Vice-Marshal the Hon. R.A. Cochrane also quoted McMullen's figures, adding that six aircraft had been forced to abort. Most contemporary sources agree with Cochrane that twenty-one Lancasters (fifteen with Tallboy, six with JW mines) attacked *Tirpitz*.

Appended to another report about Operation Paravane by 5 Group to HQ Bomber Command, dated 15 October, was a 'Plot of Calculated Strike Position of Tallboy Bombs'. It confirmed that *Tirpitz* was at the eastern berth of the western sleeve of Kaa Fjord, opposite the western anchorage occupied during the X-craft attack and immediately north of a tongue of land protruding westwards from the central peninsula. Approaching from the south-west, seven Lancasters from 617 and three from 9 Squadron evidently released their bomb approximately 2,000–2,500yds from the target, three others dropped Tallboy from widely different directions. Two aircraft (U/617 and J/9) were credited with hitting the German battleship, two more (T/9 and J/617) with near misses. 5 Group explained that 'the majority of bombing frame photographs contained very little ground detail, owing to the smoke-screen which had been put into operation. A plot has therefore been made of the calculated strike position of the Tallboy bombs, taken from the release point photographs which could be plotted. It has not been possible to plot the release point frames of the J.W. aircraft.' Complete accuracy was not, therefore, claimed – 'this indicates that two direct hits may [sic] have been obtained, and two near misses' – and 5 Group acknowledged that other intelligence information showed only one hit. On closer examination, the plot also conflicts with certain aspects of the crew reports. For example, J/617 is shown as one of the ten Lancasters to release Tallboy from the south-west, but its navigator tells another story: 'We were flying as his [Tait's] Number 2 and as Tirpitz was practically covered by smoke we over-ran the anchorage. . . . We [then] crossed the anchorage, weighing up the situation for . . . the bombing team of "J for Jig" had resolved that we hadn't put [in] all this effort . . . just to kill a few Norwegian fish.' Tirpitz continued firing and 'the almost continuous flashes from the muzzles of these large guns gave a pretty fair indication of her position. . . . We commenced the bombing run on an almost due west heading'; that is, from the east and almost 100 degrees from the spot shown on the 5 Group plot.

On 3 November, the Naval Intelligence Division reviewed the position in the light of further confirmation from Norway that Tirpitz had indeed sustained 'a direct hit forward' on 15 September. 'Technical Departments' had calculated that the bomb hit 'on the middle line about 110 feet from the bow'. Had the Tallboy not broken up as it penetrated the ship, 'there was a reasonable chance' of it reaching the keel before detonating. 'If this occurred, it would be expected to result in immediate flooding of the bow compartments up to and including "A" turret magazine and shell rooms, and a trim by the bow of about 15 feet. The structure within about 40 feet radius of the burst would be expected to be ruptured or badly distorted.' Near misses within 100ft might cause 'dishing of the plating, starting of seams and rivets and possibly consequent flooding'. The nearer the explosion, the heavier, but less extensive, would be damage. However, no firm photographic evidence backed up damage by near-misses. In another summary, compiled after the final Lancaster attack in November, the NID claimed that on 15 September 'one hit destroyed 100 feet of her bows'. This would prove to be a fairly accurate assessment. Delighted to have been posted to such a prestigious warship, Midshipman Alfred Zuba was horrified on his arrival at Kaa Fjord to see *Tirpitz*'s badly torn starboard bow. He did not know, nor did the Allies till post-war, that the vessel had officially 'ceased to be a fighting unit'.

During Operation Paravane, *Tirpitz*'s main, secondary and flak armament, backed by the numerous shore batteries totalling ninety-eight guns, put up a brisk fire. The approach of the attacking aircraft had been reported by an army post at Kautokeino, which allowed the 380mm guns to open up at long range, but the bombers loss of height and increase in speed foiled the guns. German records discovered post-war showed one hit near the battleship's bows that exploded close to the starboard side of the ship after penetration and damaged the engines, as well as causing the other damage already noted by the Allies. The Tallboy had struck the main deck forward of the anchor cables, passed through the ship at an angle and exploded close to the vessel about 35ft aft of the bow. The starboard side of *Tirpitz* sustained a large gash (estimated some 48ft long and 32ft deep) that led to flooding in adjacent compartments and damage to at least two decks. Damage also occurred to the radio masts and fire control system, but only eight men were injured.

At the time of the attack, Ultra was able to glean a certain amount of information about the German reactions, but only about 50 per cent of the enemy transmissions could be decyphered. At 1255 DBST on 15 September, the First Battle Group reported an attack on Kaa Fjord by 40–50 Lancasters (an estimate arrived at after confusion caused by so many aircraft repeating runs over *Tirpitz* above the smoke-screen), but mentioned no damage. At 1320, the harbour defence vessel V. 6303 reported 20–25 Lancasters attacking, optimistically adding that two had crashed. A number of messages could not then be decoded until 1618, when the Battle Group re-emphasised that fighters must be allocated for Tirpitz's defence. At 1652, the Commandant of Alten Fjord made his submission: at about 1300 (GST, equivalent to DBST) 40–50 four-engined bombers had attacked at high level (4,000-5,000m) from the south-south-east. The smoke-screen had been laid down already, but due to the unfavourable wind and need to keep to 'strictly economical consumption [of fuel] there were gaps'. At 2225, the First Battle Group reported that several parachute mines (the JW mines) had been dropped. Four days later, 19 September, a directive to all military attachés admitted that the battleship had been struck by a heavy bomb. Wrongly, the Germans believed that the aircraft could not have seen this and, therefore, only slight damage should be conceded. They also claimed only five casualties. Unknown to the Allies, a German conference of the naval staff attended by Dönitz on 23 September estimated that it would take nine months to make *Tirpitz* operational once more, which the C-in-C considered unacceptably long. He decided that the battleship should no longer be considered for action at sea, but be moored in shallow water further south, west of Lyngen Fjord (near Tromso) and used as a floating battery to deter invasion.

Dönitz's intercepted 'war review', transmitted on 25 September, made interesting reading: 'After successfully defending herself against many heavy air attacks the battleship *Tirpitz* has now sustained a bomb hit, but by holding out in the operational area the ship will continue to tie down enemy forces and by her presence to confound the enemy's intentions.' She certainly continued to do that. The Allies could not know about her parlous state, and a more favourable opportunity to settle *Tirpitz*'s account once and for all would soon present itself.

5

COUP DE GRÂCE, OCTOBER–NOVEMBER 1944

On 13 October 1944, the British naval attaché in Stockholm sent word that '. . . dredging is being carried out possibly for southwards passage of "T"'. That same afternoon, the SBNO in North Russia signalled that although 'photographs not satisfactorily obtained owing to cloud . . . visual air reconnaissance of Altenfiord on 13.10 showed Tirpitz in same berth'. Nevertheless, the battleship's imminent departure was suggested on 14 October by intercepted messages ordering U-boats to patrol off the mouth of Alten Fjord. During the morning of 15 October, the Norwegian radio operator Hans Hansen reported from his home at Nikkeby on the coast north of Tromso that five destroyers had passed him heading towards Alten Fjord.

Tirpitz slowly emerged from Kaa Fjord at 1200 LT on 15 October, to be protected by a strong flotilla ('nearly 50 ships' according to one eye-witness) and was accompanied by sea-going tugs in case her damaged bows did not hold. In mid-afternoon, an agent in the fishing centre of Skjerrvoy sent a coded phone message to Hansen with this news, but Hansen's wireless set had broken down, so he could not pass it on. The British estimated she steamed south at a maximum 10 knots, sometimes under 7. Post-war, the

German gunnery officer, Alfred Zuba, maintained she rarely exceeded 3 knots and frequently had to be towed. At 0130 on 16 October, *Tirpitz* reached 70 00N 20 20E and five hours later (0636) was waiting at the entrance to Sandesundet for high tide. The battleship anchored off the island of Haak west of Tromso at 1500, and Dönitz congratulated all involved in the move at 1548. The Norwegian 'chief wireless of the special [clandestine] information service' in Tromso, Egil Lindberg, sent a series of signals to London about *Tirpitz*'s arrival. On 16 October, he announced that she had been towed to the Tromso area that day, 'is now lying between Haskoe [Haakoy] and Lille Grinby [Grindoy] . . . [and] cannot use her engines'. Two days later, this information was amplified. 'The air cable across Sandessund was taken down on Saturday (14 October)' – it was 'now being hung up again' – and *Tirpitz* had then been 'towed through Sandessund to Haakoybotn and Grindoy'. Lindberg confirmed 'a large rent forward', already noted by Zuba in Kaa Fjord. The immediate result of these revelations was a signal from the Admiralty to the SBNO in North Russia during the evening of 17 October: 'Reconnaissance for Tirpitz in Altenfiord no longer required.'

Aerial surveillance at Tromso, on the other hand, certainly was. At 1053 GMT on 17 October, C-in-C Home Fleet ordered Capt L.D. Mackintosh, commanding the aircraft carrier *Implacable*, which had left Scapa the previous day after *Tirpitz*'s departure from Alten Fjord was known, to 'proceed as requisite to fly off and carry out armed reconnaissance with Fireflies for enemy major units in Tromso area'. Because the precise location of *Tirpitz* was not known, adjacent fjords should be covered as well. This would be strictly a reconnaissance operation: 'It is not repeat not intended that your force as at present constituted should carry out strikes . . . W/T silence is to be broken to report results. Obtain photographs if possible.' *Implacable* 'should return to Scapa by A.M. Sunday 22nd at latest'. That evening, C-in-C Home Fleet amended his instructions: 'Admiral von Tirpitz reported anchored 3mls 260degs from Tromso. Photographic cover required of this area. PRU Mosquitoes may be met.' The Admiralty had hedged its bets by asking RAF Benson, Oxfordshire, at 1924 GMT on 17 October also to locate and photograph the battleship.

Implacable carried twenty-one Barracudas of 2 TBR Wing (828 and 841 squadrons) and eleven Fireflies of 1771 Squadron. Shortly after midday on 18 October, the carrier sent off its Fireflies to search the Tromso area, Malavgen, Nord and Bals fjords for *Tirpitz*. Four detached to attack the German air base at Bardufoss, approximately 60 miles south (finding only Ju 52s there), and the seaplane station at Sorreisen in Solberg Fjord. Meanwhile, at 1300 GMT the remainder took several oblique photos of the German battleship unhindered by the cacophony of flak guns around her. Three-quarters of an hour earlier, a 540 Squadron Mosquito XVI NS641 (piloted by Fg Off H.C.S. Powell with F/Sgt J.W. Townshend as navigator) flying from RAF Dyce in Scotland, had secured high-level photos and managed to return to base despite flak damage, incidentally proving that an 11hr round trip to Tromso was feasible. Briefed for an hour from 0746 BST about where to search for *Tirpitz*, the crew took off at 0938 and landed again at 1618, having refuelled at Scatsta on both legs of the flight. Noting, too, four 'medium sized vessels steaming north, south of the target area', Powell reported photographing the battleship from 14,500ft at her berth 4 miles from Tromso, not without discomfort. 'Twelve bursts of heavy flak fairly accurate. Fire from pom-pom type a.a. observed from shore positions but well below.'

Flying at 14,000ft, the Fireflies found *Tirpitz* at the 'south end of Haakoy . . . lying some 350 yards off shore with bows heading east'. But with 'no full sterio cover', the NID concluded 'detailed statement on condition impossible'. None the less, once developed and evaluated, the several photos obtained by the Mosquito and Fireflies gave an invaluable basis on which to plan *Tirpitz*'s destruction. Philip Westlake (a 1771 Squadron TAG) recalled that, after the Fireflies' photos had been developed, ops room staff had to be persuaded that white dots on the film were not blemishes, but 'explosions from the A.A. bursts'. The Fireflies' achievement would be recognised by the award of a bar to his DSC for 1771 Squadron's OC, Lt Cdr H.M. Ellis.

At 1631 GMT on 18 October, *Implacable* signalled to C-in-C Home Fleet: 'German battleship *Tirpitz* photographed in position 69deg 38'08"N 18deg 47'07"E. South of Haakoy, surrounded by nets, new gun positions all round, no smoke but heavy flak.' Macintosh confirmed that the Fireflies had attacked Bardufoss and Sorreisen, destroying one He 115 and claiming another He 115 and a Ju 52 'probables'. No fighters had been seen in the air or on the ground. *Implacable* intended to retire from its position at 69 30N 10 00E at 1900, but 'am prepared to bomb *Tirpitz* to-morrow'. At 2145, the aircraft carrier sent a further message: 'Request permission to attack'. Admiral Sir Bruce Fraser replied swiftly: 'Well done. Return to Scapa. Do not repetition [*sic*] not try to bomb in face of heavy flak with your inadequate anti-flak fighter strength.' This referred to the absence of the Seafire wing, which had not sailed with *Implacable*, leaving the Fireflies as sole fighter cover. Fraser would also have been aware of the post-Goodwood criticism that the Barracudas were too slow to beat the smoke-screen. For whatever reason, the Fleet Air Arm could not immediately deal with *Tirpitz*, so RAF Bomber Command – and 5 Group in particular – must try again. C-in-C Home Fleet might conclude that 'photographs show no sign of activity', but that could not be guaranteed to last.

For, despite the battleship's slow speed southwards, reports of structural damage and loss of engine power, the Allies were not convinced that she had been disabled. Her withdrawal from Kaa Fjord may even have been tactical. The October edition of *'V' Group News* revealed *Tirpitz*'s new location, adding that perhaps 'the move was prompted by the Germans' fear of the ship falling into the hands of the Russians, who were rapidly over-running the Petsamo area, or possibly because they wished to get her back by stages to a German base, where major repairs and a refit could be carried out'. A contemporary Ministry of Information pamphlet, *Arctic War*, similarly argued that *Tirpitz* had left Alten Fjord because the Soviets threatened to capture Kirkenes airfield 150 miles to the east (actually taken on 23 October). This would not only eliminate a valuable Luftwaffe asset, but also give the Allies a nearer base from which to attack the battleship.

Following Lindberg's sighting on 16 October and the aerial photographs taken two days later, the Allies built up a detailed picture of the *Tirpitz*'s position and her surrounding defences. She was protected by the double-net anti-torpedo barrage, which had come south with her, but effective deployment of the smoke canisters proved difficult. No longer was the battleship berthed in a narrow fjord with steep confining hills, lack of which would not only hamper rapid formation of a smoke-screen but also threaten its dispersal in adverse wind conditions. The fishing port of Tromso lay on the eastern side of an island in the north–south fjord bearing its name, sheltered from the North Sea by the outer islands of Kvaloy and Ringvassoy. Haakoy [island] was 1 mile wide and 1½ miles long, its western tip almost touching the shore of the fjord. Divided from Tromsoy [island] by a 2 mile channel, Haakoy was 1 mile south-west of the small island of Grindoy, and the shore of the fjord lay ¾ mile off its starboard beam. The warships's stern was pointed towards Haakoy, its bow eastwards towards Grindoy. Flak ships, certainly two and possibly more, lay in the vicinity. Other flak batteries were stationed on the islands, the adjoining shorelines and approaches, especially on Tromsoy, and covering the line of the fjord from the North Sea.

Apart from the relatively flat and open terrain, the Germans encountered another serious problem. The anchorage did not meet the specifications that they had expected: 1.2m (3.9ft) of water beneath her keel and a rocky sea-bed topped with about 1m (3ft) of sand. In theory, in these conditions, the battleship could not be sunk, and would fulfil Dönitz's role of a floating battery to dominate the land and sea approaches to Tromso. However, the minimum depth within the anti-torpedo booms turned out to be 17m (18ft) and the bottom mud, not rock, topped with sand. The full extent of these deficiencies did not emerge until a fortnight after the battleship anchored. It was then decided to reduce the depth below and around the ship by piling more rubble onto the seabed, especially into the deep trough amidships. Such was *Tirpitz*'s paranoia about bombers that at 1301 on 18 October, she reported the Fireflies' reconnaissance as a carrier-based air raid, not until 1532 admitting that no aggressive action had occurred. To boost the morale of the men, who sensed, perhaps, that their sea-going days were over, on 22 October a visit from Admiral Polar Coast was promised 'as soon as possible'. Nor were the battleship's crew alone in dreading air attack. As a later deputy mayor of Tromso recalled, the appearance of *Tirpitz* made the port 'a focal point in the war in the north'. Almost certainly, the Allies would attempt to sink her from the air, and a few stray bombs would cause havoc in a community largely unaffected by the war so far. 'Tromso with its congested and inflammable wooden buildings was at that time full of people', its population swelled by civilian refugees and soldiers withdrawn from the north. 'Catastrophy' might well occur.

The Admiralty's Naval Intelligence Division, like the Ministry of Information, argued that 'her transfer must be regarded as a direct reaction to the menace of air attack'. In reality, it exposed *Tirpitz* to even greater risk from the air. At Tromso, 120 miles north of Narvik, she was within range of Scotland, 200 miles closer to Britain than she was at Kaa Fjord. Urgency was injected into the planning process by news from the Norwegian wireless operator, Hansen, on 22 October of rumours that *Tirpitz* might be on the move: 'It is supposed that she will go to Bogen, Ofoten, and dredging is going on at Gisund.' *'V' Group News* summarised some of the operational problems facing planning staff. 'Time and weather were the chief adversaries. Tromso is on the Gulf Stream, and the prevailing westerly wind causes persistent stratus cloud. The sky is only clear when the wind is easterly, and about five such days' could be expected at this time of the year. After the end of November, 'the sun does not rise above the horizon' although for 'a few days after, there would be enough twilight at mid-day to bomb'.

None the less, the pressure to eliminate *Tirpitz*

intensified in the autumn of 1944. Protection of the Arctic convoys and troopships crossing the Atlantic undoubtedly remained important, but the centre of Allied naval gravity had now shifted firmly to the Pacific. Capital ships tied to Scapa Flow were urgently needed to boost British presence and enhance political influence in the Far East, as powerful American fleets closed on the Japanese islands. Movement of *Tirpitz* to Tromso had certainly brought the battleship within range of Lancasters from Scotland, but even so the round trip amounted to an estimated '2,252 track miles'. With the maverick JW mines discredited, all attacking aircraft were to carry the 12,000lb Tallboy. Rolls-Royce Merlin 24 (1,640hp) engines, more powerful than Type 22, were installed in all Lancasters detailed for the operation. Their fitting, according to 5 Group, represented 'a magnificent feat in a few days' and entailed special flights to different Maintenance Units and other operational airfields. Furthermore, every attacking Lancaster would carry an extra Wellington long-range tank and Mosquito drop tank in the fuselage (which entailed removal of the rear turret to insert) – a combination planned, but not fitted, to Force B aircraft involved in Paravane – to give a total fuel load of 2,406 gallons. To reduce weight, mid-upper turrets, superfluous oxygen and nitrogen bottles, 3,000 rounds of ammunition from the rear turret, the front gun and ammunition, the tri-cell flare chute and pilot's armour plate were removed. A proposal to take out the Elsan toilet was allegedly stymied by rebellious aircrew facing a long flight.

The codename 'Obviate' was allocated to the projected attack on 24 October, the day that 5 Group Operation Order B.432 was issued. This opened by noting that *Tirpitz* was 'known' to have 'suffered severe damage' during the attack on 15 September, making it 'unfit for seagoing operations'. The text continued: 'It appears likely that the Germans may attempt to get the battleship back to a base in Germany, where the necessary repairs and re-fit can be carried out'. Crucially, however, 'so long as the Tirpitz remains afloat it continues to be a threat to our sea communications with Russia; it has therefore been decided that a further attack shall be made against this ship'. Well-known information about coastal radar stations and met. conditions followed, together with specific note of *Tirpitz*'s new location. She was 'lying anchored off the small island of Haak some three miles west of the town of Tromso'. Apart from the battleship's own 16 heavy and 16 light guns, her defences comprised '12 heavy and 20 light guns, disposed within a radius of 6½mls' of Tromso. No smoke apparatus had yet been identified, but installation must be expected shortly. Even 'if not so effective as that in existence at Tirpitz's former berth', it would 'certainly be adequate to screen the ship'.

Details of *Tirpitz*'s armoured protection, less the passage about vulnerability of the keel to JW mines, were repeated from Operation Order B.393, with the assertion that 'the Tallboy (medium) bomb . . . with its strong body and very high terminal velocity has every chance of penetrating the horizontal armour and bursting deep inside the ship'. The aim again was 'to sink the Tirpitz': this time eighteen aircraft each from 617 and 9 squadrons would be accompanied by a film unit Lancaster of 463 Squadron. Modifications to the operational aircraft were then listed with strict instructions that 'mid-upper gunners are not to be carried', only a crew of six – no passengers. The all-up weight of the Lancasters would be 68,200lb, including the Wellington overload tank and Mosquito drop tank (together giving 252 extra gallons of fuel) fitted in the rest bed area, although several flight engineers insist that only the Wellington tank was actually installed. The film unit aircraft would carry two long-range tanks (each with a 400-gallon capacity) fitted in the bomb-bay. All the extra tanks had to be carefully attached to the main fuel system. 'Particular attention' must be paid to the maintenance and testing of bomb sights, to which 'final checks' were to be made at the advanced bases. As with Paravane, 48hrs were set aside for 'thorough' briefings. A secure room was to be allocated at Bardney and Woodhall 'access to which is to be limited to crews detailed for the operation and a minimum planning staff' and from which nothing should be taken before the squadrons took off for the advanced bases. When favourable weather at Tromso was likely, the aircraft would be bombed up and proceed to Lossiemouth, Kinloss and Milltown to await further orders. For the operation itself, pilots were warned to make the intervals between aircraft taking off 'as short as possible'. The route would lead the Lancasters from Lossiemouth via North Unst (A), 63 00N 02 00E (B), 65 00N 06 47E (C), 65 34N 15 00E (D), 69 00N 19 50E (E), the target (69 39N 18 50E), returning via point B and North Unst to Lossiemouth and the other advanced bases, making a total of 2,250 miles. All aircraft were to carry 'daylight cameras'.

Scatsta on the north mainland of the Shetland islands, close to the Coastal Command station of Sullum Voe, would be the emergency airfield on the route back, though this was later changed to RAF Sumburgh. If any aircraft were to have fewer than 900 gallons of petrol at the target, or engine trouble, it should make for Yagodnik or, alternatively, Vaenga. The film unit would return to Northolt, Middlesex. All bombing aircraft were to carry one 12,000lb 'Tallboy medium bomb, fused T.D. (time delay) 0.07 secs'. 617 Squadron would attack at H–H+1, 9 Squadron H+5–H+6, the operation taking place on the morning of 28 October 'or on the first day thereafter when weather conditions are suitable'. Three DC-3 Dakota aircraft were to transport maintenance and headquarters personnel and equipment to Lossiemouth, with men and necessary equipment then sent by road to the other two advanced bases. The film unit machine, six 9 Squadron and seven 617 Squadron Lancasters would go to Lossiemouth; fourteen from 9 Squadron to Kinloss; thirteen of 617 Squadron to Milltown.

Having taken advantage of a gap in the enemy radar chain along the Norwegian coast, identified by 100 Group, the whole force would rendezvous at 67 37N 17 50E, 'where there is an easily-recognisable lake on the route at a convenient distance from the target'. The rallying point would be marked with smoke bombs. No mention was made of the fact that it was inside neutral Sweden, which would allow the attacking aircraft to be shielded by convenient hills and to approach *Tirpitz* from an unexpected, south-easterly direction. At the rendezvous, four 9 Squadron Lancasters with the API attachment would join 617 aircraft, orbit in the vicinity of 69 15N 19 26E to assess 'wind velocities', pass this information to 9 Squadron commander and fly with him for the attack. If cloud conditions were favourable, surprise achieved and no smoke-screen encountered, aircraft should bomb visually. If cloud or smoke obscured the target to that extent that 'a good bombing run' could not be made, Tallboys were to be taken back to the advanced bases. However, 'if the target itself is obscured, but clearly identifiable features in the immediate vicinity of the ship remain visible, bomb aimers are to drop their bombs, provided they are satisfied that they know the exact position of the target relative to the unobscured landmarks'. Gp Capt C.C. McMullen was to take charge of the groundcrew (due to travel ahead of the bombers) and aircrew connected with the operation from a temporary HQ at RAF Lossiemouth; Wg Cdr J.B. Tait and Wg Cdr J.M. Bazin would 'command and control' their own squadrons in the air. The indicated air speed on the outward leg would be 180–190mph.

Ground staff at Woodhall were instructed on 25 October to reposition the IFF, TR 1196 and TR 5043 (new American VHF radio) equipment on 617 Squadron Lancasters as a matter of urgency. By working a 24hr shift system, they did so in time for the operation. RAF Bomber Command informed the Admiralty on 26 October that Obviate would be launched from the advanced bases in Scotland as soon as possible after the night of Friday 27 October, asking that three destroyers be positioned along the return route for rescue purposes. On 26 October, also, 5 Group told the squadrons to prepare for the operation and more groundcrew laboured to ensure that the overload tanks were made secure. Around the tanks were fitted wooden retaining structures in the fuselage, on which unamused aircrew would soon be painfully barking their shins. And Tallboy was loaded.

During the evening of 27 October, aircrew were briefed at their own stations (Woodhall and Bardney) and warned that the following morning they would fly north to the advanced bases on the Moray Firth. They were told that, once in the air for the operation, aircraft would navigate independently at low level over the North Sea to fly along the Norwegian coast below radar level. The aircraft would then turn east through the reputed gap in the coastal radar chain, across the narrow waist of Norway into Sweden, before flying north to the rendezvous lake. There they would form into gaggles and fall in behind each squadron commander, climbing to 16,000ft before the steady bombing run at designated heights. After the attack, the aircraft would head west, coming down to 1,000ft once the coast was cleared. Crews were warned, however, about offshore islands, many of which had flak defences and had troubled Fleet Air Arm machines in the past. Radio frequencies were issued and procedures explained for contacting the rescue destroyers.

Meanwhile, earlier on 27 October, 5 Group had requested the Air Ministry to inform 30 Mission in Moscow of the intention to bomb *Tirpitz* in the early hours of the first suitable day after 28 October. The Soviets should be told that damaged aircraft would make for Yagodnik or Vaenga or 'in emergency nearest Russian territory'. As with Paravane, this seemed extremely short notice and a shade peremptory.

At 1150 GMT on 28 October, a PRU aircraft found *Tirpitz* still off Haakoy, but a 'detailed statement [was] impossible owing to haze'. However, as arranged, that morning 20 (not the planned 18) aircraft plus a reserve left Woodhall for Lossiemouth and Milltown, 20 from Bardney (14 to Kinloss and 6 to Lossiemouth). With a reconnaissance Mosquito reporting favourable weather in the Tromso area and the forecast good, the operation was set for 29 October. Last-minute preparations included the traditional pre-operational meal of egg, bacon and chips, before between 0103 and 0210 BST on 29 October, nineteen Lancasters from 617 Squadron and between 0118 and 0255 twenty from 9 Squadron took off from the advanced bases. Sgt F.L. Tilley, flight engineer of 617 Squadron's KC-T, recalled 'how compressed the tyres were on take off and how slowly the a/c accelerated down the Milltown runway which terminated in a drop over the sea'. 9 Squadron recorded that it flew to and from Tromso in 'good weather' both ways, but 'unfortunately there was considerable medium cloud in the target area with tops at about 6,000ft, and a number of crews had to make more than one run'. S–Sugar (Fg Off C.R. Redfern) returned early at 0724 with engine trouble, V–Victor and R–Roger were unable to identify the target, so only seventeen 9 Squadron aircraft bombed 'and one hit is claimed on the battleship'. 'Moderate to intense light and heavy flak from battleship and shore batteries' was encountered, but no fighters. Four 9 Squadron Lancasters were damaged by flak. Flt Lt J.D. Melrose observed that 'the cloud couldn't have been formed more accurately if it had been done deliberately', and he admitted to being 'absolutely furious'.

Like 9 Squadron, 617 met 'adverse weather conditions' at Tromso, with the ship visible 'at the start of bombing run', but obscured before the release point. 'A possible hit and one or two near misses were claimed.' Flt Lt B.A. Gumbley's W/Op (Plt Off S.V. Grimes) thought that when the battleship's main armament opened up on them during the bombing run, 'the size of the bursts was quite dramatic'. In Flt Lt R.E. Knights' words, on releasing Tallboy the Lancaster 'jumped up like a bucking stallion', and he struggled to keep it level at a constant speed for the 31secs until the camera operated over the target. A convenient break in the cloud occurred at that moment and Knight's bomb-aimer yelled that KC-O had hit the battleship. Justifiably the pilot remained unconvinced, though this Tallboy may have caused the visible rocking of the target. F/Sgt A.W. Cherrington, Sqn Ldr Fawke's flight engineer, summarised his feelings, and quite possibly those of others. The fact that *Tirpitz* had not been sunk 'after 13hrs boring flight did not make for happy thoughts'.

Flt Lt T. Bennett, now Station Navigation Officer at

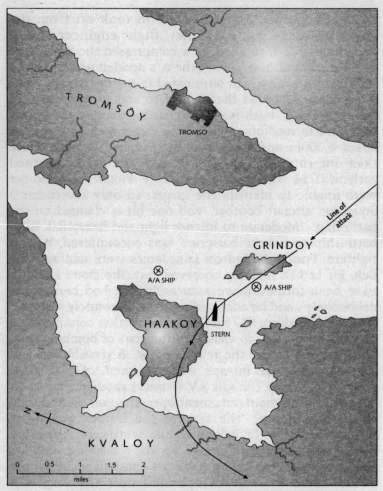

Tirpitz off Haakoy, near Tromso, during Operations Obviate and
Catechism, 29 October and 12 November 1944

Woodhall and therefore not actively involved at Tromso, gave more details in his summary: 'weather conditions were very poor over the first part of the trip', which took place at 1,000ft. The low altitude 'combined with the very heavy static in the cloud' rendered Gee useless for most crews at 62 00N 01 00E. Cloud conditions made astro fixes 'very difficult', so the flight to the Norwegian coast was largely achieved by dead reckoning. The wind velocity changed, and landfall mostly occurred 15 miles south of the briefed track. But accurate pinpoints were then made 'and no further navigational troubles were experienced'. At the rendezvous, Sqn Ldr G.E. Fawke rallied the aircraft by firing green flares, before Tait arrived to waggle his wings and lead the force north-east towards Rosta Lake (69 00N 19 50E), then north-west to the target near Tromso 54 miles away. Bennett agreed that 'low cloud seriously interfered with the bombing and results were disappointing'. The return trip proved 'uneventful', with crews flying a course of 253 degrees true for 3½hrs to North Unst, the average time in the air being 13hrs.

The American Fg Off J.H. Leavitt flew his first operation as second pilot ('passenger') with Fg Off F.H.A. Watts and recounted KC-N's experiences. He did not agree that the return trip was 'uneventful'. The Lancaster flew from Woodhall to Lossiemouth on the morning of 28 October, where its tanks were topped up and final briefing occurred before take-off 'in horrible visibility' in the early hours of Sunday 29 October. After crossing the Norwegian coast as dawn broke, the crew 'soon spotted others all over the sky and formed up behind the Winco' eventually to arrive over the target in 5/10ths strato cumulus. 'Moderate flak of all types . . . and all the Tirpitz's guns including the 15in heavies' were firing. Soon after Tallboy was released on the second run, KC-N was hit: 'fortunately no vital damage, daylight through port wing-tip, starboard tire [sic] burst, rear turret holed and several other small holes through fuselage', but nobody hurt. The flight back was 'agonisingly drawn-out and deadly tiring, until the crew realised the aircraft was short of fuel, so Watts 'brilliantly' put down at

Sumburgh with one flat tyre. Tait personally flew up a new wheel and Watts eventually reached Lossiemouth at 1900 on 30 October, stayed overnight and landed at Woodhall during the afternoon of 31 October. 'In conventional terms, it was one of the most exciting operations I ever went on. Being shot up and landing at Sumburgh on one tire.' His pilot confirmed the crew's experiences. As he approached the target in the gathering cloud, 'the recall or abandonment was given', but with a Nelsonian touch his wireless operator was unable to hear it 'plainly' and KC-N pressed on. Ahead Watts saw Fg Off Carey hit by flak: 'I saw pieces of the aircraft coming off (the only time I had previously witnessed that was in Hollywood films).' Then his own Lancaster suffered 'similar treatment . . . and [I] temporarily forgot Carey's plight'. Reflecting on *Tirpitz*'s position, Leavitt wrote: 'I'm afraid they'll send us again, but I'm damned if I can see what damage the boat can do anymore.'

Many Norwegians witnessed the events on Sunday 29 October, and some recorded their impressions. Egil Lindberg, the clandestine wireless operator, wrote that 'the detonations produced a deep trembling in the ground all over the city of Tromso', over 3 miles from the battleship. Hans Hansen, the wireless operator who had moved south from Nikkeby to the island of Senja, watched the action from afar and saw the bombers fly overhead towards the North Sea on the way home. Their determination in the face of heavy flak particularly impressed him. Lars Thoring, town clerk of Tromso, heard the air-raid warning shortly before 0900 LT and soon afterwards saw aircraft clearing the highest peak in the area, Tromsdalstind. A 'deafening noise' then came from a mass of flak guns ashore and on *Tirpitz*. Thoring estimated that the cloud base was about 6,000ft, as he observed Lancasters flitting in and out of clouds while flak shells erupted around them. 'When the bombs were dropped and exploded it sounded like thunder in the midst of the other infernal noise'. He thought that the attack lasted 15mins, but that the ship was not hit.

Including the reserve aircraft, eighteen 617 Squadron Lancasters returned to Woodhall from the advanced bases

on 30 October, the remaining two the next day (Fg Off
D.W. Carey RAAF's KC-E having been lost from the
twenty-one, which left the home base on 28 October). All
twenty 9 Squadron aircraft landed again at Bardney on
30 October. For Plt Off R.J. Harris this signalled the end of
his first tour, and he would not revisit Tromso. A message
from Cochrane awaited both squadrons: 'Congratulations
on your splendid flight and perseverance. The luck won't
always favour the Tirpitz. One day you'll get her.' Prophetic
words. He also signalled to the appropriate authorities:
'Most grateful for excellent air sea rescue arrangements
organised by Admiralty and the Coastal Command.'

The crew reports added detail to the official summaries,
but at the same time showed the fallacy, and to some
extent the confusion, of eye-witness accounts especially
those reflecting a split second during battle conditions.
Clearly, though, the sudden change of wind direction,
which caused cloud swiftly and unexpectedly to swirl above
the target as the bombers commenced their final approach,
did severely disrupt the planned gaggles of five aircraft.
From 617 Squadron, Fg Off D.F. Oram (Z) bombed at 0749
GMT from 15,000ft, Sqn Ldr T.C. Iveson (F) at 0750 from
15,500ft (both 'results unobserved'), Sqn Ldr G. Fawke (J)
at 0751 from 13,400ft, 'bomb overshot – otherwise results
unobserved'. Flt Lt J.L. Sayers RAAF (X) attacked at 1751½
from 14,200ft 'saw big flash from ship, believed to be
bomb burst, otherwise results unobserved'. Flt Lt R.E.
Knights (O), at 0752 from 13,200ft, was more specific:
'Bomb seen to enter water and explode about 20 yards off
starboard bow and ship rocked considerably. Made several
circuits after bombing and saw thick brown smoke
billowing from vicinity of midships. Shortly after bomb
exploded, observed explosion from starboard bow, followed
by thick black smoke.'

Wg Cdr J.B. Tait (S) released his Tallboy at 0754 from
13,000ft, noting 'ship seen clearly on approach but
obscured by cloud when bomb dropped'. Tait, who had led
the Squadron to the target, had been forced to make a
second run before bombing. Fg Off A.W. Joplin RNZAF (T)

bombed at 0757 from 13,400ft and 'saw what was believed to be bomb burst on forward end of ship followed by explosion and brown smoke'; Fg Off P.H. Martin RAAF (H) at 0758 from 15,000ft reported 'direct hit seen on stern [*sic*] of ship. Bombed on third run after trying runs from east and south-west.' Fg Off J. Gingles (A) also bombed at 0758 from 15,000ft, 'results unobserved'. Fg Off J. Castagnola (V) and Flt Lt L.M. Marshall (Y) dropped Tallboy at 0759, respectively from 14,450ft and 13,900ft. Castagnola 'saw bomb fall towards Tirpitz followed shortly afterwards by flak and column of smoke'; Marshall noted: 'One bomb seen to enter water just outside boom on starboard side of ship. Otherwise results unobserved'. Fg Off F.H.A. Watts (N) bombed at 0800 from 15,800ft, 'results unobserved'; Flt Lt M.D. Hamilton (G) at 0800½ from 16,000ft. Hamilton reported: 'Own bomb believed direct hit on bows followed by big flash. Saw two bombs, followed by another, drop close to Tirpitz, believed to be near midships'. Flt Lt L.S. Goodman (B) released his bomb at 0803 from 13,400ft and Fg Off J.A. Sanders (K) at 0805 from 15,000ft, both 'results unobserved'. Fg Off D.W. Carey RAAF was known to have bombed, 'was last seen heading towards Sweden' and officially 'missing'. So, in all, of the nineteen 617 Squadron Lancasters that set off from Scotland, sixteen had attacked *Tirpitz*. Three others – Flt Lt H.J. Pryor (W), Flt Lt B.A. Gumbley RNZAF (P) and Fg Off A.E. Kell RAAF (M) – were prevented from dropping Tallboy and brought it back. Gumbley did so after four abortive runs over the target area from different directions and secured permission from Tait not to go round again, incidentally showing that the 617 Squadron commander remained in the Haakoy region after dropping his own bomb.

9 Squadron revealed a similar pattern of events. Six minutes behind the first 617 Squadron aircraft, at 0755 Flt Lt J.D. Melrose and Fg Off R.F. Adams bombed from 14,200ft and 15,200ft respectively. Melrose experienced 'moderate to intense heavy and light flak over target area. Tirpitz seen clearly on approach and did not appear to be in distress. Cloud obscured target at time of bombing, making

it impossible to assess result.' Adams had 'battleship in graticule of bomb sight immediately prior to bombing. Target obscured by cloud at time of release, but position easily estimated.' An odd remark followed: 'All crew except the Captain were without oxygen and results of bombing could not therefore be accurately assessed.' Fg Off J.J. Dunne RAAF and Fg Off L.E. Marsh released Tallboy at 0756 from 14,000ft and 15,000ft respectively. Dunne noted 'one bomb seen to hit stern of ship. Hole in bomb-aimer's compartment at 0755 at 14,000ft on run up to target.' Laconically, he concluded, 'no other results observed'. Marsh noted: 'Ship seen to be hit by one bomb near forward mast and billows of smoke resulted. Guns in forward section of ship then ceased firing.' Fg Off J.E. Stowell attacked at 0757 from 13,000ft, 'three explosions seen, two in bows and one in stern'; Fg Off A.F. Williams RAAF released his bomb a minute later from 12,000ft, similarly recording that 'two hits were seen on battleship, one in centre near superstructure and the other on bows. A third bomb seen to fall very near the bows.' All these timings, like those of 617 Squadron, were GMT. Thereafter, for some unexplained reason, 9 Squadron reports must be BST (retained throughout the winter, DBST operating during the summer months), as the whole attack lasted only 18mins.

The OC, Wg Cdr J.M. Bazin, reported dropping Tallboy at 0854 (almost certainly BST and 0754 GMT, the same time as his opposite number, Tait) from 15,500ft, admitting to being 'late at the rendezvous point'. He observed 'wind at target westerly causing low stratus over fiord' and, surprisingly, 'the ship appeared to be beached at one end'. Fg Off D. MacIntosh and Fg Off B. Taylor followed at 0855 from 14,200ft and 12,000ft. MacIntosh stated 'results not observed', but went on: 'At 0854hrs at 14,000ft nearly over the target, part of battleship observed in small cloud-break and what appeared to be a direct hit on port side aft from another aircraft.' Taylor saw bombs 'entering water in several directions about half a mile from ship. Bomber on third run owing to cloud. Thick yellow/brown smoke appeared to be coming from amidships.' Fg Off A.L. Keeley and Sqn Ldr

A.G. Williams also dropped Tallboy at 0855 from 14,000ft and 15,000ft. Keeley registered 'gun flashes from Tirpitz, but target obscured by cloud. Bombs were seen to fall all round but none on target.' Williams had 'centre of ship in bomb sight. Light and heavy flak moderate to intense from shore batteries and Tirpitz, which was also firing heavy guns from aft. Rear gunner saw direct hit on bows of Tirpitz, followed by big explosion and column of brown smoke'. Fg Off S. Laws attacked at 0856 from 14,000ft, but 'broken cloud prevented detailed observation of general attack. Two bombs seen to slightly undershoot'. Fg Off A.F. Jones RAAF followed a minute later from 14,000ft, as well, noting 'red flashes on ship thought to be explosions rather than flak. Small vessels were seen round Tirpitz' and his bomb aimer 'thought target pranged'. Three 9 Squadron aircraft bombed at 0901: Fg Off G.C. Camsell RCAF and Fg Off W.D. Tweddle from 15,000ft, Fg Off R.J. Harris from 14,000ft. To Camsell 'bombing appeared scattered. Trip considered fairly good. Scattered bombing due to cloud cover'; Tweddle 'one large yellow cloud seen after bombing and column of brown smoke. Not possible to assess results owing to broken low cloud.' Harris noted that 'Tallboy was aimed at bow of battleship allowing for wind drift. First run-up target not visual, and on second run only two aircraft left and earlier bombing not seen.' His bomb aimer, Plt Off H.F.C. Parsons, in calling a second circuit, angrily reflected that he 'hadn't come all that bloody way for nothing'. The last Lancaster to bomb was that of Flt Lt A.M. Morrison from 14,800ft at '0807 [sic]'. Tallboy was released on the fifth run, 'as target obscured by cloud at last minute on previous run. When on fourth run orange explosion seen on stern of battleship. Own Tallboy not seen to explode owing to cloud.'

Thus, of the twenty 9 Squadron aircraft that took off from the advanced bases that morning, seventeen dropped Tallboy. One (Fg Off C.R. Redfern) returned early, Fg Off S. Arndell RAAF and Fg Off R.C. Lake were prevented by cloud from bombing and took their bomb back with them, Arndell after making two unsuccessful runs. If, as seems reasonable, several of the 9 Squadron times are converted to GMT, the whole attack off Haakoy [island] took place between 0749 (Oram, 617 Squadron) and 0807 (Morrison, 9 Squadron). This makes a spread of 18mins, which fits in with reports on the ground about the duration of the attack.

The fate of 617 Squadron's missing crew, that of Fg Off D.W. Carey RAAF, did not emerge for some time. Like other bomb-aimers, Plt Off D.H. McLennan RCAF lost *Tirpitz* at the last moment as the cloud closed in. His pilot, therefore, circled to port for another try and continued to do so until, at the sixth attempt, McLennan saw the battleship clearly enough to release Tallboy. However, the Lancaster had been hit in the port inner engine, which was feathered as Carey turned westwards for home. As the aircraft crossed a small offshore island, flak also damaged the port outer engine and shattered the wireless set. The W/Op miraculously escaped injury as at that precise moment he was making his way through the fuselage towards the Elsan toilet. A quick check established that with so much loss of fuel Carey could not reach the emergency field at Sumburgh. Sweden was the only option. Movable equipment, even the Gee navigation set and bomb sight, went out of the aircraft and, losing height rapidly, Carey put down in a bog at Porjus, close to the southern end of the rendezvous lake. The machine pitched precariously on its nose before settling onto an even keel, and the pilot dislocated his knee. When asked by an interrogating officer why the Lancasters had violated the airspace of a neutral country en route to *Tirpitz*, Carey explained earnestly that the navigation of the force commander had been faulty. The very pistol signals were fired by him to gather the aircraft, so that he could lead them away from Swedish territory. A decided case of economy with the truth. Carey and his crew were eventually repatriated, but to their chagrin reached Woodhall too late for the third *Tirpitz* operation.

More details also came out about 9 Squadron's Fg Off A.F. Jones' time over Tromso. Apparently, the 'flak broke [the] left hand panel of his cupola' and the pilot was badly hit in the face. His bomb-aimer then flew the aircraft across the North Sea before Jones managed to put down safely in Scotland. Fg Off A.E. Kell RAAF of 617 Squadron was not injured, but very nearly came to grief when, short of fuel and with Tallboy still aboard, he was forced to land at RAF Sumburgh. Nor did the BCFU Lancaster in reality enjoy its declared 'uneventful' trip. During the operation, in which poor weather and unsatisfactory light conditions restricted film footage to 150ft, before reaching Haakoy the aircraft sustained damage to the starboard wing, engine nacelles and main undercarriage. On approaching Waddington, the pilot therefore ordered the crew into crash positions and put down successfully on one wheel after 14hrs 20mins in the air. It had been an interesting, at times frustrating, but certainly not 'uneventful' flight. Flt Lt B.A. Gumbley RNZAF brought back his Tallboy and, similarly short of fuel, put down on the short runway of RAF Scatsca, 20 miles north of Lerwick on Sullum Voe.

A PRU flight over *Tirpitz* at 1210 GMT on 29 October found no evidence of damage and Ultra interceptions later found that no hits had been obtained, though a near miss caused an estimated 800 tons of water to seep into the battleship. It later emerged that this Tallboy had 'damaged the port shaft and rudder and flooded almost 100ft of the after end of the ship on the port side'. Just three casualties were recorded. 5 Group summarised the PRU evidence as showing *Tirpitz* still off Haakoy 'lying inside booms as before the attack. She is believed to be on an even keel. No satisfactory damage assessment is possible.' An analysis of the photos taken by attacking aircraft did not help. All were 'badly obscured by cloud and smoke but stern of battleship seen on one photo in usual berth. Nearest identifiable burst was 300 yards off.' On 3 November, the Naval Intelligence Division noted that thirty-two Lancasters had attacked *Tirpitz* on 29 October in 'light cloud [that] made accurate bombing difficult'. It stressed that 'photographic evidence is not conclusive. Strike reports state that there were a number of near misses, and the ship may have sustained damage'; a hope not altogether vain. At 0845 LT on 29 October, *Tirpitz* had reported being under attack by forty heavy bombers, and subsequently that no hits had been suffered, only a near miss which caused 'slight damage'. Several aircraft had been shot down. No doubt this claim, and the fact that *Tirpitz*'s crew apparently once more prevented the battleship being sunk, raised morale. Post-war, Midshipman Alfred Zuba confirmed that the gun crews believed that their weapons had foiled the attack, not the clouds.

Wishful thinking was not confined to the enemy. The number of RAF crews that reported multiple hits on the battleship made assessment back in the United Kingdom extremely difficult and this led, initially at least, to exaggerated claims which were later disproved. From the outset, though, '*V*' *Group News* more soberly reflected 'without doubt one very near miss', but no evidence of a hit, concluding: 'Once again, these two squadrons were cheated of their prey, and this time by a trick of the weather which was wholly unexpected, and certainly undeserved'. 5 Group expressed 'disappointment' that 'cloud intervened at the crucial stage in the bombing run', but added a mixture of hope and caution. 'The doomed battleship, with her protecting zareba of booms and nets against surface and below surface attacks and her smoke protectors from aircraft, was safe for another short spell; safe until the incidence of fair weather should give the bombers their required pre-conditioning of "drawing a bead on her".' *Tirpitz*'s 'hope of survival' rested on unfavourable bombing weather 'and this was likely on five days out of six owing to the prevailing westerly wind'. Only an east wind would clear the sky 'and as the sun would not rise above the horizon again after November until Spring, there was but a narrow margin of time for success'. 26 November signalled the onset of perpetual winter darkness. F/Sgt C.B.R. Fish later recalled how Cochrane addressed 617 Squadron at Woodhall after Operation Obviate, emphasising that *Tirpitz* must be sunk. The Lancasters would be sent back 'again and again' until the job had been done.

Surviving sources are clear about neither the precise date

when surplus crew left the warship (on arrival off Haakoy or following Operation Obviate) nor the exact number of men involved (400–600); one later commentator claimed only 100. But by early November, with *Tirpitz* no longer capable of steaming any distance, the bulk of the engineering staff had undoubtedly been put ashore. In keeping with her new static role, the battleship now concentrated on gunnery and maintenance duties. Of this reduced function, the Allies remained ignorant.

The task of filling the trough under *Tirpitz* with rubble officially began on 1 November (though Capt Junge would later state that 'the first dredging took place on the 2nd or 3rd'), with the objective of creating 'an even 2m [6.56ft] below the keel'. The original problem had been exacerbated by Tallboy near-misses on 29 October, which not only scoured the sea-bed further but incidentally revealed the mud, not rock, bottom. By 12 November, British Naval Intelligence estimated that about 14,000 cubic metres (half the required total) 'had been filled in at both sides below the midship section'. The dredgers had no mean job still to do. On 4 November, although still its Commanding Officer, Junge left Capt Robert Weber in charge of *Tirpitz*, and Weber immediately instituted a survey of the battleship. Three days later, a comprehensive list of required spares was drawn up.

On 3 November, the Royal Navy's Intelligence Division estimated that 'to make the ship operationally seaworthy it will probably be necessary to re-build forward of turret A, a major operation involving docking for a considerable period'. It was 'unlikely' that this work could be done 'at a northern base, and a period of at least 4 to 6 months at a main base (including docking) would probably be necessary to make her fully operational'. On this basis, *Tirpitz* could not be left alone. She was still a potential menace that must be dealt with – soon. Only twenty-three days remained before winter darkness, and a lot could be done to recondition her under its protective cloak.

Plans to relaunch Operation Obviate, under the codename Catechism, were therefore begun almost as soon as the

Lancasters touched down at their home bases. On 2 November, HQ 8 Group informed Bomber Command that to ensure 'feasible weather conditions' for an attack on *Tirpitz*, it was 'essential to station Pampa Mosquito at Vaenga near Murmansk immediately'. Although the Soviets were evidently approached, instead two days later two met. Mosquitoes were deployed to RAF Sumburgh. Meanwhile, on 3 November, 5 Group formally warned Nos 53 and 54 Bases that Operation Order B.432 (dated 24 October) would be repeated under the codename Catecism and renumbered B.439. H-hour would be morning civil twilight plus 90mins in the target area on 5 November.

So, on 4 November, twenty Lancasters from 9 Squadron and nineteen (including one reserve) from 617 once more flew to the advanced bases in Scotland. Sqn Ldr T.C. Iveson of 617 Squadron had to put down at Carnaby for running repairs en route, eventually reaching Milltown after the others. He need not have hurried. That evening a gale warning was issued, and at 1000 on 5 November the operation was cancelled 'through adverse weather'; the aircraft returned to Woodhall and Bardney. On 6 November, the Air Ministry informed 30 Mission in Moscow that, due to the uncertain weather, Catechism had been postponed 'until further notice'. The Soviets should be thanked for their offer of assistance and advised that the possibility of operating a Mosquito from Vaenga had not been finally discounted. That day, too, 617 and 9 Squadrons were warned to stand-by again, and the following day 9 Squadron Lancasters landed at Lossiemouth and Kinloss, 617 at Lossiemouth and Milltown, with the 463 Squadron film unit machine putting down at Lossiemouth. As *'V' Group News* later put it: 'This was the third week-end in succession this avalanche had descended upon them, [and] the inhabitants of the advanced bases had mixed feelings, which they courteously concealed.' A legend has persisted that at Woodhall on Saturday 11 November, clad in striped jersey and football boots, Tait was summoned from the playing field to be told that the Lancasters were to fly at once to the advanced bases for another attempt to mount Catechism. Variations of the story have the AOC instructing the perspiring squadron commander in person or, more likely, over the phone. However, if this incident did happen, it must have been on 10 November, after which the crews were briefed, for they were in northern Scotland by the afternoon of 11 November. The provisional weather forecast read: '. . . threatening convection cloud over the Norwegian coast . . . [with] high icing index, while there was no guarantee of the target being clear of strato-cumulus'. Specifically, icing conditions were likely over the Swedish mountains. Shortly after midnight 11/12 November, a met. Mosquito landed at Lossiemouth to report a slight improvement: 'No convection cloud, but there were patches of stratus.' 'Not very promising', Bomber Command admitted. Nevertheless, the operation was on. In the light of their previous disappointment over Tromso, one participant noted that the 'crews were determined, but not optimistic'.

For this operation, the American Fg Off J.H. Leavitt piloted KC-R and again recorded his experiences. 'After a late lunch on Saturday I went to bed, and though I didn't sleep much, got up at 10pm feeling refreshed and in spite of a "butterfly feeling" in the pit of my stomach rather hungry.' Following 'a very short last-minute briefing' and 'a good meal', he went out to his Lancaster to find the ground crew working frantically to defrost it. Although the windscreen was cleared outside, 'the inside kept freezing from our breath, so that our take off was done almost completely by instruments'. With an all-up weight of 68,500lb 'it was a bit of a mental hazard'. Keeping navigation lights on until near to the Norwegian coast, Leavitt had the company of other Lancasters, but then lost them. Now completely alone, KC-R found itself 50 miles north of the briefed track 'in the first light of dawn' and saw flak ahead. This indicated that another aircraft had strayed off track and encouraged Leavitt to skirt the enemy position as he climbed. 'The terrain below was bleak, precipitous and barren, and at the same time magnificent. . . . I have never felt so completely alone in my life'. Eventually, as the sun rose, other Lancasters gradually materialised on the horizon, KC-R joined them and successfully reached the rendezvous.

After turning north close to Tarna inside Sweden (65 34N 15 00E), as with Obviate on 29 October, crews navigated individually to Akkajaure Lake, 150 miles south-south-west of Tromso (67 37N 17 50E). The eighteen operational 617 Lancasters, with the pilot of the reserve aircraft (Flt Lt H.V. Gavin) flying with Sqn Ldr T.C. Iveson as 'a passenger', took off between 0259 and 0325 BST. Thick hoar-frost on the wings grounded seven 9 Squadron Lancasters, the other thirteen taking off between 0300 and 0335. B flight commander, Flt Lt J.D. Melrose, was livid that the maintenance crew had not defrosted the aircraft, and as a result his and the OC's Lancaster were among those grounded at Kinloss. Fg Off D.A. Coster's WS-T did get away, but the pilot 'held the Lancaster down an awfully long time' before it eventually got airborne. Flt Lt B.A. Gumbley RNZAF of 617 Squadron managed to take off, because his flight engineer helped the groundcrew by sweeping the Lancaster's control surfaces with a broom.

Fg Off W.R. Lee's navigator, Fg Off H. Watkinson, praised Gee as 'a real godsend'. It inevitably failed due to range, 'but by then we had calculated the winds accurately and DR was made simpler'. Fg Off A.W. Joplin's navigator, F/Sgt C.B.R. Fish, who would bang his head against the fuselage to help keep awake during the subsequent 'boring, tedious' flight back, found Gee helpful though limited in range. Crossing the Norwegian coast, with no other aircraft in sight, he took an astro shot of Polaris and, to his amazement, found the aircraft north of the briefed track. After swift course adjustments, Fish 'heaved a sigh of relief' when he saw another Lancaster ahead. After that 'everything else was pretty well hunky dory', except that when he eventually got back to base he 'literally slept round the clock' and was not the only one to do so. Piloting KC-O, Flt Lt R.E. Knights recalled: 'After turning out over the Moray Firth, we set course north-east for the Norwegian Sea at 1,500ft. We saw the Shetland Isles pass by on our left, and when we reached 46degs N turned eastwards towards the Norwegian coast at low level. We crossed the coast, climbing rapidly to clear mountains, and flew over the Swedish border. We turned north, and keeping on the Swedish side of the border proceeded to our assembly point.' The film unit Lancaster took off at 0324, having been delayed 'owing to heavy frosting of the aircraft'.

Approaching the Norwegian coast in darkness, as the first glint of light pierced the horizon Iveson made out a Lancaster shape ahead. Closing on it, he saw Tait's grinning rear gunner (WO H.D. Vaughan) gesticulating rudely in his direction. The two Lancasters then flew together to the rendezvous, on which 'miraculously' after 'wonderful navigation' a swarm of four-engined gnats appeared from the west within minutes. The lake, according to Bomber Command later, 'was identified by the cloud that hung over it like an identical twin in shape'. After orbiting twice in the bright morning light, Tait fired very lights and led the armada off towards their target. Aircrew remarked on 'the beautiful sky . . . could see for 100mls . . . startlingly clear, absolutely startling . . . a gin-clear sky', but they were also acutely aware of Bf 109 fighters, reported to be at the nearby Bardufoss air base. Tait mused that there was 'nothing I could do if they did appear and I got on with the job in hand'; Iveson, one of his flight commanders, admitted to being 'very wary', others to anxiously scanning the sky. Climbing steadily towards their allocated bombing heights in their separate gaggles, they flew along the north–south Bals Fjord. *Tirpitz* stood out nakedly: no cloud, no smoke-screen, though some effort was being made with limited equipment on the vessel itself. Too late. Tait thought she 'looked like a spider in a web, trapped in the anti-torpedo nets which spread around her'. The German gunners had seen the bombers, too, and opened up with the main armament, whose shells pitted the sky with 'orange puffs', to some more like menacing 'orange clouds'. These were soon left behind and the more familiar black curtain of flak explosions lay ahead.

Bomber Command remarked that, 'every lake was covered with stratus, the surprise was great therefore when Tromso was seen clear of cloud or smoke'. To Plt Off S.V. Grimes, Gumbley's W/Op, the long bombing run required by the SABS bomb sight 'seemed interminable'.

Flt Lt R.E. Knights focused on the 'black shape' of *Tirpitz*, which he could see 'quite clearly contrasting with the surrounding snow-covered ground'. About five minutes away, the bomb doors were opened and he held his aircraft steady at the required height and air speed. Fg Off A.B. Walker, his bomb aimer, saw Tallboy begin to spin before Knights turned to port. Iveson, like all pilots, lost the target under the nose of his Lancaster as he lined up for the bombing run. 'Then I thought to myself that this time we had a very good chance, as conditions were ideal. So I carried on, moved in through a lot of flak, but not so much as at Alten, because there was not so much shore-based as there.' He 'concentrated on the instruments and cut myself off from what was going on'. After the bomb went 'we had a little look but decided there was a long way to go and had better get the hell out of it. And that's what we did'. Iveson was not alone. After bombing, Tait claimed to have judged the environment to be 'not healthy' and, with the operation obviously going according to plan, 'didn't hang around'. This was typical modesty. He undoubtedly circled to port to watch the other seventeen Lancasters from 617 Squadron complete their attack in just three minutes before leaving the area.

The film unit aircraft, once more piloted by Flt Lt B.A. Buckham RAAF, had already started to fly westwards, having shot 700ft of film, when the rear gunner reported *Tirpitz* listing at 70 degrees and it went back to shoot more footage from 5,000ft. Independently, several 617 Squadron rear gunners confirmed the battleship's death throes. The shout of 'she's going' from Sgt B. Kent in Sanders' KC-W prompted most of the crew to crowd into the astrodome. Flt Lt I.M. Marshall's rear gunner, Fg Off D.W. Bale, called a similar warning and the pilot 'swung round so we could all witness her turning over and it was quite a sight', wrote the W/Op, Fg Off H.J. Riding. Eyeing the stricken vessel, WO W.H. Pengelly in Knight's KC-O reflected more soberly: 'Thank God for that. It's the last time we've got to come here.' Puzzled, but grateful, that no fighters had appeared, Fg Off Watts mused: 'We were fortunate in not catching the enemy on one of his better days.'

Evidence of the bombers' achievement, and, indeed, eagerly awaited success, soon mounted. The pilots' debriefing reports provided the first strand in building up a comprehensive picture of the sequence and results of the attack. The 617 Squadron timings were given in GMT. On a bearing of 340 degrees True (T) and at 170mph IAS, Wg Cdr J.B. Tait (D) dropped the first Tallboy at 0841 from 13,000ft, observing: 'We did not see our bomb burst, but the initial bombing was concentrated on the vessel. When we arrived there was steam coming out of the funnel.' Like succeeding 617 Squadron aircraft, Tait recorded 'clear visibility'. At 0842, evidently in an ordered gaggle of five, Fg Off W.R. Lee RAAF (P, 330 degrees T, 165 IAS) bombed from 14,400ft; Fg Off J.A. Sanders (K, 350 degrees T, 170 IAS) from 14,000ft; Flt Lt R.E. Knights (O, 330 degrees T, 170 IAS) from 13,400ft; Fg Off J. Gingles (A, 340 degrees T, 170 IAS) from 13,200ft; and Fg Off J. Castagnola (V, 340 degrees T, 170 IAS) from 12,650ft. Lee noted that 'the ship was obscured by smoke just after we bombed' (that is, released Tallboy from approximately 2,000yds away). 'Our bomb went straight down into the centre of the smoke. All bombing we saw appeared very well concentrated and firing from the ship ceased after the first bombs went down.' Sanders observed: 'Two bombs, one of which was ours, went down together and both appeared to hit the edge of the ship near its centre' (implying that this crew's vision was not impaired by smoke). 'Bombing appeared generally concentrated. Only one wide bomb.' Knights' report was more lengthy. 'Our bomb fell about 10yds off port quarter. We saw the first four bombs go down as follows: on or near starboard quarter; starboard bow; port bow and near funnel. We remained near target area until end of attack and saw large explosion at 0851 and a smaller one at 0853. Before we left we saw the Tirpitz listing heavily to port.' Gingles recorded: 'We think we obtained a direct hit . . . [in] centre of ship. We did not see any further results as we were hit by flak and had to turn away'; Castagnola that 'our bomb fell on the centre of the superstructure. There was a direct hit at the same time a cloud of smoke followed and the ship became completely obscured by it.'

Fg Off A.W. Joplin RNZAF (T, 320 degrees T, 170 IAS), Fg Off F.H.A. Watts (U, 332 degrees T, 167 IAS) and Sqn Ldr T.C. Iveson (F, 345 degrees T, 165 IAS) all released Tallboy at 0842½, respectively from 15,200ft, 13,800ft and 13,000ft. Joplin registered that 'our bomb fell in the smoke which covered the ship. One direct hit and two near misses were seen.' Watts said: 'We did not see our own bomb burst but saw one possible direct hit, one overshoot, one undershoot and two wides.' Iveson reported: 'Our bomb fell in the centre of the smoke pall which covered the ship when we attacked.'

Five 617 Lancasters dropped Tallboy at 0843: Flt Lt B.J. Dobson (S, 300 degrees T, 165 IAS) and Fg Off J.H. Leavitt (R, 332 degrees T, 170 IAS) both from 15,600ft; Fg Off B.A. Gumbley RNZAF (J, 325 degrees T, 165 IAS) 15,400ft; Flt Lt I.M. Marshall (Y, 330 degrees T, 160 IAS) from 14,800ft; and Fg Off A.E. Kell RAAF (M, 300 degrees T, 160 IAS) from 12,850ft. Dobson observed that 'our bomb fell into smoke concentration over target. Bombing appeared very accurate'; Leavitt, 'our bomb went down into centre of smoke over Tirpitz. Bombing very well concentrated on and round vessel. Heavy explosions seen'; Gumbley, 'one [Tallboy] seen to enter the water about 20yds off the Tirpitz. A dull red glow was observed well forward of [?on] the port bow'; Marshall, 'our bomb fell in the main concentration which appeared to be on or around the Tirpitz. The ship was covered in smoke and a fire was seen on board.' Kell was more expansive. 'We bombed along the length of the ship turning to starboard and running in on the bows. Our bomb which registered a hit or a very near miss fell in the centre of the smoke coming up from just in front of the superstructure. We saw at least one direct hit which was followed by a big column of reddish brown smoke.' At 0843½ Fg Off I.S. Ross RAAF (C, 330 degrees T,

170 IAS) from bombed from 14,600ft, Fg Off M.B. Flatman (G, 345 degrees T, 170 IAS) 13,600ft. To Ross, 'the after part of ship was obscured by smoke when we bombed. Our bomb hit on or very close to the bows'; to Flatman, 'our bomb is estimated to have fallen 25yds aft of the funnel. We also saw a very near miss near the port quarter of the ship. Immediately after the first bombs fell a red glow appeared followed by a big column of black smoke.' Flt Lt S.A. Anning (Z, 340 degrees T, 170 IAS) bombed at 0844 from 16,000ft, held that 'our bomb fell in the centre of the smoke concentration' and reinforced Knight: 'There was a big explosion on the ship at 0851.' Flt Lt J.L. Sayers RAAF (W) was the last 617 Squadron pilot to attack from 14,200ft at 0845: 'We followed our bomb down nearly to the ship when it was lost in the smoke. It was either a hit on the bows or a very near miss.'

As laid down in the Operation Order, 9 Squadron trailed 617, and its timings were given in BST (GMT+1). Sgt J.C. Pinning, Fg Off Coster's flight engineer, noted that WS-T saw no other aircraft over the North Sea, and crossed the coast with dawn breaking, as the navigator pointed to 'the fingers of cloud in the fjords'. Breasting the last ridge before the target, Pinning saw *Tirpitz* ahead 'like a dinky toy'. The peaceful scene was soon shattered when his starboard outer engine was hit by flak. Eventually the flames were doused, but the starboard inner was also running rough and, having lost fuel, the crew decided to make for Sweden. In all the confusion, Tallboy was released. Every pilot noted 'clear visually' in the bombing area. Sqn Ldr A.G. Williams (D, 300 degrees T, RAS 175) and Fg Off C. Newton RCAF (R, 320 degrees T, 200 IAS) both dropped Tallboy from 16,000ft at 0945 (0845 GMT), the same time as the last 617 Squadron pilot (Flt Lt Sayers). Williams recorded 'very near miss on starboard side aft seen just before bombing and about three other bombs seen to burst close to the ship. One hit believed as a column of smoke enveloped the ship and its guns stopped firing', a development already mentioned by Fg Off Lee of 617 Squadron. Newton noted 'centre of smoke covering ship which was seen on run-up. One large explosion seen amidships and 2 to 3 close near misses.' Interestingly, and uniquely, he added: 'Two E boats at 69.38N 17.20E at 0958 hours, 7,000ft approx fired at a/c. Rear gunner returned fire damaging one E boat', an exchange that took place south-west of Tromso during the withdrawal.

Fg Off W.D. Tweddle (Y, 320 degrees T, RAS 195) attacked at 0945½ from 14,600ft: 'on run up one bomb seen to hit fjord side of ship and only one gun on fjord side continued firing afterwards. After leaving the target a large explosion was seen at 0947 hours'. Fg Off M.L.T. Harper RNZAF (Q, 345 degrees T, 185 IAS) followed at 0946½ from 15,000ft: 'a near miss seen on starboard side of ship. Bombing concentrated but difficult to assess owing to smoke. Rear gunner saw large fire amidships.' At 0947, Flt Lt R.C. Lake (V, 334 degrees T, RAS 185) bombed from 16,000ft, Fg Off A.E. Jeffs (E, 305 degrees T, RAS 170) and Fg Off J.E. Stowell (B, 325 degrees T, 180 IAS) both from 14,000ft. Lake reported: '5 bombs seen to fall. No 1 – 50yds off bow of ship. No 2 slightly undershot centre of ship. No 3 – about 30yds from stern. No 4 overshot centre of ship by about 150yds. No 5 overshot to the right about 150yds. In addition rear gunner saw own bomb which he considers hit the ship as a big explosion and fire followed immediately.' Jeffs noted 'ship seen on run-up, but just before release of bomb smoke obscured target. Bomb was aimed at centre of smoke. No hit seen, but bombs seen bursting all round ship.' Stowell reported: 'one bomb seen to fall approximately centre of port side. Explosion followed by reddish smoke seen through smoke [sic] and another amidships by rear gunner when leaving target area. This followed by large fire. 2 or 3 near misses on port side of bows and one on starboard side.' Stowell further explained that 'flak from ship ceased temporarily, started again and then ceased altogether', and that his Lancaster had been hit: 'Rudder control port tail plane damaged by heavy flak over target immediately after bombing.'

Two minutes after Lake, Jeffs and Stowell, at 0948 (in final typed report, but 0945 in one draft) Flt Lt L.E. Marsh

(G, 310 degrees T, RAS 195) attacked from 16,500ft. 'Crew stated bombing very well concentrated around the ship and a large fire was seen burning amidships after leaving the target area from some distance away. A great deal of smoke was also seen.' The last two 9 Squadron aircraft known positively to have bombed were those of Flt Lt H. Watkins (W, 354 degrees T, RAS 185) and Fg Off D. Macintosh (C, 360 degrees T, RAS 180), both at 0949 from 16,000ft and 14,500ft respectively. Watkins, like Marsh a minute earlier, recorded 'glow seen amidships' and also 'a pillar of smoke both from bows and stern. Two near misses seen but difficult to assess owing to distance from target. Own bomb fell in smoke at stern.' He added: 'Considerable amount of smoke from ship about ⅓ size of battleship lying alongside the latter', which was not mentioned by another crew and presumably omitted by the squadron intelligence officer from the final typed version of Watkins' report. MacIntosh saw 'many near misses . . . and one hit believed just forward of centre of ship. Two explosions occurred after bombing, followed by plume of white smoke which covered the ship. Bomb sight was u/s on first run. Emergency computer used for second run.' Excised from the final version was the passage: 'Only one gun seen firing from ship when aircraft made its bombing run and ship appeared to be listing to starboard with a fire amidships.'

Ten 9 Squadron Lancasters thus reported attacking *Tirpitz*. An eleventh, piloted by Fg Off D.A. Coster RAAF, was missing. It soon became known that, after releasing Tallboy over the battleship and being severely damaged as noted by Sgt Pinning, it had landed without casualties at Vandnasberget, near Kalix in Sweden. The crew would later be repatriated. Flt Lt G.C. Camsell RCAF and Fg Off C.E. Redfern both individually reached the rendezvous after the others had gone. An empty sky greeted them. Camsell did glimpse Redfern in the distance, but was not seen by him. So, independently, the two Lancasters returned to their advanced base with Tallboy. In total, therefore, twenty-nine Lancasters bombed *Tirpitz* on Sunday 12 November. From their reports, it appeared that several Tallboys had either hit the battleship or been near misses, and that smoke from *Tirpitz*'s own on-board system had taken effect almost as soon as the Lancasters began to bomb. This almost certainly meant that it was activated as the attackers breasted the last 1169m high ground near Vikran at the head of Bals Fjord, 10mins flying time away.

Several Norwegians witnessed the attack, and the gist of what they saw was quickly transmitted to England by Egil Lindberg. His first brief message that day ran: 'Tirpitz capsized after a series of hits. A little of her side and keel show above water.' Lindberg himself heard an air-raid warning at 0850 LT and, slightly inaccurately, held that the first bomb fell at 0935. He believed that three hits were achieved: the first on the port side, in front of the forward turret; the second behind this turret, and this caused a substantial fire; the third approximately 8mins after the first, again forward on the port side. There were two near misses to starboard, which he thought caused the battleship to capsize as she went 'bottom up' shortly afterwards. 'The explosions simply blew the water away from under the ship, the bomb on the port side of the deck at the same time pressing her down to port. . . . The detonations produced a deep trembling in the ground all over the city of Tromso.' Lars Thoring, Tromso's town clerk, put the alert at 'about 0900' on 'an unusual day considering the time of the year'; a clear, bright sky with 'not a breath of wind'. He saw the aircraft at approximately 12,000ft approaching out of range of batteries on Tromso island, but 'the guns of the Tirpitz put in a veritable display of fireworks, aided by powerful anti aircraft [guns] on Haakoy'. Thoring watched the raid unfold from the first floor of the weather office in Tromso. After the bombs dropped in the sea, 'columns of water rose several hundred yards [sic] into the air like a gigantic fountain in the middle of splendid fireworks'. The blast, even 3 miles away, was so strong that windows were broken and Thoring feared that the wooden building would be 'lifted off its foundations'. *Tirpitz*'s forward flak guns were soon silenced, but those aft continued to fire. So did those on Haakoy, until a stray

Tallboy hit the island and simulated a 'volcanic explosion' with stones spitting upwards. Then the shore battery also stopped firing. Thoring ran up to the roof to see 'a dark thundercloud in the sky' above the German warship, which was 'lying there stripped of masts and tower and everything on deck. She looked rather like an unfinished construction on the stocks.' The behemoth began to keel over and finished up 'like a stranded whale'. Other watchers saw the battleship list about 20 degrees to port, then an explosion lifted C turret aft into the air and *Tirpitz* heeled over until her starboard side was clearly visible from the shore. Unlike Thoring, observers on Haakoy reported that, although battered, the upperworks were still evident. Once the smoke cleared, one saw *Tirpitz* 'lying almost capsized in the anchorage, looking like a silver island', another focused on the matchstick figures crawling across the upturned hull, clinging to anti-torpedo netting or flailing to survive in a water temperature of minus 8C. Many homeowners, though, experienced immense personal relief. Requisition orders to accommodate crew members ashore had patently been overtaken by events. The warship's fate led to 'great enthusiasm' in Tromso, but unwary public demonstrators quickly found themselves in a Gestapo cell. Forty years later, Olav Sandmo, the deputy mayor of Tromso, recalled this 'fateful day . . . an incredible drama', when people came out of their shelters and 'discovered to their relief that Tromso had been spared, but that *Tirpitz* had been sunk'. The experience of Egil Akre, a former forced labourer who had witnessed the warship's fate from the window of a cellar on Tromsoy, added a comical postscript. Walking back to the fishing port through forestland, he met a group of sailors who had been playing football close-by. Realising that the wind direction had carried the sound of the battle, which was visually concealed by the terrain, away from them, he said: '*Tirpitz* has been sunk'. 'Crazy Norwegian' came the laughing response.

The return trip for the Lancasters, unchallenged by the enemy but lengthened by adverse winds, did not pass without incident. For 617 Squadron, overcast conditions caused Ross (landed 1529), Gingles (1602), Castagnola (1546) and Anning (1558) to divert to Milltown from Lossiemouth. Sanders (1514), Lee (1530), Gumbley (1537), Marshall (1550), Watts (1607) and Sayers (1620) did, however, return to Lossiemouth. Short of fuel, Flatman (1447) put down at Scatsca and Joplin (1459) at Sumburgh, to the plaudits of his navigator. 'Cookie [Sgt G Cooke, the W/Op] got the bearing and then a wonderful bit of flying by old Jop to get in, because there was a large hill at one end.' Iveson (1528), Leavitt (1558) and Dobson (1659) diverted to Fraserburgh; Knights (1539) and Kell (1614) to Peterhead. Also diverted from Lossiemouth, Tait (1545) landed at the small fighter airfield of Dallachy, where on touching down he was asked curiously whether he had been on a cross-country exercise. Redfern and Camsell of 9 Squadron, who reached the rendezvous point too late to join the attack, returned to their advanced base at 1420 and 1455. The other ten Lancasters landed between 1512 and 1609, but their precise destination is not clear. Excluding the film-unit Lancaster, from the thirty-one aircraft that left Scotland on Operation Catechism during the early hours of Sunday 12 November 1944, only one from 9 Squadron had failed to return.

On 13 November ten 617 Squadron aircraft returned to Woodhall, according to the Station ORB, to confirm that *Tirpitz* had been sunk and be 'welcomed by ground staffs and the band of the Border Regiment'. The musicians, possibly of the Kings Own Scottish Borderers, were supposed.to have rendered 'See the Conquering Hero Comes' to greet them, but that joyful scene may be a confusion with stories of the triumphant blasts from Soviet instruments during the celebrated football match at Yagodnik in September. In any case, eight crews missed the performance after their diversions to other airfields in Scotland, some arriving on 14 November, Joplin a day later. Similarly, 9 Squadron returned to Bardney 13–14 November. Tait flew to London on 14 November 'to make a broadcast on the attack'. He returned from the capital on 15 November with the Secretary of State for Air, Sir

Archibald Sinclair, who, following lunch in the Officers' Mess, 'addressed the aircrew personnel in the briefing room in the afternoon'. Tait went back to London again, and 'all aircrew [were] granted a 48-hr pass'. Precisely one week later, 22 November, Gp Capt M.G. Philpott held a station commander's parade at Woodhall, attended by the aircrew and at which the military regimental band 'provided martial music'. G.F. Handel may well have appeared on its programme on this occasion.

Bomber Command, 5 Group and the two squadrons were almost literally showered with telegrams, telephone messages and letters. From King George VI came, 'please convey my hearty congratulations to all those who took part in the daring and successful attack on the *Tirpitz*'. Sinclair sent the War Cabinet's 'congratulations on the brilliant achievement of Bomber Command in sinking the *Tirpitz*. The series of attacks on Germany's most powerful battleship were pressed home with great skill and determination against formidable opposition. The destruction of the *Tirpitz* must rank with finest feats of Bomber Command and marks a further stage in the crumbling of German Power.' After a succinct message from Harris, '*Tirpitz* sunk this morning. Bert', in Paris Churchill replied equally briefly: 'Heartiest congratulations to all.' Lord Trenchard, the doyen of RAF history, sent 'his heartiest congratulations to all who took part in sinking of *Tirpitz*'. Harris signalled Cochrane: 'Congratulations to you and all ranks of the squadrons concerned in the destruction of the *Tirpitz*. The skilful planning and courageous and determined execution of these operations put precisely that end to this ship which was inevitable as soon as the squadrons got a clear bead on her.' Wallis in turn wired Harris: 'Very very hearty congratulations to you on magnificent success due entirely to your courage and determination to persevere.' C-in-C Bomber Command replied: 'Many thanks for your message. On the contrary, success entirely due to your perseverance with your bomb.' 4 Group, so closely involved in the Halifax operations in 1942, sent congratulations 'on your magnificent achievement in sinking the *Tirpitz*'. The

Admiralty offered 'thanks to those concerned in this very successful attack on *Tirpitz*. . . . It was a job well done.' *Furious* signalled 'should be grateful if you will pass on to the Air Ministry "well done"'.

The Chief of the Air Staff expressed 'warmest congratulations . . . unbounded admiration . . . [for the] skill, courage and perseverance now so happily crowned with success'. He also underlined broader implications: 'Apart from the effect on the war at sea of the permanent removal of the most powerful unit of the German Navy, this exploit will fill the whole German Nation with dismay at a critical time and will enhance the fame of Bomber Command throughout the world.' Churchill also took up the international theme. He telegraphed Stalin, 'let us rejoice together', and three days later Roosevelt: 'It is a great relief to us to have this brute where we have long wanted her.' General H.H. Arnold, Commanding-General of the US Army Air Forces, passed a message to Portal through Eisenhower: 'Congratulations on positive and permanent disposal of that troublesome thing at Tromso.' The CAS's response took a side-swipe at those doubting the effectiveness of the Allied strategic bombing campaign on Germany. 'I am confident that all our headaches will yield eventually to the same treatment as applied by the well known firm of Spaatz and Harris' (commanding respectively the American and British heavy bombers). On 14 November, in offering 'warmest congratulations' to those 'whose skill and tenacity have been so fittingly rewarded', 30 Mission signalled Bomber Command: 'Russians most impressed and grateful that this menace to the convoy route has been disposed of.'

Portal responded unsympathetically to a suggestion from Harris that his congratulatory message should be publicised: 'I have never agreed to publication of my messages and I don't want to start now. They are for the squadrons, not the public!' Others were less reticent. The Air Ministry issued a communiqué on 13 November that received wide cover on radio and newsreels, in newspapers and periodicals. 'The *Tirpitz* has been sunk. Yesterday morning 29 Lancasters of RAF Bomber Command led by

Wing Cmdr J.B. Tait DSO DFC and Sqdn Ldr A.G. Williams attacked the German battleship *Tirpitz* with 12,000lb bombs. There were several direct hits and within a few minutes the ship capsized and sank. One of our aircraft is missing.' The following day the national and provincial press went wild. Headlines in the *Daily Telegraph*, for instance, ran: '*Tirpitz* sunk by 29 Lancasters 3 Direct Hits by 12,000lb bombs. Battleship Capsizes: one plane lost'. The accompanying text described 'a triumph of aerial precision attack from a great height, possibly about 16,000ft. . . . Yesterday only the keel and some part of the bottom of the *Tirpitz* could be seen above water.' One hit had been achieved amidships, another in the bows and a third towards the stern, with near misses probably causing the battleship to turn turtle, 'so violent is the explosive effect of these bombs when they burst in the water', and Barnes Wallis was named as the designer of the destructive weapon. The film unit pilot, Flt Lt Buckham, described seeing three hits and further explained: 'Her guns had been firing like blazes when we first arrived, but after the first bomb hit her the guns stopped firing. Not a shot came up after that. Smoke began pouring up.'

Even as the early leader writers were fashioning their script, photographs taken by a PRU Mosquito at 1150 on 12 November were presenting spectacular proof of success. *Tirpitz* had undoubtedly 'capsized to port', with about 700ft of her hull exposed, and was lying in 8–9 fathoms of water. 'The centre and starboard propellor shafts are visible, and quantities of oil cover the fjord.' Correlation of this evidence with other visual sources took time. The NID concluded that the cameras carried by attacking aircraft 'clearly showed two direct hits and one near miss all on the port side. A cinematograph film also showed the *Tirpitz* capsized to port.' Copies of a comprehensive 'confidential' interpretation report dated 21 November, 'Bomber Command Attack on Battleship Tirpitz at Tromso on 12.11.44', from the Central Interpretation Unit (CIU) at RAF Medmenham was distributed to 544 addressees and vastly expanded the NID summary. In several respects, not least lack of smoke in the

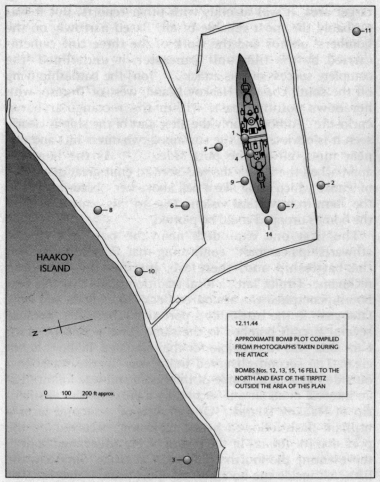

12.11.44

APPROXIMATE BOMB PLOT COMPILED
FROM PHOTOGRAPHS TAKEN DURING
THE ATTACK

BOMBS Nos. 12, 13, 15, 16 FELL TO THE
NORTH AND EAST OF THE TIRPITZ
OUTSIDE THE AREA OF THIS PLAN

HAAKOY
ISLAND

0   100   200 ft approx.

Operation Catechism, final Lancaster attack, 12 November 1944 target area, it was at odds with other reports. But it was probably the most reliable of all. Based narrowly on the bombers' photos and the work of the three cine cameras carried by the film unit Lancaster, it underlined 'the complete success of this attack . . . [on] the battleship lying off the south coast of Haakoy Island, west of Tromso, with her bows pointing east, within the rectangular boom enclosure'. 'Although only the after part of the ship is clearly seen it is obvious that she sustained two direct hits and one near miss, all on the port side. . . . As the bombers approached the *Tirpitz* she was seen to emit great quantities of smoke which hung like a pall above her, obscuring all but the stern from vertical vision.' Due to this, only sixteen of the bombs dropped could be plotted.

The first one exploded 'near the port end of the athwartships catapult', confirming that Tait did indeed hit the battleship and, therefore, justified his squadron nickname 'Tirpitz Tait': a local tradition holds that this first bomb penetrated the armoured decks to explode and rip a fatal gash in the battleship's port side. Thereafter, because several aircraft bombed at the same time, precisely which Lancaster was responsible for the tabulated Tallboys is not clear. The second observed burst was 'in the water just outside the southern side of the boom and was followed at an interval of about one second by a burst on the southern tip of Haakoy Island'. 'One eighth of a second later a brilliant flash followed by an explosion' occurred 'on the port side [of *Tirpitz*] in the region of the after range finder', representing the fourth bomb seen to strike. Similarly, the fifth 'fell inside the boom off the port beam'; 'two seconds later' the sixth 'fell between the boom and the shore'; 'a quarter of a second' after this the seventh 'fell inside the boom off the starboard quarter of the ship'. The eighth 'fell close inshore near No. 6'. Then, referring to a specific print, 'during the time interval between the falling of bombs No. 8 and 9 vertical photographs show that the *Tirpitz* plunged to starboard. A line of white froth is seen along the port side of the hull and four ripples on the starboard side of the stern'. The ninth, 'about one and a half seconds' after the eighth, 'made a near miss off the port quarter, close to Y turret. The bomb burst quickly developed into a high column of heavy black smoke. No other bomb that fell into the water produced a similar disturbance. . . . One and a half seconds later a bright flash was observed amidships which did not develop as a bomb burst and therefore may have been due to exploding ammunition . . . [though] a burst boiler or the inrush of sea water into the boiler rooms would probably produce a similar result.' The tenth bomb 'fell close inshore' causing a 'great disturbance of water', the eleventh, twelfth and thirteenth 'fell in the water at least 1,000ft to the east of the ship'. The fourteenth bomb examined 'fell at a late stage of the attack and is estimated . . . to have been close to the stern'. 'Bomb No. 15 fell inshore on east side of Haakoy Island and No. 16 fell slightly south of No. 12.'

The final photos taken by the film unit Lancaster 'show the *Tirpitz* capsized in her boom protected berth, with the greater part of the smoke having blown away'. The photographic evidence as a whole showed that 'regular gunfire appears to come from the central part of the ship until bomb No. 4 has fallen, and then spasmodically until a very late stage of the attack'. Two flak ships, 'one S.W. of Grindoy Island and one off the east coast of Haakoy Island', fired continuously, so did 'a medium sized vessel west of the battleship and . . . a large vessel, possibly the floating workship *Neumark*, off the N.E. tip of Haakoy Island'. 'Land batteries' were active on Haakoy. Late film unit aircraft shots 'show that a medium vessel has moved near to the boom enclosure where the *Tirpitz* had turned over onto her port side'. The report concluded: 'As only the after part of the ship is visible during that attack and even that becomes rapidly obscured in smoke and explosions, more bombs may well have fallen on the target.'

A month after the operation, HQ 5 Group undertook its own 'most careful analysis of release point photographs, and the positions of the bomb strikes tally almost exactly with the evidence of C.I.U. Medmenham and with evidence from other sources'. It concentrated, however, on the distribution of the bombs, not their relation to the target. In forwarding the detailed plots to the SASO Air Cdre S.C. Elworthy on 13 December, Wg Cdr D.S. Richardson felt that a change between the point at which the wind was found and bomb-release would explain 9 Squadron's pattern: 'I suggest that only the first 50 per cent of the aircraft to attack will have had a clear run and a reasonably clear AP and that smoke must have made subsequent aiming very difficult.' This took into account the fact that 9 Squadron bombed after 617. Richardson thought that 9 Squadron aimed 'with a 20 mph vector error set on their bombsight at a target probably obscured by smoke'. Presumably Richardson had not seen the post-operational crew reports, and Elworthy was not impressed. The following day, he observed to the AOC that 'three bombs out of ten, with an error of less than 300yds, does not appear reasonable'. Cochrane responded on 16 December by instructing him that 'the Squadrons should not see the bomb plot of the other Squadron' and approving his SASO's draft individual letters to them, which he sent two days later. The 9 Squadron plot showed only one bomb within 200yds of the Mean Point of Impact, seven of the remaining nine within 700yds. Cochrane pronounced this 'highly unsatisfactory'. In his letter to the squadron, Elworthy 'noted that the M.P.I. is some 300 yards offset from the target, equivalent to a vector error of 20 miles per hour or a wind of 340deg/17 instead of 028deg/27, which was found by the aircraft'. In spite of Richardson's plea, Elworthy considered it 'unlikely' that 'so considerable a change' should have occurred over the target and believed that bomb aimers would have noticed 'a vector error of 20 miles an hour'. Moreover, even if this vector did exist, 'the pattern of bombs round the M.P.I. should have been much closer than that plotted'. The SASO wanted 'a thorough investigation' to determine the cause of the errors: '. . . all crews in their raid reports claimed that the ship or a portion of the ship was in their sights when they released their bombs'.

Using the SABS Mark IIA sight, 617 had a more satisfactory distribution. No ground detail appeared on Tait's 'release point frame' but 'the bombing frame is centred almost exactly over the target and shows that the bomb must have fallen very close to it'. Furthermore, 'strong evidence from various sources' indicates that this bomb did hit the ship. K-King of 617 had a photographic malfunction, but seven bombs were calculated to have fallen within 200yd of the MPI and the rest within 700yd. There were, though, a number of line errors, and this tendency had been experienced during 'recent practices with the SABS'. Elworthy explained to both squadrons that 'each individual plot is likely to be accurate to within 200 yards', or put another way liable to a radial error of 200yd. This does seem to undermine the precise conclusions of the analysis.

An interesting personal account of the operation appeared in November's *'V' Group News*. The writer noted that, in 'pleasant contrast' to the pouring rain of 29 October, 'the weather was fine and clear for take-off . . . [which] was to prove an omen'. He went on to explain that with aircraft distributed over three airfields and to avoid congestion, individual Lancasters set off immediately for the first turning point at North Unst. In an effort to maintain some sort of force cohesion, each aircraft had its navigational lights on and flew at 'the most economical cruising speed' of 185 RAS during the first part of a 'route studded with flame floats'. Nevertheless, aircraft did get isolated and off track. Twilight at the Norwegian coast allowed accurate map reading to replace dead reckoning and in broad daylight the attackers crossed mountains only for 'large areas of strato-cumulus' to become 'depressingly evident' and every lake (including that detailed as the rendezvous) to be covered in stratus. The navigator's task became more complicated. 'Map reading in the mountains, particularly when they were snow-covered and the lakes frozen, is tricky.' 'The first view of Tromso therefore, with no cloud and no smoke, and the *Tirpitz* in her anchorage, massive, black and unmistakable, was better than any crew had dared to hope for, and the job was then as good as done'. Thus 'the inglorious career of one of the largest and most heavily armed and armoured ship afloat . . . was brought to an end'.

Later, the NID produced a more precise summary of that 'end'. During the attack with 'heavy calibre bombs', *Tirpitz* sustained two direct hits on the port side at 0942, 'one on the A/C catapult and one abreast of B turret. A few seconds later she listed 15deg–20deg to port. By 0945 she was listing about 30deg or 40deg. At 0950 the list was 60deg–70deg and the list was increasing rapidly.' Two minutes later, the battleship 'capsized to port at an angle of 135deg'. She had 'grounded fore and aft and sank amidships into the hollow which had not been sufficiently filled up, causing the port bilge keel to carry away'. The report speculated that 'considerable changes had occurred in the sea bottom' due to near misses – Wallis's projected camouflet effect – 'particularly in the artificial filling of the hollows'.

No full account or balanced judgement of the sequence of events off Haakoy [island] on 12 November 1944 could be complete without German reports and assessments, many of which were not examined until post-war. In the immediate aftermath, fragmentary information became available, and the picture gradually built up over the following two years. An intercepted wireless message at 2330 on the fateful day indicated that 596 survivors had thus far been rescued, but that loss of life was undoubtedly high. The final, official German count would be 971 dead, though several German and English sources maintain 1204. Twenty-eight of those were the acting captain and his senior staff (including the second-in-command, senior signals officer and chaplain) who were trapped in the armoured command centre, when buckled exit doors could not be opened. Sub Lt Bernhard Schmitz, one of those to study the approaching bombers through binoculars or telescope while they remained beyond range of the main armament, had a lucky escape. Before the ultimate disaster, he left the bridge for the chartroom. Although several explosions had already occurred and structural damage on and around the bridge was severe, Schmitz remained convinced that in shallow water *Tirpitz* could never sink. When orders to abandon ship came, he managed to swim clear of the stricken vessel, almost two hours later being picked up from the buoy to which he was clinging. Around him flotsam and dead bodies swirled and the 'terrible sight' of the capsized vessel some 150m away faced him. Unlike him, many men who had escaped the carnage on board failed to survive in the water.

The clearest account of the battleship's death throes came from another survivor, Lt Fassbender, the senior flak officer, who wrote a detailed account on 4 December of her last hours. He acknowledged that non-essential personnel and equipment, such as torpedo warheads and the ship's aircraft, had been disembarked. Damage sustained from the Tallboys on 15 September and 29 October meant that 'a considerable amount' of water was still being carried fore and aft, and Fassbender calculated that *Tirpitz* was already listing 1 degree to port before the attack.

At 0800 LT (0700 GMT) 'clear, cloudless, very good visibility' prevailed, with a light south-west wind. Shortly afterwards a report came through from the observer organisation that a single Lancaster had been seen in the Bodo area 200 miles to the south; 15mins later three more were observed near Mosjoen flying east (a further 100 miles south and 300 miles from Tromso). Given that the bombers were dispersed and all heading towards Sweden, the possibility of an overflight to the USSR could not be discounted. But *Tirpitz* feared a repeat of the 29 October raid: 'the circumstances are similar – time of day, weather and approach'. So flak guns were put on preliminary alert and urgent efforts made to secure clarification of the situation from the observer authorities. Fighter protection at this early stage (0815) was sought, too. Ten minutes later, four more Lancasters were reported on a north-easterly course in the Mosjoen area, which 'strengthened our suspicions that the enemy intended to attack'. Urgent consultation now took place between the battleship's flak commander and 'the main observer post' and another request for fighter protection was sent to the divisional control centre at Bardufoss – in vain. Some secondary sources state that Weber telephoned the Luftwaffe commander, Maj Ehrler. No direct threat to *Tirpitz* had yet been decreed. Nevertheless, at 0840 the flak alarm was sounded 'as a precaution'. A curious report, originating from an army coastal battery at 0854, that seven single-engined monoplanes were approaching from the north-east 50km (31.25 miles) away, raised additional fears of a simultaneous carrier attack, and led to an air-raid alert not only for *Tirpitz* but also Tromso a minute later. Although the observer organisation signalled at 0900 that the situation remained unclear, at 0902 *Tirpitz* went to action stations. Three minutes later, 20–25 Lancasters in 'open formation' were identified 120km (75 miles) south of the battleship flying on a north-easterly course. Almost 70km (43.75 miles) away, the aircraft turned towards *Tirpitz*. This was 617 Squadron in the van. Fassbender held that 'from the time of the first sighting, fighter protection had been requested continuously via the main observer post', which at 0912 spotted a second formation (9 Squadron). Both enemy formations were flying at an estimated 2,500–3,000m (7,500–9,000ft) – a gross underestimate, which may well explain the subsequent inaccurate salvoes from *Tirpitz*'s main armament. Finally, at 0915, a signal arrived: 'Enemy formation over Bardufoss, therefore impossible for fighters to take off'. With the Lancasters now clearly visible, Capt Weber told the ship's company that fighters had been requested. More economy with the truth. Ten minutes later, at 0925, according to *Tirpitz* the first fighter was reported airborne with more set to follow. At 0927, Weber broadcast once more: 'We are expecting a heavy air attack. The Ship's Company of the *Tirpitz* will fulfil its duty again this time and prepare a hot reception for the four-engined bombers.' Exactly at that moment 'smoke flares' were seen from the first formation 40km (25 miles) distant, and the attack developed from starboard on a bearing of 60–70 degrees.

At 0938, Weber ordered the gunnery officer to open fire at will, and two minutes afterwards the main armament did so at 21km (13.1 miles) to produce the 'orange puffs' or 'orange clouds' noted by 617 Squadron crews. The secondary armament and heavy flak guns joined in at 15km (9.4 miles). Fassbender admitted that, although correct for range, the main armament's shells burst too low, and the secondary armament proved ineffective. The Lancasters flew steadily on, although one aircraft 'was observed to be shot down' on the approach, probably Fg Off Coster of 9 Squadron – the aircraft did survive. The battleship's medium and light flak guns 'came into operation mostly only after the bombs had been dropped' and the aircraft came within effective range.

Fassbender then produced details that were quoted verbatim in the NID report and therefore date the latter firmly as post-war. At 0942 'a stick of bombs' fell 'mostly inside the net enclosure'; 'two direct hits are observed on the port side, one on the aircraft catapult and one abreast B turret. . . . A few seconds later [*Tirpitz*] listed heavily [15–20 degrees] to port'. A 'marked decrease in defensive fire' ensued, but never entirely ceased until shortly before the warship capsized. When the first bombs hit, damage control parties were instructed to correct the trim by flooding. At about 0945, the list became 30–40 degrees and Weber ordered evacuation of the lower decks. Within five minutes the list increased to 60–70 degrees.Then, dramatically and mortally, the 700-ton C turret exploded and arched upwards into the water. No hits had been recorded in that area, so Fassbender assumed that 'armaments' (ammunition) had caught fire.

Almost immediately, at 0952, *Tirpitz* capsized to lie at an angle of about 135 degrees. A few men balanced precariously on the upturned hull, but many (including Schmitz) 'tried to reach land by swimming or with the assistance of floats or objects drifting around'. The first rescue boats were on the scene in about fifteen minutes. No more bombs were dropped after the battleship capsized, although one aircraft (the film unit Lancaster) continued to circle at an estimated 2,000m (6,560ft). Fassbender concluded tersely: 'Armament was on the whole efficient. Fighter protection lacking. There was no smoke cover.' However, Midshipman Willibald Völsing from the Gunnery Fire Control Section later maintained that 'the radar elements of the Fire Control system had been adversely affected by the buffeting received in the [previous] attacks

Tirpitz had endured, plus the effect of the topography of the Tromso area'. He held that accurate information could not therefore be relayed to the senior gunnery officer on 12 November and was 'amazed' when the main armament opened fire. Völsing concluded that the salvoes had been 'laid manually into the designated Zone One', which explained why they exploded below and behind the bombers. Inspection teams found that bomb 'craters' (*sic*) – indication of more than one 'wide' – on Haakoy measured 30m wide 3 10m deep in rocky ground. This gave an indication of the massive holes blasted in the seabed below the battleship by near misses. On 1 April 1945, Zuba, who was on duty in the Gunnery Fire Control Section throughout the attack, compiled his account of events during Operation Catechism. Inevitably the bulk of his recollections concerned his personal experiences in the upturned hull. But he also independently supported much of what Fassbender wrote, though without his precise timings or clear sequence of events. After breakfast, Zuba had settled down to read a history book when a warning came of 'aircraft in the west', quickly followed by 'identified as German'. However, *Tirpitz* was not complaisant and Zuba noted that the flak alert was sounded, in spite of the reassuring message. An announcement followed which swiftly heightened tension: '20 [*sic*] four-engined [aeroplanes] 100km to the west. When these were then reported as Lancasters, Zuba reflected that they would inevitably be carrying '6 ton' (*sic*) bombs like those dropped '14 days earlier [when] we had driven off 30 British aircraft . . . [and] suffered only light damage'. Capt Weber told the ship's company that fighters had been requested and 'after a short while, which seemed to us along time, came the news that fighters had taken off'. Meanwhile, Zuba passed on information relayed to him by telephone: range 30,000m, 29,500m; height 3,000m, 2,900m. He concluded that the attackers 'were flying relatively fast'. At a range of 20,500m Anton and Bruno turrets fired the first salvo, followed by a second, after which the secondary armament opened up. Shortly afterwards came two severe jolts 'and everything [movable] flew past us in disarray . . . now the ship took on a heavy list, slowly and irresistably'. Very soon the angle was an alarming 18 degrees. As he and others in the section hung on to equipment to avoid falling, the electricity failed and Lt Mettergang in vain sought permission to get out. 'Suddenly, new terrible banging noises, new sounds of bombs falling, a more pronounced list, which resulted in the order "evacuate".' Taking off his headphones and grabbing his gas mask, Zuba rushed to the emergency exit. Agonising hours of entombment lay ahead.

Ashore on Kvaloy [island] preparing to set up an observation post, similar to that on high ground overlooking Kaa Fjord, Sub Lt Adalbert Brunner helplessly saw the air-raid warning flags hoisted on *Tirpitz* half an hour before the attack, the subsequent bombing and end of the battleship. He noted in particular the red lead on its exposed hull. Whether establishment of the post, for which equipment had arrived on 5 November, would have been decisive or not, lack of its installation showed uncharacteristic lassitude among the Germans. It was fortunate that Lt Cdr Walter Sommer was on Tromsoy awaiting a boat back to *Tirpitz*, when the raid developed. He managed to gather cutting equipment from Tromso and organised boats to carry it and its operators out to the stricken vessel. Largely due to his efforts, eighty-seven men were brought out from the hull; and the rescue efforts went on until 15 November, two days after the last person was found alive. The experiences of men trapped in the upturned vessel added poignancy to the story. Alfred Zuba was in a party that responded to tapping on the hull and established contact with rescuers above. He was comforted by the sound of oxyacetylene equipment being used, but terrified in the chilly confines of his metal tomb when it suddenly stopped. Eventually, it restarted and he squeezed through a narrow gap to look in relief at stars shining brightly in the crisp darkness. His panic, he learnt, had resulted from the need to change exhausted rescue teams, relays of which were required to complete the arduous task. Zuba was lucky. Not every trapped group could be reached before its oxygen ran out. For an estimated 100hrs rescuers attempted to cut their way through to fifty men with Lt

Lutz Mettergang, but were ultimately frustrated by *Tirpitz*'s thick, protective armour. Of those recovered, 165 bodies would soon be buried with full military honours in Tromso.

Captured documents showed that the naval communications office at Tromso reported rather inaccurately at 0946 that *Tirpitz* had blown up and capsized after being hit amidships. Virtually at once a series of investigations were instigated and attempts to escape blame launched. Failure to install and make workable the smoke-screen units that had been moved south came under close examination. But the terrain in the Tromso area would never have allowed an effective smoke-screen like that deployed at Kaa Fjord, so this avenue was not vigorously pursued. Lack of fighter cover was much more serious. The papers of Admiral Polar Coast confirmed that requests were made repeatedly by *Tirpitz* from 0815 onwards.

The British had learnt that one gruppe (wing) from a Jagdgeschwader (fighter group) of Bf 109Gs apparently flew into Bardufoss, 10mins flying time from *Tirpitz*, on 8 November. Planners then assumed the proverbial worst case scenario that III/JG 5 was at full nominal strength of forty, the number quoted in pre-operational briefings and associated documents. Movement of units between Luftwaffe airfields frequently took place, and one contemporary Norwegian report placed fifty-five aircraft at Bardufoss, not all of them fighters. That figure possibly included Ju 52s spotted by PRU flights, He 111 bombers and Focke Wulf Fw 189 reconnaissance machines also known to use the base. They certainly included a squadron of Ju 87s, whose commander had until recently exercised administrative control of Bardufoss. One of III/JG 5's squadrons (No. 10) had remained in the north at Alta and there is strong evidence that only one full squadron (No. 9) plus a number of raw newcomers under training, nominally formed into a 'commando' squadron, were at Bardufoss during Operation Catechism. The former was on 3min alert, the latter 15, but an additional 5–6mins taxiing was required from the fighters' distant dispersal points. Hence Lt Werner Gayko, 9 Squadron commander, estimated an astonishing 9min delay after the order to take off. His squadron, however, had been re-equipped with the Fw 190 armed with two 20mm cannon. About 20–24 single-engined Bf 109 and Fw 190 fighters may have fallen short of the number predicted by British intelligence, but they still posed a formidable threat to Lancasters with no mid-upper turret, even if flown by inexperienced pilots. One explanation for the fighters' tardy response, that a hill at one end of the runway restricted take-off, in reality could have proved no major handicap to aircraft with a fast rate of climb and sharp turning capacity. An undoubted drawback, though, was the inability of the different aircraft types to communicate with ground control and one another when airborne.

Unlike the RAF, the Luftwaffe did not grant temporary promotion to officers holding appointments, so it was not unusual to find Maj Heinrich Ehrler, a 28-year-old, much decorated veteran of the Arctic air war and Eastern Front with 199 'kills', as commander of III/JG 5. Ehrler's actions and the performance of his pilots on the day have come under close scrutiny ever since 12 November 1944 and remain controversial. Several commentators in after-years and many Luftwaffe colleagues from the time believe Ehrler became a convenient scapegoat for the incompetence of others. He was afterwards court-martialled in Oslo, charged with contravening standing orders by leaving a non-commissioned officer in control of the fighter command centre. Threatened with death, Ehrler was sentenced to three years imprisonment, but released after a month. Nevertheless, he was demoted and found himself posted to a Messerschmitt Me 262 jet squadron in Germany, where he showed signs of depression. On 4 April 1945, according to official records, Ehrler was shot down over Berlin during an American air raid. Anecdotal evidence, however, maintains that, out of ammunition, he told ground control he intended to ram a bomber, signing off: 'We'll meet again in Valhalla.' In later years, many under his command on 12 November 1944 expressed lingering dismay, verging on guilt, that they failed to save *Tirpitz*. Luckily for the

Lancaster crews, it seems increasingly clear that they were never given a reasonable opportunity to do so.

Precisely what happened to III/JG 5 at the crucial time, and why, remains obscure, mainly because comprehensive records have not survived. Written three weeks later, Lt Fassbender's account gives an incomplete patchwork of activity – and inactivity. Over two hours before the Tallboys started to fall, the first radar report of an incoming Lancaster to the south was logged, and *Tirpitz* learnt at approximately 0815 that more bombers had been detected at 0738 LT (0638 GMT). The time-lag of 40mins before that information reached the Haakoy anchorage indicates either slackness in the communication system or disbelief that *Tirpitz* was the target. Midshipman Zuba's revelation that the aircraft were initially thought to be friendly may partly explain this. But this could only have been a fleeting error. However, at no stage after learning of the first sighting did the battleship show complacency. As other information arrived piecemeal, Weber concluded that a repeat of Operation Obviate seemed likely. Clearly, nobody else did. Urgent contact between the warship, local and regional observer posts engendered no reaction. An hour after the initial radar reports, others identified aircraft flying northwards inside the Swedish border, heading for Norway. The celebrated 'fog of war' then came into play: watching eyes saw what they expected to see, enemy aircraft overflying Sweden to the Soviet Union. So, at 0900, 'the main observer post' informed *Tirpitz* 'situation still not clear'. Five minutes afterwards, officers on *Tirpitz* using powerful binoculars visually identified one enemy formation (617 Squadron) 75 miles away and a second (9 Squadron) in the same area at 0912. Not until 0925 did Fassbender record 'one fighter reported to have taken off, shortly afterwards more fighters'. No other mention of fighter activity appeared in his summary.

The sequence of events at Bardufoss may only be provisionally and sketchily deduced from fragmentary surviving reports, later personal recollections and the lengthy transcript of Ehrler's military trial, at which Fassbender and

Gayko were called to testify. Some of the timings appear illogical and contradictory, accounts at the court martial not easy to equate with the known facts. In one version, the siren at the air base sounded at 0910, with fighters beginning to take off 10mins later. Another, implying that the first firm information sent through Luftwaffe channels to Bardufoss arrived at 0918, holds that an NCO with inadequate maps at his disposal wrongly plotted the enemy aircraft far to the north near Hammerfest in the vicinity of *Tirpitz*'s old berth in Kaa Fjord. Not until this error had been corrected did Ehrler order his pilots into the air, at 0923. But Ehrler himself reported taking off in a Bf 109 at 0925 and, once aloft, looked back to see the other aircraft still 'parked'. He could not know that they were being further delayed by a Ju 88 or Ju 52 (recollections of the type vary) coming in to land. Subsequently, one of the five charges levelled against Ehrler was that he failed to provide leadership by waiting for more fighters to take off. For, undoubtedly, he now set off for Bals Fjord alone. He later claimed to have carried out a wide search but failed to locate any bombers, could not contact anybody else because his radio malfunctioned (an assertion not believed at his court-martial), but did pursue a Lancaster to the Swedish border, which would put him east of Bardufoss at approximately 1015. He then evidently flew on to Alta, his original destination before putting down at Bardufoss that morning. Gayko, though, maintained in after years that his gruppe commander landed at Bardufoss again immediately, which seems more likely given his time in the air, distance covered and fuel capacity.

In the meantime, other fighters had taken off. Gayko, still suffering the painful after-effects of the previous night's mess party, heard the alert in his quarters and dashed to dispersal in a car. There he discovered that eighteen fighters had already gone, but one machine remained on the ground with engine trouble. Gayko pulled rank and eventually got airborne at 0930, according to his log book, some 10mins after the others. But this does not square with the report that the order to take off came at 0923, with an ensuing time-lag of about 9mins. This would put the respective takeoffs of the seventeen aircraft (not including Ehrler) and Ehrler himself at around 0932 and 0942, which seems more likely. A non-commissioned officer in his squadron, Heinz Orlowski, noted circling for some time before the arrival of his commander and then setting off towards 'smoke' in the north. Gayko had shared a car from his headquarters with Capt Franz Dörr who, after visiting the command centre to assess the situation, took off with the adjutant Lt Kurt Schulze to lead the 'commando' *ad hoc* squadron of trainees. Even given that his diversion to the command centre overlapped with Gayko's commandeering of a troublesome aircraft at dispersal, Dörr could not have taken off before about 0945. Fassbender's contention that several fighters were in the air shortly after 0930 seems reasonable, therefore: 9 Squadron and the 'commando' squadron were already up awaiting leaders. Fassbender's assertion, based on an unidentified source, that the departure of fighters had been delayed because an 'enemy formation [was] over Bardufoss' and Gayko's subsequent claim that he had seen four-engined aircraft 'above the airfield' seem corroborative and conclusive. However, visibility was extremely clear on 12 November and *Tirpitz*'s officers undoubtedly identified the bombers 75 miles away. In his statement, Gayko used the word 'über' which can mean 'beyond' as well as 'above'. Fassbender may well have misunderstood, others mistranslated the word. This would fit the known facts. Bardufoss lies about 60 miles south of Tromso, and RAF records put the Lancasters no closer than 25 miles east of the German base as they flew north from the rendezvous lake.

Once the German pilots became airborne, the orders issued to them become important. Bardufoss appears not to have launched the fighters until specific Luftwaffe orders at 0918, followed by a 5min hiatus due to inaccurate plotting. One later report holds that fighters were initially sent to the Norwegian border (which would be consistent with them being despatched before the bombers turned along Bals Fjord towards *Tirpitz*); a second says that they were sent 200 miles north to Kaa Fjord. Gayko and Schulze reported reaching the vicinity of Tromso. They saw no enemy, but Gayko identified 'a huge ship lying hull upwards'. He had seen flak bursts in the distance during his climb and flew immediately towards them. Scanning the sky from altitude, it would have been possible to miss single bombers below, but if Gayko did go straight to Haakoy his declared take-off time must indeed be suspect. Leaving Bardufoss at 0930, he would have been there before the last aircraft bombed and *Tirpitz* capsized; the 0910–0930 version of events at Bardufoss thus lacks credibility. Orlowski in Gayko's squadron also recalled flying to Tromso and seeing no enemy. After rallying his clutch of trainees, if he did so, Dörr would have arrived even later.

Gayko's further assertion that his primary aim was not to defend the battleship, but to re-equip 9 Squadron, was apparently supplemented by his later claim that Tromso represented a restricted area and that *Tirpitz*'s position was not known to the Bardufoss units. This is not necessarily contradicted by reports that two fighters were fired on during training when they strayed into the Tromso defence zone. That zone was extensive, covering the various approaches and fjords, and the incidents did not necessarily occur close to Haakoy. After this débâcle, a liaison visit to the Tromso defence authority resulted in a special telephone being installed in the Bardufoss command centre. Even if there were no contingency plans to defend *Tirpitz*, it remains a bizarre outcome that in a 'gin-clear sky' no interceptions were made in the target area. Belated take-off, with the exception of Ehrler, and lack of clear orders seem the most feasible explanations.

Only one Lancaster pilot even saw a fighter, and that was after the attack finished. On 24 November, having been repatriated from Stockholm, Fg Off D.A. Coster RNZAF of 9 Squadron revealed that 'crossing to Sweden we were attacked by two Me 109s but were not hit'. His flight engineer, Sgt J.C. Pinning, later elaborated. Having decided to make for Sweden on 2½ engines, following the damage incurred attacking *Tirpitz*, Coster took the briefed withdrawal route south-west from Tromso, then hugged the Norwegian coast flying south before turning to port across desolate ground. This took the Lancaster 'close to' Bardufoss and shortly afterwards a Bf 109 made two passes from behind as the rear gunner engaged it and Coster corkscrewed to safety. When the bomber levelled out 'I saw another Me 109 coming straight at me', Pinning recalled. 'It made one pass from starboard, but didn't press his attack possibly because he thought we were a dead duck.' Coster flew on skilfully to put down his damaged machine in a small clearing on a pine-covered island.

The account of WS-T's crew members gives substance to sketchy reports ascribed to Gayko and Ehrler. The former held that he made two attacks on a four-engined bomber, but after managing a few shots each time was foiled by malfunction of his guns. Ehrler described pursuing a Lancaster to the Swedish border, but he deliberately did not overfly neutral territory in order to avoid a diplomatic incident; shooting down of Swedish aircraft by Gayko's wingman had recently 'generated much paperwork' according to Maj Knut Store. Coster's report, 'two Me 109s', raises another issue. Gayko's squadron may not after all have converted to Fw 190s. It is inconceivable that an experienced gunner like Sgt W.J. Jones would have mistaken one of those distinctive machines, with an air-cooled radial engine, for a Bf 109. Astonishingly, yet another version of events maintains that the German pilots did not learn of the whereabouts of *Tirpitz* until official recriminations gathered pace that evening. With Gayko, Schulze and Orlowski undoubtedly known to have been near Haakoy, it is utterly inconceivable that fellow pilots would have remained ignorant of their experiences after they landed. However, if 10 Squadron were indeed at Alta where III/JG 5 staff remained, this report could apply to it. Furthermore, if Ehrler flew on to Alta after the operation, this might also explain the story that fighters from Bardufoss were sent to that region (Kaa Fjord being close-by). To say the least, unravelling the movements of Bardufoss fighters on 12 November remains a challenge.

An interesting postscript surfaced in 1967. In a conversation with Plt Off A.E. Kell's W/Op, Fg Off D.E. Freeman, a former Norwegian resistance member, claimed responsibility for the non-appearance of the German fighters. When the Lancasters 'appeared over the mountains', as ordered via a coded message, he and others 'cut the timeline [*sic*] between the boat [*Tirpitz*], the shore radio station and the air base'. However, if they did so it need not have been decisive. The Germans had ample other sources of information about the developing attack.

Failure of the Luftwaffe to come to the battleship's aid remains both critical and debatable. Ehrler could not have been solely responsible. Significantly, several observer, flak and naval personnel were also court-martialled and sentenced to imprisonment after Operation Catechism. Not recognising that the bombers were closing on *Tirpitz*, in spite of the radar evidence and the precedent of 29 October, was the key. Whatever information reached Bardufoss, it did so belatedly. The weakness in the German administrative system appears to have been rigid adherence to dedicated Service chains of command. Information had to be passed up each line before being transmitted to another authority at the appropriate level. Thus, even if Weber did personally contact Ehrler before the attack developed – and there is tentative collateral evidence that the special phone in the Bardufoss ops room did ring that morning – the Luftwaffe commander could not have acted at that stage without orders from his own service. Furthermore, misplotting of the radar reports did not help. Fassbender recorded no positive reaction from 'the main observer post' until 0912. Overall, the confusion of reported and alleged messages has contrived to muddy the waters of understanding – possibly deliberately to protect the guilty.

To the British all of this had absolutely no relevance. At his morning planning conference on 13 November 1944, Air Vice-Marshal the Hon. R.A. Cochrane could announce that, after five years of effort, the beast had finally been slain.

EPILOGUE

THE CHASE IN
RETROSPECT

'**O**ur Tirpitz sunk', began an intercepted message
to German forces in the Aegean Islands on
16 November. It continued with acknowledgement
of the severity of the loss, but sought also to highlight
the warship's strategic achievements. 'Twelve [*sic*] super-
heavy bombs against the ship's side ripped the battleship
wide open and made it capsize. The ship is lying in shallow
water. The loss of the ship, which through its presence
in north Norway for two years tied down powerful
enemy forces and scored numerous defensive successes
against the British Air Force, is a severe blow to us.
The British state in their press that *Tirpitz* was always a
serious impediment to the freedom of movement of British
naval forces.'

PRU flights unequivocally confirmed *Tirpitz*'s fate, and
their graphic photographs of her upturned hull were soon
widely publicised. Referring to the final operation in *The
Listener* on 30 November, Sqn Ldr John Strachey wrote: 'You
will have seen from the pictures in the newspapers and on
the news-reels what a tiny target the *Tirpitz* looked. . . . The
sinking . . . has struck the imagination of the world.' He
scarcely exaggerated. Like the dramatic photos of the

breaching of the west German dams in May 1943, those of *Tirpitz*'s end had international, as well as national, impact. They were spectacular.

Excluding aborted attacks and those mounted more generally on dockyard areas in Wilhelmshaven and Kiel, RAF Bomber Command carried out nineteen operations in 1940–1, four in 1942 and three in 1944 specifically against *Tirpitz*; the Fleet Air Arm carried out one in 1942 (the attack at sea) and six in 1944. Overall, therefore, during the period May 1940–November 1944, British aircraft bombed, attempted to mine or torpedo the battleship on thirty-three occasions. Including approximately 300 twin-engined Whitley, Hampden and Wellington bombers 1940–1, over 700 RAF and FAA aircraft attempted to sink *Tirpitz* in harbour, another twelve to torpedo her at sea. Some 250 fighters acted as escorts for some of these raids. Still more fighters, flying boats and bombers mounted simultaneous diversionary operations. A wide variety of destructive schemes had been mooted, including separately the use of American B-17s and RAF Mosquitoes with a smaller version of Barnes Wallis's celebrated 'bouncing bomb'. On one occasion, two squadrons of Hampdens were despatched to the northern Soviet Union to attack *Tirpitz*. A special curio was that, as with the Dambusters Raid, one American pilot flew on each of the three 617 Squadron raids.

In the immediate aftermath of triumph, one newspaper leader concluded that 'she [*Tirpitz*] has had a luckless career'. Perhaps. The Germans were right to emphasise that she had tied down a considerable number of capital ships and escorts that could have been usefully deployed elsewhere. This, after all, was a root cause for Churchill's constant pressure to sink her. Grand Admiral Räder eschewed commerce-raiding and deliberately sent the battleship to Norway primarily to fulfil the role of containment. His plea to Hitler, in January 1943, for retention of the German capital ships and *Tirpitz* in particular, centred on the maritime concept of 'The Fleet in Being'. Räder's subsidiary aim of threatening Allied shipping in the Arctic was also successful. The battleship may have only made one aggressive foray, to Spitzbergen, but her sortie against PQ12, phantom operation on PQ17 and enforced suspension of Arctic convoys when insufficient naval escorts were available demonstrated her effectiveness in this respect. At the Admiralty, the Naval Intelligence Division lauded the destruction of *Tirpitz* 'just four years and two days after her completion'. Indirectly, it acknowledged Räder's achievement. 'Throughout the whole of her career she neither sank nor damaged a single British warship. She did, however, succeed by her mere presence in northern waters, in pinning down important British naval forces during a critical period of the war'. A hidden bonus for the Germans was inter-Allied friction over failure to run promised, regular convoys to the Soviet Union, which on occasions spilt over into expressions of outright anger from Stalin.

That the battleship was at length sunk, despite nit-picking that she was not totally submerged, is indisputable. But which Service, indeed which squadron and even which individual aircraft, did so has been and remains a matter of quite bitter contention. A generation later, a Ministry of Defence civil servant (Clive Ponting) revealed that acid memos between the two Services were still crossing his desk. And, to this day, 9 and 617 squadrons not only dispute which of them delivered the decisive blow, but also disagree over ownership of part of the battleship's bulkhead acquired after the war. Over the years, that item has been physically and ingeniously purloined by one squadron from the other on several occasions.

The important months for *Tirpitz* were April–November 1944. Despite the bravery of the X-craft crews, the battleship had only been temporarily disabled in September 1943. By March 1944 she was steaming again at 27 knots in trials. The Fleet Air Arm attack on 3 April (during which the Germans acknowledged sixteen hits or near-misses) undoubtedly did permanent damage to the battleship, though to what extent is unclear. That having been said, no report puts her speed above 20 knots thereafter.

Much has been made of the relatively slow speed of the Barracudas and their unsuitability for attacking a target like

Tirpitz. But Fleet Air Arm pilots, while accepting the machine's shortcomings, believed it provided 'a stable bombing platform'. The inadequacy of available bombs, until the arrival of Tallboy, has also been widely aired. None the less, on 24 August 1944 a 1,600lb AP might have been decisive if its defective fuse had worked and the full amount of explosive (instead of about half) had been contained in it. The potential of the Barracuda and the 1,600lb AP bomb was thus demonstrated and with luck could have succeeded.

What the four-engined Lancaster bomber and deep-penetration 12,000lb Tallboy did was to remove any element of luck, provided accuracy could be obtained. Without doubt a critical blow was struck on 15 September, when a large hole was made in the battleship's starboard bow. *Tirpitz* never again exceeded (possibly did not even attain) 10 knots; extensive and prolonged repairs would be required to make her operational once more, even if that were technically possible. For this operation, aircraft of 9 and 617 squadrons bombed close together – which particular Lancaster dropped the relevant Tallboy remains a matter of doubt. The post-operational bomb plot is inconclusive, visual observations sparse and uncorroborated. To pinpoint one of the Lancasters, therefore, must be a matter of faith. Wg Cdr Tait of 617 Squadron has been credited with the feat, but at least one other crew from that squadron holds that it was successful and another (later lost) could have been responsible. Nor should Flt Lt J.D. Melrose of 9 Squadron be forgotten. He did release Tallboy 'fractionally' after Tait in the van of the bombers.

Barnes Wallis had initially designed Tallboy to drop beside a target and burrow underneath it before exploding. On 3 November 1944, the NID believed that one dropped up to 100ft away could affect plates, seams and rivets to cause internal flooding. A near-miss during the 29 October operation, noted by the Germans, did cause underwater damage to *Tirpitz* and further reduce her effectiveness. But without doubt, Operation Catechism delivered the coup de grâce. There is a preponderance of evidence from the CIU

Medmenham photographic analysis, from local eye witnesses and from crew reports that up to three of the first gaggle's bombs hit the target. On this occasion, 617 Squadron undoubtedly did bomb first, followed by 9 Squadron. Admiral Polar Coast attributed the battleship's capsizing to 'a stick of bombs falling in the water on the port side', which caused her to adopt a fatal 135 degree list. 'Stick' may reasonably be interpreted as more than one bomb, though damage to the hull on the port side and an adjacent crater found in the sea bed could point to one decisive near-miss, as Wallis predicted in 1941. Post-war the Directorate of Naval Construction referred to the effect of direct hits 'aided by one near miss'. The German survivor, Lt Fassbender, recorded a 15–20 degrees list to port 'a few seconds' after two direct hits at 0942 LT. That list had increased to 30–40 degrees by 0945 and 60–70 degrees five minutes later. At 0952 *Tirpitz* capsized to lie at an angle of 135 degrees. The NID in its later summary added: 'Apparently considerable changes had occurred in the sea bottom from the effect of bombs which had fallen in the vicinity, particularly in the artificial filling of the hollows.' Consideration of both the hollow amidships and the sandy nature of the sea-bed would become central to attempts to determine precisely how the battleship capsized.

Interviewed post-war Rear-Admiral Peters, Flag Officer of the 1st Battle Group in Norway until October 1944, spoke of the 'official opinion . . . that the greatest initial damage was caused by five or six near misses, which blew in a considerable length of the port side below the waterline'. He held that a direct hit would not have 'opened up a sufficient extent of the ship's side to admit rapidly the large quantity of water necessary to cause this [capsizing]'. Capt Reinecke, chief of staff to Admiral Polar Coast until January 1944, also pointed to near misses off the port bow, which 'caused extensive unsymmetrical flooding and resulted in the ship capsizing to port'. Both Peters and Reinecke were relying heavily on a high-level naval investigation, albeit with narrow terms of reference, to which Peters contributed.

On 13 November 1944, Dönitz signalled Hitler that he

had already instigated an enquiry into the battleship's loss. The C-in-C believed that 'contrary to orders and reports *Tirpitz* had not been anchored sufficiently securely'. Four officers made lengthy submissions to that enquiry. On 16 November, Peters recalled that soundings of *Tirpitz*'s berth off Haakoy [island] after she arrived there had put 2m of water below the battleship's bow and stern at low water, 5–6m (16.6ft–20ft) under the keel. This led the warship's officers to conclude that she would at worst take on 'a heavy list' if bombed. Nevertheless, 'the relatively great depth below the middle of the ship was undesirable' and two solutions were considered: moving the warship south 'into more shallow water' or filling in 'the deep hollow under the midship section' using dredgers. Subsequent discovery that soft sand constituted the sea bottom proved highly significant. It seemed 'possible . . . in my opinion' that during the fatal attack *Tirpitz*'s keel 'did not meet sufficient resistance in the sea-bottom when the ship began to list'. This caused 'the inertia moment to increase and the ship to capsize' or, alternatively, that restraining cables had broken, which allowed the battleship to slip into deeper water. Peters admitted that this was supposition. Peter's figures were greatly at odds, however, with those put forward by Capt Junge and Vice-Admiral Nordmann.

Junge's report of 15 June noted that a planning conference in Tromso 28–30 September had recommended an anchorage off Haakoy. More detailed discussions were subsequently attended by *Tirpitz*'s navigation officer: 'When choosing the berth, the question of the arc of fire came into the foreground, as well as safeguards against sinking or capsizing.' During a conference on the battleship in Kaa Fjord at the beginning of October, Junge learnt that it was intended to position his ship 'in approximately an east–west direction . . . [to] enable all her guns to be brought to bear on the main lines of fire'. The day before *Tirpitz* moved south, he discovered that 'the desired arc of fire' would indeed prevail over safety. More than 8½ fathoms [51ft] would be beneath the battleship at the selected berth. Another berth with a maximum 6 fathoms depth existed closer to Haakoy, but this would unacceptably restrict the arc of fire. 'The safeguards against sinking or capsizing seemed to me to be very questionable', Junge protested, but was told that further tests would be carried out when the warship reached her new anchorage. Once there, 'the unfavourable contour was confirmed'. Dredgers would take about a week to fill in the required 30,000 tons of rubble, and this work had only just started when Junge left the ship on 4 November. Like Peters, he believed that 'the soft nature of the sea bed . . . possibly did not give the ship sufficient support on touching the bottom'.

Admiral Polar Coast (Vice-Admiral Nordmann) reviewed *Tirpitz*'s circumstances on 17 November. In the designated area, 'no uniformly level berth' existed. The first planned one would have placed the battleship along a deep channel, lying north–south. This was changed to another spot, where *Tirpitz* would be east–west with a hollow of 45ft beneath her amidships. But the warship did not 'take up the exact position . . . therefore the hollow was now 51ft' (Junge's declared depth), the fault being the responsibility of *Tirpitz*'s own officers. Dredgers did not commence work until 2 November, according to Nordmann – over two weeks later. Once their task had been completed, even with 'a heavy hit', it was thought that *Tirpitz* would right herself once she touched the bottom. But the job had not been done by 12 November.

The Sea Defence Commandant at Tromso, Capt Krüger, prefaced his remarks by drawing attention to eye-witness accounts 'that the portside outer hull was ripped open by a direct hit and several near misses'. He held that the ship keeled over 60–70 degrees following the lifting of C turret 20–25m from its mounting after an explosion, which caused 'heavier [*sic*] inrush of water and further rapid heeling over of the ship'. On 27 January 1945, the shipbuilding section of the German navy drew attention to reports that the sea-bed under *Tirpitz* comprised 5–6m of mud topped by 1m of sand, which contradicted claims that she had 3.5m of water beneath her and above firm ground: 'The different construction of the sea-bottom . . . [was] an obvious cause for the capsizing.' Before January 1945, however, Dönitz's inquiry had already decided that 'the actual depth of the prepared berth did not conform to the requirements and directions of the commander-in-chief'. Thus it was evidently agreed how *Tirpitz* capsized, but not why; specifically at which point flooding reached critical proportions.

On 21–22 May 1945, an RAF team led by Air Cdre C.N.H. Bilney carried out an investigation into the sinking of *Tirpitz*. Apart from examining the wreck, it interviewed the Chief of Staff to the Admiral Polar Coast (Capt Lieseman), Chief of Staff Coast Defence, Tromso (Lt Cdr Monsen) and the Chief Engineer Tromso Dockyard (Barade Voss), in the absence of members of *Tirpitz*'s crew, who were then back in Germany. The three Germans confirmed that *Tirpitz* had been so severely damaged in Operation Paravane on 15 September that it would have been impossible to get her back to Germany for major repairs. She was therefore 'moved to the Tromso Fjord to be used as a floating fortress at the position in which she was sunk'. They maintained that the battleship made the journey from Kaa Fjord under her own power at 8–9 knots. That slow speed was 'due to the very heavy damage to the vessel's bows caused by a hit from a 12,000lb bomb, supplemented by damage to the starboard propeller shaft tunnel from midget submarine attack'. A warning of the Lancasters' approach on 12 November had been issued when they were near Bodo, giving ample time to alert the defences, but 'no smokescreen apparatus was available at the ship's new anchorage'. Failure of the Bardufoss fighters to intervene thus becomes even more puzzling. The only logical explanation remains that information was passed through different chains of command and that of the Luftwaffe did not function quickly enough. A similar delay of 2½hrs had occurred during the Albacore attack on 9 March 1942.

The German officers agreed that the first bomb struck 'almost amidships' quickly followed by a second hit 'abaft and to port of C turret', the latter starting a fire. 'Immediately after being hit' the ship began to list to port.

'Considerable damage' then occurred to the ship's side, presumably through near-misses. 'Owing to the number of casualties [1,000 out of the 1,900 crew on board at the time of the attack], shock and the rapidity of events, no clear-cut picture was available as to the exact sequence of events or damage sustained.' Those interviewed had not seen copies of reports sent via Oslo to Berlin. But they were able to supply valuable and, in some respects unique, details from information that had come to them. 'The bomb hits pushed the armoured decks downwards and opened a gap between the side of the ship and the decks. Twenty minutes [all other accounts put this at about 10mins] after the first hit, an explosion occurred and the cumulative damage tore a hole 120ft long on the port side of the ship from deck to keel'. 'Very shortly' after this, the battleship 'turned turtle to port, rolling through approximately 140degs, with the superstructure embedded in the sea bottom'.

The RAF investigating team summarised the position in May 1945. The superstructure and turrets remained buried in the mud. The starboard bilge keel was 'almost vertical', and most of the starboard side armour had been removed and taken back to Germany. So far as visible damage was concerned, the Tallboy at Kaa Fjord had destroyed 100ft of the bow 'and the plating [was] dished for a further 50ft aft'. An intriguing passage about the effect of a near-miss then appeared in Bilney's report. It had 'severely dished in the outer bottom over a length of approximately 50ft just above the bilge keel'. An analysis of the effect of this damage incidentally gave a good indication of the strength of Tirpitz's construction. 'The main frames are badly sprung inwards, and had it not been for the welded construction of this vessel, serious leakage would have occurred. In this ship the plates are butt welded together, and they are also welded to the stringers thus making a homogeneous but flexible structure.' The outer bottom had been 'driven in to a maximum depth of approximately 4ft', yet no significant leakage had happened and no plates had been 'torn apart'. A close examination of the dishing led to the conclusion that the Tallboy had exploded about 60ft away, but 'the ship's structure has stood up remarkably well'. This is, of course, contrary to the NID's expressed opinion that a near-miss up to 100ft from the ship would cause internal flooding. 'Some slight dishing' about 120ft forward of the propellers was also observed.

Bilney acknowledged that cracking in the starboard propeller shaft and its being out of alignment were legacies of the X-craft attack. By implication, therefore, that operation had permanently reduced the battleship's capability. There was evidence of underwater repairs in this area having been carried out in Kaa Fjord. This is consistent with intelligence reports at the time and the reasonable conclusion that the warship was being restored to operational efficiency. The investigation team noted that a fuller report could not be presented until divers had 'thoroughly' inspected the port side, most of which was totally submerged. No trace of concrete had been found in the wreck and this supported the three German officers' assertion that, contrary to intelligence reports, none had ever been used to repair damage.

Looking more widely, Bilney stated that ten Tallboy craters were visible from the air and a 'broken' Tallboy had been found lying in the mud: 'This bomb was scored on its nose, and the body was slightly flattened, the fracture having occurred a few inches behind the spigot hole in the body.' When interviewed, the German bomb disposal officer responsible for dealing with it in 1944 said he believed that the Tallboy had hit the side of the ship and ricocheted 200yds to the present position. Bilney concluded: 'This seems to be a highly probable explanation, as it is most likely that the bomb would have broken up on the muddy foreshore and as the rear half of the bomb would have detonated in close proximity the ship with .07 secs delay fuzing, this would account for the third apparent hit shown on the strike photographs.' He added : 'The informants expressed the opinion that the ship would not have capsized had not an internal explosion occurred, caused by a fire stared from the second bomb hit' – a contentious belief.

Another team of investigators, from the Directorate of Naval Construction, examined the wreck 4 September–15 October 1945 and similarly interviewed witnesses. Two Norwegian residents of Kvaloy (Anton and Edmund Rikkardson) explained that a hit just forward of the bridge, slightly to starboard, devastated the superstructure, another on the port side about 20ft inboard caused the battleship initially to list and a third occurred on the starboard side of the quarter deck after *Tirpitz* had listed some 25 degrees. The Norwegians reported two explosions, one in the region of C turret. None of this conflicted substantially with other observations.

In his evidence, the master of the German salvage vessel *Scheibenhof* admitted to considerable dismay at finding only thirty-six intact bottles in the wine store after an elaborate operation to gain access following removal of intervening plating on the wreck. More seriously, he agreed that several of the battleship's officers, liberty men and technical staff were ashore during the final attack. He had spoken to Lt Schulz, who had escaped from the engine room and believed that a direct hit on the port side had caused the warship to list 45 degrees, where she remained until C turret blew up. When the order came to abandon ship, watertight doors and hatches were flung open and this probably led to a fatal influx of water that caused *Tirpitz* to capsize – yet another explanation for that final movement. Explosions, however severe, would not have been decisive without an unacceptable flood of water. The DNC team concluded by warning that the '16 craters' found around the battleship may not all have been made during the November attack.

Analysis of aircrew reports of 12 November, not least that of the film unit Lancaster pilot who specified three hits, is consistent with Bilney's conclusion that two bombs penetrated the armoured deck and a third ricocheted from the port side. Nor does it conflict with other evidence contained in the German or British reports. The Central Interpretation Unit, after examining still and film photographic evidence, put the decisive strikes among the first releases of Tallboy. Excluding Flt Lt R.E. Knights, who reported his own near miss, five 617 Lancasters bombed between 0841 and 0842: Tait and Lee (whose crew did not see their bomb burst), Gingles and Castagnola, who both claimed direct hits, and Sanders, who believed that two bombs including his own 'appeared to hit the edge of the ship'. Undoubtedly, the three successful strikes came from these aircraft. Knights, who remained in the area until the last bomb had been dropped, observed two internal explosions at 0851 and 0853, which roughly coincides with several German reports and that of Fg Off D. Macintosh from 9 Squadron. There is no dispute that the ship did capsize at about 0852. The lingering doubt must be whether the final movement resulted from these internal explosions, as Bilney's witnesses averred, one near-miss intimated by the naval staff or the series ('stick') of near-misses reported by Admiral Polar Coast.

Tirpitz capsized approximately 11mins after the first Tallboy fell. For her to do so, an extraordinary amount of water must quickly have flooded the ship. Once she began to list, the shaky nature of the sea-bed became particularly relevant, its lack of grip accentuating further movement. Many contemporary reports and later investigations point to one or more near-misses holing the port side, and this would account for the early progressive listing. The violent explosion, which lifted C turret and clearly stemmed from a direct hit, seemingly induced the final lurch.

It is quite possible, however, that by then *Tirpitz*'s fate had already been sealed through the lack of watertight integrity, established by the Directorate of Naval Construction. For Tallboy, read iceberg, and a doomed passenger liner comes to mind. Claims of 'twelve' or even 'a stick' of lethal bombs opening up the port side of the German warship lose credibility on examination of the photographic evidence presented by RAF Medmenham. Only two near-misses were plotted to port. But by 0945 LT (0845 GMT), the battleship had been so badly holed that she was listing 30–40 degrees and the lower decks were evacuated. Watertight doors between bulkheads, identified by the DNC report, would then have been opened. Not all may have been closed again in the haste to escape and the flooding produced by underwater damage on the port side may thus have been exacerbated. The explosion of C turret, gaps opened up by the structural separation of decks from ship's sides and loosening of the unstable sea-bed all accelerated the process.

There was, thus, no single cause of *Tirpitz*'s ultimate loss. Lack of watertight integrity in her construction, which provokes a tantalising image of a military *Titanic*, was exploited by a combination of Tallboy near-misses (nos 2, 5, 7, 9 and 14 on the Medmenham plot) and hits (nos 1 and 4) which induced a mortal amalgam of rapid, unacceptable flooding and shifting of the sandy sea-bed below. The speed of *Tirpitz*'s sinking remains astonishing, though, for unlike *Hood* her back was not broken.

Another salient question is not when the battleship sank (undoubtedly on 12 November 1944), but at what point she ceased to be a viable fighting unit. In this context, reliable intelligence is literally vital. As the Naval Intelligence Division explained in a post-war analysis, captured German documents showed that many reports about *Tirpitz* were 'inaccurate', 'misleading', 'untrue' – words that pepper the entire comprehensive survey about 'Admiral von Tirpitz'. However, critically, not all the fallacies had been detected at the time and this led to 'erroneous' conclusions in good faith. A combined British and American assessment of 4 March 1944 believed that 'the repairs the Germans have in hand . . . are evidently undertaken with the object of enabling the ship to steam under her own power. She could maintain a speed of 18 knots on one engine.' Noting that information received in the weeks prior to 15 October 1944 was 'on the whole reasonably accurate', even in retrospect, the analysis quoted a NID report of 13 September 1944: despite known damage, 'the possibility of her carrying out a limited operation cannot, however, be ruled out'. As late as 3 November, the NID agreed that more serious damage had been sustained, but still referred to repairs 'necessary to make her fully operational'. *Tirpitz* apparently still posed a substantial threat and the strategic arguments deployed since 1939 remained valid, based on contemporary, available information. Whether that should have or, indeed could have, been more rigorously interpreted is not the issue. The Allies feared until her battered bridge nosed into the sand off Haakoy [island] that she might yet regain sea-worthiness.

It all began in the United States with Brig-Gen William Mitchell's contention that bombers could sink battleships, as Bomber Command inferred with a touch of hyperbole: 'A new stage in the aircraft versus battleship was reached on 12 November [1944]'. Inter-Service and inter-squadron disputes should not obscure the fact that, in the words of 'V' Group News, this was a 'magnificent achievement'. However, without in any way undermining the skill and determination of the Lancaster crews during autumn 1944, the escalating nature of damage inflicted by the X-craft and Fleet Air Arm aircraft, in the face of formidable opposition, prior to the final trio of operations needs to be underlined. Nor should the bravery of the early bomber crews, 1940–2, and the constant contribution of PRU personnel be forgotten. The passive but invaluable work done by the Norwegian resistance should certainly not be overlooked. Ultra intercepts were priceless, but not always accessible. Men and women on the spot plugged gaps by supplying details of movements and dispositions not obtainable from intercepted transmissions. The facilities and assistance of the Soviet authorities ought not be lightly discounted either.

With the information available to them at the time, Allied planners were entitled to believe that *Tirpitz* remained a potent threat right to the end. Furthermore, not until September 1944 did the Germans admit to themselves that she could no longer be made operationally active. Even then, some hoped that she might yet be repaired. After Operation Catechism, those dreams were irrevocably dashed. With 'a great relief', Winston Churchill could then announce that we 'have this brute where we have long wanted her'.

On 22 March 1945, a PRU aircraft undertook 'a post mortem sortie' to bring back 'remarkable low oblique photographs . . . [showing] capsized hull of battleship decently draped in snow'. 'Sic transit gloria mundi', (So passes away earthly glory), a staff officer ironically added.

APPENDIX

BOMBERS INVOLVED IN ATTACKS, 1942–4

Notes:
(i) Figures do not include early returns or aborted operations, nor the reported Soviet attack of 10/11 February 1944.
(ii) 'Lost in Action' does not include ditched aircraft from which crews were saved or several badly damaged machines subsequently scrapped.
(iii) Under 'bombers' are included bomb-carrying fighters, which directly attacked *Tirpitz*. Excluded are Hellcats and Corsairs that carried bombs but strafed and bombed adjacent positions during the Goodwood operations.
(iv) Precise fighter figures are impossible to determine, but approximately 250 Corsairs, Fireflies, Fulmars, Hellcats, Seafires and Wildcats supported the Fleet Air Arm operations during 1944. Of these, 5 Corsairs, 1 Firefly and 1 Seafire were lost. In addition, 1 Corsair and 1 Hellcat ditched, all crew members being saved.
(v) During the 1942 Halifax operations Hudsons, Beaufighters and a Catalina carried out diversionary attacks. Seafires and Swordfish flew fleet protection patrols during the Fleet Air Arm operations.
(vi) Overall, 1940–4 the RAF used 16, the FAA 11, types of aircraft against *Tirpitz*.

APPENDIX

Date	Command	Aircraft	Location	Lost in Action
1942				
30 January	RAF	7 Stirling 9 Halifax	Foetten Fjord	0[1]
9 March	FAA	12 Albacores	off Lofoten Is.	2
30/31 March	RAF	33 Halifaxes	Foetten Fjord	6
27/28 April	RAF	30 Halifaxes 11 Lancasters	Foetten Fjord	4 Halifaxes[2] 1 Lancaster
28/29 April	RAF	21 Halifaxes 12 Lancasters	Foetten Fjord	2
1944				
3 April	FAA	41 Barracudas	Kaa Fjord	3
17 July	FAA	44 Barracudas	Kaa Fjord	0[3]
22 August (1)	FAA	9 Hellcats	Kaa Fjord	1
22 August (2)	FAA	7 Hellcats	Kaa Fjord	0
24 August	FAA	33 Barracudas 10 Hellcats 5 Corsairs	Kaa Fjord	2 Hellcats
1944				
29 August	FAA	26 Barracudas 3 Hellcats 2 Corsairs	Kaa Fjord	0
15 September	RAF	27 Lancasters	Kaa Fjord	0[4]
29 October	RAF	39 Lancasters	Tromso	1[5]
12 November	RAF	31 Lancasters	Tromso	1[5]

Total: 14 ops (7 RAF, 7 FAA)   412 bombers   23 Lost

1. Halifax ditched, crew saved.
2. Two Halifaxes crash-landed in Norway. Crews (less one injured, became POW) escaped to Sweden and repatriated.
3. Two Barracudas ditched, crews saved.
4. Six Lancasters written off in crashes in USSR, crews safe. One Lancaster lost on flight back to England (11 on board).
5. Both crash-landed in Sweden, crews repatriated.

BIBLIOGRAPHY

1. Notes on Sources

When consulted by the author, the Barnes Wallis Papers were together at White Hill House, Effingham. Since Sir Barnes' death, they have been dispersed to several different locations, including: the Science Museum; Barnes Wallis Memorial Trust; Churchill College, Cambridge; RAF Museum Hendon; as well as to members of the family. References would, therefore, be meaningless. Apart from this problem, footnotes in general have been omitted on the grounds that they deter the non-specialist. I have, therefore, opted for a detailed bibliography as a starting point for researchers and those seeking further information.

Unfortunately, not all official records have survived, even squadron ORBs. Furthermore, squadron diaries are patchy, depending as they do on the skill and commitment of the writer. Some, regrettably, are linguistically profane and grammatically informal, detracting from their value.

The timings given in documents preserved in the Public Record Office need to be watched carefully. From February 1940 until October 1945, the United Kingdom was permanently on Summer Time (GMT+1) and during the summer months on Double British Summer Time. However, the dates at which DBST operated during these years varied. Germany and the Occupied countries similarly used Central European Time (GMT+1) and German Summer Time (GMT+2). The western Soviet Union had permanent Summer Time (GMT+3). PRO Readers' Guide No. 8, *RAF Records in the PRO*, and the annual editions of *Whitakers Almanack* are particularly helpful for sorting out confusion. Extra vigilance is necessary, though, when different types of timing appear in the same document. Entries in 9 and 617 squadrons' ORBs for Operation Paravane illustrate this.

BIBLIOGRAPHY

2. *Public Record Office, Kew*

The following classes were consulted:

Air 1   Air Historical Branch, 1862–1959
Air 2   Citations and Awards, 1887–1985
Air 4   Flying Log Books
Air 6   Air Council Minutes, 1916–1973
Air 7   RAF Personal files
Air 8   Chief of the Air Staff
Air 9   Directorate of Operations and Intelligence
Air 14   Bomber Command
Air 15   Coastal Command
Air 22   Returns and Intelligence summaries, 1936–1963
Air 24   Operations Record Books: Commands
Air 25   Operations Record Books: Groups
Air 26   Operations Record Books: Wings
Air 27   Operations Record Books: Squadrons
Air 28   Operations Record Books: Stations
Air 34   Central Interpretation Unit
Air 45   RAF Delegation, Washington
Air 50   Combat reports, Fleet Air Arm

Adm 116   Fleet Air Arm operations
Adm 199   Fleet Air Arm operations
Adm 207   Fleet Air Arm, squadron records
Adm 223   Naval Intelligence summaries

AVIA 15   Ministry of Aircraft Production

Cab 23   War Cabinet minutes
Cab 65   Confidential annexes to War Cabinet minutes
Cab 69   War Cabinet Defence Committee (Ops)
Cab 79   Chiefs of Staff Committee minutes
Cab 80   Chiefs of Staff Committee memos

Defe 3   Intelligence from Enemy Radio Communications (Ultra intercepts)

WO 216   No 30 Mission to Moscow

Of specific interest are:

Adm	116/5468	Operation Tungsten
	199/941	Operation Tungsten
	223/50	Summary of operations against Tirpitz, 1941–4
	223/87	Tirpitz: intelligence digest
Air	14/917	Operation Paravane
	14/1973	Operation Obviate
	14/1972	Operation Catechism
Air	24/204	Bomber Command Operations Record Book, 1942
	24/264	Coastal Command Operations Record Book, 1939–42
Defe		3/79, 86–8, 110–1, 305–6 and 342 Ultra intercepts

3. Department of Aviation Records, RAF Museum Hendon

Highball papers and technical data
Capt J. 'Mutt' Summers' log book
Barnes Wallis diaries
Gp Capt F.W. Winterbotham's correspondence

4. Imperial War Museum, London

DEPARTMENT OF DOCUMENTS
Memoirs, recollections or log books of:
Sqn Ldr T.P.E. Barlow; E.C. Dabner (captured by *Tirpitz* on Spitzbergen); Lt H.J. Davidson RNVR; Flt Lt A.F.P. Fane; Lt C. Friend RN; Lt Cdr R.P. Raikes DSO RN; Sqn Ldr F.A. Robinson DFC

SOUND ARCHIVE
Tapes of varying lengths preserve relevant accounts and memories of:
J.N. Bazin (FAA); D.C.T. Bennett (RAF); T. Bennett (RAF); R.L. Bigg-Wither (FAA); R.A. Briers (RAF); B.A. Buckham (RAAF); G. Byam (RAF); L.W. Curtis (RAF); I. Easton (FAA); J. Herrald (FAA); I. Hewitt (RAF); T.C. Iveson (RAF); A. Kimmins (FAA); R.E. Knights

(RAF); S. Klouman (Norwegian); O.R. Olsen (Norwegian); P.M. Scott (FAA); E.J.W. Sherlock (FAA); H.J. Spiller (RAF); A.W.F. Sutton (RN); E.W. Sykes (FAA); J.B. Tait (RAF); D.G.J. Wilkey (FAA).

5. Miscellaneous Data

Barnes Wallis Papers
Director of Naval Construction, 'Tirpitz', vols 1&2 (1948)
Fowler, S. (et al), RAF Records in the PRO
Naval Staff, Battle Summary No 27 (Operation Tungsten) Nov 1944
Westbrook, C., Crichel Down Bombing Range Report

6. Published Books

(Place of publication London, unless stated)

Anon., *A Formidable Commission* (1947)
Apps, M., *Send Her Victorious* (1971)
Beesley, P., *Very Special Intelligence* (1977)
Bekker, C., *The Luftwaffe War Diaries* (Eng trs) (1966)
Bennett, D., *Pathfinder* (1958)
Bennett, T., *617 Squadron: the Dambusters at War* (1986)
Boyle, A., *No Passing Glory* (1957 edn)
Brickhill, P., *The Dam Busters* (1952)
Bridgman, L. (ed.), *Jane's All the World's Aircraft 1943–4* (1945)
Brennecke, H., *The Tirpitz* (Eng trs) (1963)
Broome, J., *Convoy is to Scatter* (1972)
Brown, D., *Tirpitz: the Floating Fortress* (1977)
Burns, J., *Roosevelt: the Soldier of Freedom 1940–1945* (1971)
Busch, F.-O., *The Story of Prince Eugen* (Eng trs) (1967)
Cameron, I., *Wings of the Morning* (1962)
Canning, H., *Borderers in Battle* (1948)
Churchill, W., *The Second World War*, Bks 4–9 (1969)
Collier, B., *A History of Air Power* (1974)
Crosley, R.M., *They Gave Me a Seafire* (1986)
Curtis, D., *A Most Secret Squadron* (1995)
Dönitz, K., *Ten Years and Twenty Days* (Eng trs) (1959)
Frere-Cook, G., *The Attacks on the Tirpitz* (1973)
Gilbert, M., *Winston S. Churchill*, vol 7 (1986)
Golovko, A., *With the Red Fleet* (Eng trs) (1965)
Green, W., *Avro Lancaster* (1959)

——, *Famous Bombers of World War II* (1959)

Grenfell, R., *The Bismarck Episode* (1969)

Gunston, W., *Bombers* (1978)

Harris, A., *Bomber Offensive* (1947)

Harrison, W., *Fairey Firefly* (1992)

Hastings, M., *Bomber Command* (1993 edn)

Herwig, H.H., *The German Naval Officer Corps 1890–1918* (1973)

Higham, R., *Air Power: A Concise History* (1972)

Howarth, D., *The Shetland Bus* (1951)

Humble, R., *Fraser of North Cape* (1983)

Hurley, A., *Billy Mitchell: Crusader of Air Power* (New York, 1964)

Hurren, B., *Perchance. A Short History of British Naval Aviation* (1949)

Jackson, A., *Avro Aircraft since 1908* (1965)

Kennedy, L., *Menace, the life and death of the Tirpitz* (1979).

Killen, J., *The Luftwaffe: A History* (1967)

——, *A History of Marine Aviation, 1911–1968* (1969)

Lawrence, W., *No. 5 Group RAF (1939–45)* (1951)

Levine, I., *The Story of General Mitchell, Pioneer of Air Power* (1943)

MacBean, J. & Hogben, A., *Bombs Gone* (1990)

Macmillan, N., *The RAF in the World War*, vol 4 (1950)

Morpugo, J., *Barnes Wallis: a Biography* (1972)

Peillard, L., *Sink the Tirpitz* (Eng trs) (1973)

Powers, B., *Strategy without Slide Rule* (1976)

Price, A., *Sky Warriors* (1999)

Probert, H. *Bomber Harris* (2001)

Ready, J., *Forgotten Allies*, vol. 1 (1985)

Robertson, B., *Lancaster – the Story of a Famous Bomber* (1964)

Roskill, S., *The War at Sea*, vols 1–3 (1954–6)

——, *Naval Policy Between the Wars*, vol 1 (1968)

——, *Churchill and the Admirals* (1977)

Saward, D., *Bomber Harris* (1984)

Schofield, B., *The Russian Convoys* (1964)

Scott, J., *Vickers – A History* (1962)

Shears, P.J., *The Story of the Border Regiment* (1948)

Smith, N., *The Halifax Raids* (1994)

Soward, S., *A Formidable Hero* (1987)

Sturtivant, R. & Balance, T., *Squadrons of the Fleet Air Arm* (1984)

Thetford, O., *Aircraft of the Royal Air Force since 1918* (1968)

Tuleja, T., *Eclipse of the German Navy* (1959)

Vincent, D., *Mosquito Monograph* (1982)

Wagner, R., (ed.) *The Soviet Air Force in World War II* (Eng trs) (1974)

Webster, C. & Frankland, N., *The Strategic Bomber Offensive against*

Germany, vols 1–3 (1961)

Wilmot, C., *The Struggle for Europe* (1956 edn)

Winton, J., *Find, Fix and Strike* (1980)

Woodward, D., *The Tirpitz* (1953)

7. Articles and Pamphlets

Bell, D., 'The Tirpitz Raid', *Canadian Aviation Historical Society Journal*, (Summer 1980)

Capsey, G., 'Assignment Archangel', *Air Clues*, vol. 4, no. 12

Griffiths, R.M., 'Fleet Air Arm Attacks on the Tirpitz', *Navy News*

Jepson, J., 'Tirpitz Plaque', *TABS (IX Squadron Association)*, (1998)

Knights, R.E., 'Sinking of the Tirpitz' (unpublished)

Leach, R., *'Tirpitz', Fly Past* (Dec 1999)

Lindberg, E., 'Tirpitz' (unpublished)

Ministry of Information, 'Fleet Air Arm' (1943)

——, 'Arctic War' (1945)

Mortimer, B., 'Sunderland Strike Force', *Wingspan*, Feb 1992

Orbis, 'HMS Tirpitz', *War Machine*, vol. 2, no. 18

——, 'Attacking the Tirpitz', *War Machine*, vol. 7, no. 78

Powell, J.W., 'Tirpitz Missed or Attack Torpedoed' (unpublished)

Strachey, J., 'Big Bombs and V2', *The Listener*, 30 Nov 1944

Thoring, L., 'The Sinking of the Tirpitz, eye witness account' (unpublished)

Zuba, A., 'Tirpitz' (1945, unpublished)

8. Other Material

Information has also been drawn from past correspondence and conversations with: Air Vice-Marshal S.O. Bufton (former DB Ops at the Air Ministry), Air Chief Marshal Sir Ralph Cochrane, Dr A.R. Collins (former scientific officer at the Road Research Laboratory), Marshal of the Royal Air Force Sir Arthur Harris, Air Vice-Marshal H.V. Satterly (former SASO, No. 5 Group, Bomber Command), A.D. Grant, H. Jeffree and R.C. Handasyde (Vickers-Armstrong, Weybridge).

INDEX

Note: Italic page numbers refer to maps.

INDEX

INDEX

INDEX

INDEX